Peter Maggs grew up in Ealing in West London. He left school with one 'O' level and spent several years playing rock 'n' roll with various bands. Following a spell of conventional work and night school, he studied physics at university, and followed a career in the engineering industry. He developed an interest in 19th century social history through investigations into the genealogy of his family, and took early retirement to spend more time doing research. *Smethurst's Luck* is his second book. He has also contributed articles on genealogy and sailing to various magazines.

Smethurst's Luck

The story of Dr Thomas Smethurst
"The Richmond Poisoner"

By Peter Maggs

To Graham,
with best wishes,
Peter

Published by Mirli Books, 2013

© Peter Maggs 2013

Published in the UK in 2013 by
Mirli Books Ltd,
21 Highfield Road
Chelmsford CM1 2NF

ISBN 978-0-9562870-1-4

A catalogue record for this book is available from
the British Library

Also by Peter Maggs, *Henry's Trials*

Design: Gill England
Print: MBC Print Consultancy

I dedicate this book to my mother,
Annemarie Maggs, the original *Mirli*.

Ill were it to be just
If to the more unjust falls stricter justice

Hesiod

Acknowledgements

I would like to offer my sincere gratitude to the many archives and libraries that have provided me with resources and assistance in assembling material for this book. In particular, The British Library, at King's Cross and Colindale, The National Archives at Kew, the Surrey History Centre, The London Metropolitan Archives, Middle Temple Library, the Library of the Royal College of Surgeons, The Cheshire Record Office, The National Library of Wales, The Richmond Local Studies Library and the Archives of the Society of Apothecaries. I wish to thank Essex Libraries for their splendid suite of on-line resources, the Elsevier Corporation for providing me with access to *The Lancet* on line, and 'Old Bailey on Line' at www.oldbaileyonline.org, v 7, for permission to quote from the Old Bailey transcripts.

Many grateful thanks are also due to Hilary Grainger, Diane Hardy and Dr George Knox MD, for proof-reading the manuscript, spotting errors and offering numerous helpful suggestions. My wife Jacky has endured Dr Smethurst for several years, and has never failed to support the project. As well as providing excellent proof-reading skills, her comments on content, style, spelling and grammar have always been constructive and helpful.

Contents

Prologue   9

Characters in the Smethurst Affair   15

Beginnings   21

Isabella Bankes   40

Gathering the Evidence   50

Capital Charge   73

The Case for the Defence   112

Verdict   154

Storm in the Press   165

Sir George Considers   197

Bigamy   234

Probate   249

Aftermath   280

Epilogue   299

Appendix 1 – Family Tree of Thomas Smethurst   318

Appendix 2 – Family Tree of Isabella Bankes   319

Appendix 3 – Thomas Smethurst's letter to *The Lancet*   320

Appendix 4 – Glossary of Medical Terms   327

Sources   334

Picture credits   338

Index   339

Prologue

Friday, 2nd September 1859, and prison staff at the Surrey County Gaol at Horsemonger Lane were preparing for an event that had not happened for seven years. On the following Tuesday, there was to be a public hanging on the roof of the entrance to the prison.

The case of Thomas Smethurst, 'The Richmond Poisoner', was a story straight out of Victorian melodrama – even Charles Dickens' worst villains were hardly guilty of so dastardly a crime. Smethurst was a retired doctor in his fifties who had met Isabella Bankes at a lodging house where he was staying with his wife Mary. Isabella, a single lady of forty-two from a respectable family and of independent means, found herself to be attracted to Dr Smethurst. He was, as he claimed later, unable to resist her advances. The landlady, not unaware of what was going on, asked Isabella to leave, which she did, followed a few days later by Smethurst himself. In December 1858, they underwent a ceremony of marriage at a church in Battersea, and subsequently went to live in Richmond as man and wife. In March 1859, Isabella fell ill with sickness and diarrhoea. After Smethurst's own treatments appeared to have no effect, he called in several other doctors to try and cure her. Nothing seemed to work and Isabella grew weaker. On 1st May, Smethurst called a solicitor out on a Sunday to draw up Isabella's will in which she left virtually everything to him. The next day, two of Isabella's doctors had Smethurst arrested and accused of trying to poison her; arsenic had been found in one of her evacuations. Smethurst managed to persuade the magistrate that he was not trying to poison his 'wife', and that he should be at home with her as she appeared to be dying. The next day, 3rd May, Isabella did die and Smethurst was immediately rearrested for her murder. The post-mortem examination, as well as finding antimony in her body, established that she had been pregnant. Arsenic was found in one of Smethurst's medicine bottles. In August he was tried at the Old Bailey, found guilty of murder and sentenced to death.

Two weeks later, Horsemonger Lane Gaol was preparing for the execution, and the local houses and businesses were doing a roaring trade selling viewing space. But the anticipation in and around the gaol was tempered with uncertainty. Since the trial, much comment had been printed in the newspapers regarding the bias of the trial judge, the questionable medical evidence and the validity of the chemical tests conducted on the body of Isabella Bankes. Significant doubts had arisen regarding the verdict. A number of representations had been made to the Home Secretary on the subject and there was a rising expectation that a reprieve might be granted...

I became aware of the Smethurst affair while researching the case of Henry John Hatch.[1] He had been convicted of indecent assault against two young girls in his care. The defence case was badly mishandled; there was disquiet in the press and elsewhere about the conduct of the trial, and much debate about the need for a Court of Criminal Appeal. Time and again, comment in the newspapers compared the Hatch case to that of Dr Smethurst.

The judge in his summing up during Smethurst's trial stated that the case was

> ...one of the most remarkable in all its circumstances
> that [I have] ever remembered in [my] long experience.

---

1   His story is related in my previous book, *Henry's Trials*.

It is difficult to disagree with the sentiment, and there was much more still to come when he made that statement. Details of the case shed much light on the state of those two great liberal professions, law and medicine, in England in the mid-nineteenth century. In a very real sense, one might say that they collided head-on during Smethurst's trial for murder, and neither side survived the experience undamaged. In the quite unprecedented furore in the press which followed the guilty verdict, much criticism was made of the practitioners of both professions. The Home Secretary commented on the 'imperfection of medical science...and the fallibility of judgement', while the judge was roundly criticised in the medical press as being more like an 'advocate for the prosecution' than 'holding fairly the trembling balance of justice'.

The trial was the first in which 'expert witnesses' were to play a key role. Virtually all of the *material* – as opposed to *circumstantial* – evidence was presented by a number of highly-qualified and experienced medical practitioners and scientists. If Isabella Bankes had been poisoned, only Thomas Smethurst could have done it; but had she, in fact, been poisoned?

A number of articles and two full-length accounts have been written about the Smethurst case. Of the books, the first, in 1859, published shortly after the murder trial, was compiled by Augustus Newton the barrister who had presented Smethurst's petition for mercy to the Home Secretary. The Home Secretary, Sir George Cornewall Lewis, who had to sanction Newton's access to the trial papers in order to write the book, strongly supported publication. He wanted to ensure that all the facts of the case including his own decisions were fully publicized in order to allay public concern. Newton's book consists of transcripts of the prosecution witness statements with a few commentaries, the judge's summing-up, and various petitions and 'memorials' to the Home Secretary for mercy. There are also a number of letters relating to the case. The account is

11

most critical of the judge, Sir Frederick Pollock, in his conduct of the trial. The second book was published seventy years later by Dr Leonard Parry. He presented transcripts of the various court appearances (without comment), plus many other documents relating to the case, including petitions for mercy and letters to the press. He also included an introduction with a brief narrative of Smethurst's life up to the murder trial, and a modern assessment of Isabella Bankes' illness.

Both accounts consist mainly of edited transcripts of the legal hearings, reproduced largely (Newton) or entirely (Parry) without comment, with virtually no background information on Smethurst himself, his family, or the family of Isabella Bankes. Unsurprisingly, Newton concentrated on legal matters, Parry on medical ones. It seemed that a synthesis of the legal and medical issues was needed with the story being told in narrative form.

There was considerable press coverage of the Smethurst affair at the time (both authors, to a large extent, reported only what was printed in *The Times*), with much editorial comment as well as published letters from doctors, lawyers and others. That material provides a rich resource of information relevant to the case, some of it from those directly involved.

There is a substantial cache of contemporary documents on the Smethurst case residing in the National Archives. Parry reproduced some of these in his book, but ignored the correspondence between the judge and the Home Secretary over the question of Smethurst's guilt following the trial. Pollock's long summary of all aspects of the evidence against Smethurst not only provided information that failed to get into the newspapers, but shed much light on Pollock's own character and attitudes. The archives also include a number of police reports on various allegations made against Smethurst and his brother James which came to light following the publicity of Thomas Smethurst's first trial.

A journalistic, rather than academic, style has been adopted for this account, in the belief that a better narrative flow can be maintained in this way. References are generally kept to a minimum, except where required by copyright or for clarification. Records of the legal proceedings consulted consist of the Old Bailey transcripts together with press reports, and the transcript of the judge's summing-up in the murder trial printed by Newton. Speeches by prosecution and defence counsel are not included in the Old Bailey records; neither are the judges' summings-up. These, together with all other legal hearings, have been reconstructed from contemporary press reports.

This story of Thomas Smethurst includes details of six separate actions in court. Given the nature of the case, much of the same evidence was considered in the different hearings and elsewhere, thus presenting the chronicler with a real difficulty in avoiding repetition. Where possible this has been removed, although inevitably the same points do keep coming up. In the interests of brevity, the witness evidence presented in court has been edited to the essential facts. Where spoken or written material is quoted from directly, the original spelling and punctuation has been retained. In a few cases, for dramatic effect, addresses by barristers or judges have been changed into the first person from reported speech. Where this has been done, it is recorded in a footnote. Several of the medical witnesses were referred to in different reports variously as 'Mr', 'Doctor' or 'Professor'; Mr Bird, one of the medical practitioners who treated Isabella Bankes, was frequently referred to in press reports as 'Dr Bird'. Alfred Taylor of Guy's Hospital, whose chemical analysis evidence was central to the case, was referred to interchangeably as 'Dr' and 'Professor' Taylor. Where contemporary reports are referred to in the narrative, the title used at the time has been retained.

There is a list of sources consulted at the end of the book. The *Oxford Dictionary of National Biography* is an invaluable archive of information on the more notable personalities involved in the Smethurst affair, and is referenced as 'ODNB'. Where directly quoted from, the *Oxford English Dictionary* is referenced as 'OED'. Family trees of Thomas Smethurst and Isabella Bankes are provided in appendices 1 and 2 respectively, together with the text of Smethurst's letter to *The Lancet* from prison in appendix 3, and a glossary of medical terms in appendix 4.

Characters in the Smethurst Affair

Smethurst Family

Thomas Smethurst	*TS*, surgeon-apothecary, later MD, and proponent of the Water Cure
James Smethurst	Older brother of *TS*, sometime druggist and stock jobber
William Smethurst	Younger brother of *TS*, mentally disabled
Mary Smethurst	Née Durham, Wife of *TS*, previously Mary Johnson

Bankes Family

Isabella Bankes	*IB*, bigamous wife of *TS*
Louisa Bankes	Sister of *IB*, witness in the various actions against *TS*
Elizabeth Tomlin	Née Bankes, Sister of *IB*
Friend Tomlin	Husband to Elizabeth, witness in the action for probate
Jane Haffenden	Née Bankes, Sister of *IB*
Alfred Haffenden	Husband to Jane
George Vernon Bankes	Brother of *IB*

Laporte Family

John Peter Laporte	Artist, aka John Johnson
Martha Laporte	Née Henderson, wife of John Peter Laporte
George Henry Laporte	Artist, son of John Peter Laporte by Martha Laporte, witness in the bigamy trial

15

Charles Laporte	Artist, son of John Peter Laporte by Mary Johnson/Durham, previously known as Charles Johnson, witness in the bigamy trial
Charles Laporte, Jnr	Son of Charles Laporte, witness in the bigamy trial

Trial for Murder

Sir Frederick Pollock, Lord Chief Baron	Judge
Mr Justice Willes	Judge, assisted Sir Frederick Pollock during the latter part of the trial
Serjeant William Ballantine	Lead counsel for the Crown
Mr Bodkin	Counsel for the Crown
Mr J Clerk	Counsel for the Crown
Mr Merewether	Counsel for the Crown
Serjeant John Humffreys Parry	Lead counsel for the prisoner
Mr Hardinge Gifford	Counsel for the prisoner

Medical and Scientific Witnesses for the Crown

Dr Frederick Gilder Julius	Medical practitioner in Richmond
Mr Samuel Dougan Bird	Dr Julius' partner
Mr William Caudle	Dr Julius' assistant
Dr Thomas Buzzard	Colleague of Mr Bird
Mr Richard Barwell	Surgeon

Dr Samuel Wilks	Assisted Dr Taylor at Guy's Hospital
Dr Robert Bentley Todd	Physician of King's College Hospital
Mr Harry Smith Palmer	Surgeon
Dr Charles Metcalfe Babington	Physician at Queen Charlotte's Lying-in Hospital
Dr Lewis Squire Bowerbank	Practised medicine in Jamaica
Dr James Copland	Experienced physician and author
Dr Alfred Swaine Taylor	Surgeon and Professor of Chemistry at Guy's Hospital
Dr William Odling	Physician and Professor of Chemistry at Guy's Hospital
William Brande	Chemist, retired from the Royal Institution

Other Witnesses for the Crown

Mary Smith	Landlady at Rifle Terrace
Marian Grabouska	Landlady at Kildare Terrace
William Easter	Parish Clerk for Kennington
James Sprice	Parish clerk for Battersea
Alexander McCrosty	Clerk at the London and Westminster Bank
Ann Robertson	Landlady at Old Palace Terrace
Elizabeth Robertson	Daughter of Ann Robertson
Susannah Angelina Wheatley	Landlady at Alma Villas
Susannah Wheatley	Daughter of Susannah Angelina Wheatley

Jemima Chetwood	Nurse
Frederick Senior	Solicitor
William Tarte	Isabella Bankes' mortgagee
George Julius	Dr Julius' son
Catherine Murray	Dr Buzzard's servant
Inspector Robert Graham McIntyre	Inspector of Police at Richmond

Witnesses for the Prisoner

Dr Benjamin Ward Richardson	Grosvenor Street School of Medicine
Dr Julian Edward Rodgers	Past professor of Chemistry, Grosvenor Street School of Medicine
Dr John Lewis William Thudichum	Grosvenor Street School of Medicine
Dr Francis Cornelius Webb	Grosvenor Street School of Medicine
Dr Gilbert Finlay Girdwood	Obstetrician
Mr James Edwards	Surgeon
Dr William Tyler Smith	Queen Mary's Hospital
Mr Pedley	Dentist

Trial for Bigamy

Baron William Bramwell	Trial Judge
Mr Clerk	Lead counsel for the Crown

Mr Beasley	Counsel for the Crown
Mr Sleigh	Lead counsel for the prisoner
Mr Talfourd Salter	Counsel for the prisoner

Witnesses as for murder trial except that Joseph Smith, husband of Mary Smith, landlady at Rifle Terrace, was called instead of his wife

Action for Probate

Sir Cresswell Cresswell	Trial Judge
Dr Phillimore, QC	Counsel for TS
Dr Swabey	Counsel for TS
Mr Downing Bruce	Counsel for TS
Mr B Webster	Counsel for TS
Serjeant Ballantine	Counsel for the Bankes family
Mr Merewether	Counsel for the Bankes family

Witnesses

James Mellor Smethurst	Barrister, not related to *TS*

Other witnesses as for murder and bigamy trials

Others

Edward Penrhyn	Chairman of Surrey Magistrates
Mr Combe	Surrey Magistrate
William Carter	Coroner for East Surrey

Sir George Cornewall Lewis	Home Secretary
Horatio Waddington	Under-Secretary of State at the Home Office
Dr Robert Ferguson	Sometime obstetrician to the Queen
Dr William Baly	Physician Extraordinary to the Queen
Dr William Jenner	Future Physician Extraordinary to the Queen
Sir Benjamin Brodie	Surgeon and President of the Royal Society
Mr Charles Octavius Humphreys	Solicitor for *TS*

Beginnings

When Thomas Smethurst was admitted as a Licentiate of the Society of Apothecaries in 1834, the practice of medicine in England was diverse. The Transactions of the Associated Apothecaries and Surgeon-Apothecaries had observed not long before:

> ...the present classification of medical men is purely the child of circumstances...

Medicine was practised by *Apothecaries*, *Surgeons* and *Physicians*. Apothecaries, or surgeon-apothecaries, were the general practitioners of the time. The *Worshipful Society of Apothecaries*, having seceded from the *Society of Grocers*, was incorporated in 1617. As their antecedents suggest, apothecaries were originally shopkeepers specializing in the sale of medicines and drugs, who dispensed medicines against prescriptions from physicians. Inevitably apothecaries were asked for advice, and began to provide basic surgery to poorer people, such as the removal of teeth and lancing of cysts. In 1704, they won a famous action against the Royal College of Physicians allowing them (the apothecaries) to prescribe as well as dispense medicines.

The Apothecaries Act of 1815, the first attempt at regulating medicine in England, was the culmination of a process that had started some three years earlier. At a general meeting in July of 1812, apothecaries had aired their grievances. Some of these were financial, some concerned with status, others regulatory. The apothecary was being degraded from a '...gentlemen to a tradesman by the mode in which he is remunerated'. There were the 'encroachments of the druggists', persons just selling drugs; there were 'improper persons' practising medicine, and there was a clear need for apothecaries, surgeon-apothecaries and practitioners in midwifery to be placed '... under the direction of a proper controlling body'. Candidates for Licentiate of the Society of Apothecaries (LSA), as required by the new Act, were examined orally after having completed a course of lectures on anatomy, botany, chemistry, *materia medica* (medicines, drugs etc.), theory and practice of physic (treatment with medicines), midwifery and the diseases of women and children, and twelve months' work in a hospital.

The Company of Barber Surgeons was established at the time of Henry VIII in 1540. In 1745, the surgeons broke away from the barbers, and in 1800 became the Royal College of Surgeons by Royal Charter. In September 1834, *The Lancet* published the requirements for the Diploma of the Royal College of Surgeons that conferred membership of the college (MRCS). Candidates were required to be at least 22 years of age and have been 'acquiring professional knowledge' for six years. They had to have attended 140 hours of lectures and 100 demonstrations on anatomy and dissections over a period of at least two years, as well as lectures in surgery, the practice of physic, chemistry, midwifery, botany and *materia medica*. Twelve months' surgical practice in a hospital in London, Dublin, Edinburgh, Glasgow or Aberdeen was also required. Since the academic requirements of apothecaries and surgeons were largely the same, many 'GPs' acquired both accreditations, MRCS and LSA, 'College (of Surgeons) and (Apothecaries) Hall'. Many surgeons worked in hospitals, which provided either education for students (with plenty of dissection opportunities) or employment for those qualified. The first issue of *The Lancet* in October 1823 published some lectures given by the eminent surgeon Sir Astley Cooper. He defined the job of a surgeon:

...while it is the duty of the Physician to attend to internal diseases, it is the duty of the Surgeon to attend to those that are external; to perform operations for the removal of diseased parts; and to know how to regulate the system by the use of medicine, when local diseases are produced by constitutional derangement...

Surgeons could be very well paid. At the height of his career Sir Astley's annual income exceeded £20,000.[1]

The third type of medical practitioner was the physician. As alluded to by Sir Astley Cooper, physicians generally dealt with internal disorders which they treated with physic (medicine). Physicians required a university degree – before 1835 only a degree from Oxford or Cambridge was sufficient.[2] In 1832, the regulations of the Royal College of Physicians (of London) were printed in *The Lancet*, entirely in Latin. Accompanying these were records of the admissions to the college in the previous years – between two and three fellows per year, and around 13 licentiates. Physicians were thus an intellectual if not a medical elite. Ten years later the entrance regulations of the college were finally published in English, and some of the requirements are illuminating. Candidates for a Diploma in Medicine had to be at least 26 years old, of unimpeachable moral character and have spent at least five years studying medicine. Subjects studied should include anatomy and physiology, the theory and practice of physic, forensic medicine, chemistry, botany, *materia medica*, natural history and the principles of midwifery and surgery. After each of three examinations, a *viva voce* (oral examination) was conducted in Latin, 'unless the Board deems it expedient to put questions in English...' A knowledge of Greek was desirable but not essential. Latin was, however, essential, and at the start of each *viva voce*, a translation,

---

1 ODNB

2 A medical degree from the universities in Scotland and Ireland did not qualify before that date.

aloud, of a passage from Hippocrates, Galen or Aretaeus was mandatory. Having survived such arduous training, a physician could expect in his professional life to visit well-off patients, provide a consultation, write out a prescription in Latin to be filled by an apothecary, and collect a fee.

The practice of medicine in the mid-nineteenth century was primitive by modern standards. There were no painkillers other than cocaine, opium or laudanum (opium in alcohol), no antibiotics and no anaesthetics. Bloodletting was common practice, either by opening a vein in the arm, by cupping (applying a partial vacuum to the skin which was sometimes cut) or by the use of leeches. Bloodletting was employed to

> ...moderate vascular function, reduce [inflammation], relieve congestion, allay spasm and pain, relax the muscular system, promote absorption, and arrest haemorrhage...

With no X-rays, skilled practitioners used touch to feel internal organs and assess their condition. Dentistry without local or general anaesthetics was a nightmare, and surgery, including amputation, with the patient conscious was akin to medieval torture.

Many of the medicines in regular use would be regarded as poisons today. For example, medicines to control vomiting and diarrhoea included opium, which was administered by mouth and also as an enema. Apart from its painkilling properties, it arrested the 'secretions and peristaltic motion of the bowels'. Opium was used widely to treat dysentery and the effects of cholera. *Dover's powder*, consisting of opium and ipecacuanha (a plant emetic), was used to treat diarrhoea and dysentery. *Grey powder*, consisting of metallic mercury rubbed into powdered chalk, was used as a mild laxative. Silver nitrate solution, which has a caustic action, was used as an enema to treat dysentery by its astringent effects. Bismuth, administered as a subnitrate, and copper sulphate (separately) were used to allay vomiting and diarrhoea. Prussic acid (cyanide), in a very dilute form, was used in 'neuralgic affectations of the bowels' and in cases of chronic vomiting. This was the state of medicine in the early Victorian era, within which Thomas Smethurst made his career.

Thomas Smethurst, born on 2nd January 1805 in Budworth in Cheshire, was the second of three children born to William and Charlotte Smethurst. William Smethurst was a 'warehouseman', which in the late eighteenth century meant that he owned a warehouse, and may have been involved in the cotton industry in Manchester. William and Charlotte married by licence in London in 1798 at St Mildred, Bread Street; the £200 marriage bond indicated that William was reasonably wealthy. His wife, Charlotte, had quite an exotic background. She was Jeanne Jacobine Charlotte 'Chloee' Liardet, third daughter of Jean-François Louis Liardet and Marie Salome Kückh. There was an older sister, Charlotte Salome Liardet who had died in infancy, and Jeanne Jacobine, following her father's example, decided to adopt a more English name; henceforth she was known as 'Charlotte' Liardet. Her father was a clergyman from Vevey in Switzerland who came to England as chaplain and tutor to the Earl of Dysart.[3] Jean-François was naturalized in 1776, and as John Liardet, he was awarded a patent for a type of stucco which was adopted by the Adams brothers to use on their buildings. It is said that the family was the English branch of an old Austrian family ennobled by the Empress of Austria, Maria Theresa, presumably through Charlotte's mother, Marie Salome Kückh.[4]

---

3   Information from various sources.
4   From the Who's Who entry of Colonel Charles Liardet, one of Jean-François' grandsons.

Nothing is known for certain of Thomas Smethurst's grandparents on his father's side. There was a William Smethurst, a warehouseman of Salford who died in 1798, an event that could have precipitated William and Charlotte's marriage about nine months later, but the connection with our Thomas Smethurst is tenuous and circumstantial.

Thomas Smethurst had two brothers. James was born in 1802, and William, who was described as being mentally disabled, was born in 1810. Thomas Smethurst never spoke about his schooling, but it is clear from his subsequent book on Hydropathy and his editorials in the *Water Cure Journal* that he was articulate and well-read, and had received a classical education. He had knowledge of Latin and Greek, and was familiar with the ancient writers in those languages. His scholarship extended to literature related to the curative properties of water right through the Dark Ages, into the Renaissance and up to the period in which he was writing. It may be that his grandfather, John Liardet, who was a professional tutor helped in this regard. It also seems likely that Smethurst gained a working knowledge of French and German from his mother and her family, and this would have facilitated his subsequent travels around Europe.

According to Smethurst's own account, the family came to London around 1815. In November 1824, when he was nineteen, he was indentured as an apprentice apothecary to Mr James Hay, MRCS, of Newgate Street, a surgeon from Scotland. Nineteen was old for an apprentice, although the custom was that any age between fourteen and twenty-one was acceptable. The apprenticeship lasted five years, finishing in 1829 or 1830. In order to qualify for the Society of Apothecaries, Smethurst spent nine months at the Westminster Hospital; but it was not until 1833 that he was examined by Mr Wheeler for the Society's licence – and rejected. A year later, he applied again, and was again turned down – this time by Mr Tegart. Finally in

September 1834, on his third try, again with Mr Tegart, he was successful and was admitted as a Licentiate.

Now qualified, Smethurst practised medicine at Holland Place in Clapham Rise, styling himself surgeon. Some time later, he moved to Spencer House in Ramsgate, as he claimed later, for the healthy sea air. It is not clear exactly when he went, but he was certainly there by 1841, having dissolved his partnership with Mr C Taylor, another surgeon with whom he had a shared practice in Clapham. Smethurst was accompanied to Ramsgate by his wife Mary. He had married Mary Durham in 1828, evidently while he was still an apprentice. It was normal practice – usually an explicit condition of the indenture – that the apprentice should remain unmarried. Perhaps Mr Hay turned a blind eye although he was unmarried himself; perhaps Smethurst just didn't tell him.

In the early 1840s, Smethurst became aware of the concept of 'Hydropathy' as a treatment for a variety of ills. Vincent Priessnitz, a farmer's son of limited education, had set up a hydropathy establishment in Gräfenberg in what was then Austrian Silesia near the Polish border. The village is now Lázně Jeseník in the Czech Republic. He had discovered the apparent curative properties of water, as a result of watching a small deer which had been shot through the thigh cure itself of the wound by repeated bathing in a cold stream. When Priessnitz broke several ribs in a cart accident, doctors told him that he would be an invalid for life. He applied cold water compresses to the affected area (a method previously tested on a damaged finger), and cured himself. He started treating others, and gradually his ability to effect cures where conventional therapy had failed made him famous. His methods were simple: rich food and alcohol were banned, plenty of exercise was required, but above all up to thirty glasses of (cold) water were consumed in a day, together with cold baths and showers and sweating induced by being wrapped in blankets, followed by being rubbed vigorously with wet cloths.

Hydropathy was brought to the attention of the English-speaking world largely as a result of the book by 'Captain' R T Claridge. His *Hydropathy or The Cold Water Cure*, published in 1842, outlined the methods used and claimed that the application of water externally and internally could cure everything from toothache, heartburn and piles, to cholera, smallpox, syphilis and cancer. Claridge, whose 'Patent Asphalte Company' boasted Isambard Kingdom Brunel as a consulting engineer, had been suffering from debilitating headaches and rheumatism while travelling in Italy. He was advised to consult Priessnitz, and the success of his cure prompted the writing of the book. In February 1842, *The Lancet* announced receipt of a copy of Claridge's book and a month later printed a four page critique.

Thomas Wakley, founder and editor of *The Lancet*, was not equivocal in his appraisal:

> Hydropathy is a fine word for water-pain, a "science" which certainly rests on a better foundation than homoeopathy, or mesmerism, or any of the other mystic "sciences" which have latterly issued from that hot-bed of absurdities, Austria, where the crushed minds of men that cannot bear the healthful fruits of free investigation, run riot in the extravagancies of fantastic credulity, or ignorantly strive to breathe life into the dead superstitions, and one-idead theories, of the Middle Ages.

Then:

> We are never in a hurry to notice these novelties; as the climate of England is not very congenial to them, and they seldom make much impression here...excepting in our lunatic asylums, and in small coteries of the wrong or weak-headed.

After a rant about homeopathy and mesmerism during which Wakley conceded that there are *some* truths in their claims, he equivocated slightly on the water cure:

> So, if we condemn the humbug of hydropathy, it must not be imagined for a moment that we deny the virtues of cold water as a remedy when administered with discretion...

There followed a description of the water cure, during which *The Lancet* was highly sceptical of Priessnitz's self-cure of his broken ribs, stating that an English physician would have had him up on his feet in a few weeks. At least two more pages followed in which Claridge was accused of everything from being unable to spell in German or Latin, to suggesting the absurdity that men acquire three to four pounds weight daily – duly sweated or excreted – entirely from 'feeding on air'. The piece finished by observing that Claridge was a stupid and ignorant person, and declaring the intention to ignore his 'asphaltic squireship's aspersions' on the medical profession for not embracing hydropathy as a universal panacea.

In April, *The Lancet* published a letter entitled 'The Water-Cure Quackery', followed in June by a report on the meeting of the Hydropathic Society:

> ...a more miserable failure, a more wretched display of ignorance, it was never our lot to witness...

It is, of course, almost superfluous to observe that the claim to be able to cure syphilis and cancer by the application of cold water alone must be undiluted quackery, and this was a view very much shared by *The Lancet*.

Smethurst was an avid reader of *The Lancet* and corresponded with it regularly. In 1832, his first acknowledged letter to the journal had been rejected as 'not demand[ing] publication'. In 1836 he tried again, perhaps encouraged by

29

his now qualified status. His letter was not published but the editor, displaying his classical knowledge, printed an ironic and enigmatic response to 'Mr Smethurst', referring to 'Pythias and Damon' – loyal friends from Greek mythology – relating apparently to a suggestion about blood transfusion as a treatment for bites. In February 1841, *The Lancet* at last published one of his letters. It was a plea for correspondents to the journal not to hide under the anonymity of *noms de plume*. Perhaps encouraged by this success, Smethurst bombarded the journal with more than a dozen letters over the next year. The following month, his first letter on a medical condition was published. It described the use of leeches for the opening of 'scrofulous abscesses'. In the light of Smethurst's subsequent history, it is difficult not to be intrigued by the language of this submission. He started:

> The serious and lasting deformity usually resulting either from the lancing or bursting of scrofulous tumours in childhood, must necessarily be attended with considerable regret by the beautiful and interesting female, when so lamentably affected.

Continuing,

> ...it is often painful to observe the attempts made to conceal... the... stigma of some foul and loathsome disease...and probably [results in]...many persons refusing a matrimonial alliance in consequence of such appearances alone.

The application of leeches '...results in the wounds inflicted being of sufficient calibre for the purpose', resulting in far less scarring. He signed himself 'Thomas Smethurst, Surgeon'. In July 1841, *The Lancet* published a very interesting letter from him. He was called to attend a two-year-old child, daughter of a laundress, who had fallen into an old well and was found submerged in two feet of water. No pulse or respiration could be detected and about half an hour had elapsed since the accident had happened. He placed the child in a warm bath, gave her mouth to mouth resuscitation and two other persons rubbed her body and limbs with a flannel. He also used burned feathers applied to her nostrils in lieu of smelling salts. After two hours she showed signs of life and a full recovery followed. In January 1842, Smethurst wrote to the journal regarding the question of who pays the doctors' fees – the insurer or the insured – when a medical certificate is needed for life assurance. In the course of this letter Smethurst declared that his uncle, Sir Hugh Evelyn, took offence when Smethurst requested a fee of one guinea from the insurance company before issuing the certificate.[5]

Mentioning in 1842, that Sir Hugh Evelyn was his uncle might have rebounded on Smethurst the following year, when Sir Hugh was finally released from prison. It was a newsworthy event reported in the press, mainly because of the extraordinary length of his incarceration – he had been in a debtor's prison for eighteen years. Indeed there followed a two-year hiatus in Smethurst's correspondence with *The Lancet*, although this was probably more to do with his literary aspirations and apparent conversion to the principles of Hydropathy.

Smethurst would have read the extensive negative copy published in *The Lancet* regarding hydropathy, but having acquired Claridge's book he decided to find out for himself, and see whether the water cure would clear up the effects of an old

5   Sir Hugh Evelyn, 5th and last Baronet of Wotton, was uncle by marriage to Thomas Smethurst; Sir Hugh's sister, Phillipa, had married Wilbraham Liardet, Charlotte Smethurst's brother. Hugh had inherited the baronetcy from his brother John Evelyn, who died insane. Sir Hugh Evelyn was incarcerated in the King's Bench Prison for debt between 1825 and 1843, and had already served several years in prison before that, also for debt. In fact, certainly later, Sir Hugh had been living outside the prison, effectively on licence, in the local adjacent area known as the 'King's Bench (later Queen's Bench) Prison Rules'.

knee injury sustained when he fell down stairs as a child. In the autumn of 1842, he travelled to Gräfenberg and spent 'some months' there. There were two ways of getting to Gräfenberg from England as Smethurst detailed later. Firstly, by steamer to Hamburg, mail coach to Berlin, railway to Frankfurt (an der Oder), mail coach to Breslau (Wroclaw) then railway, mail coach and private carriage via Olau (probably Gmina Olawa) and Neisse (Nysa). The second route started with a channel crossing to Ostend, then by rail to Liège, by public stage coach to Aachen, railway to Cologne then steamer along the Rhine to Mainz, railway to Frankfurt (am Main), mail coach to Leipzig, railway to Dresden and mail coach to Neisse. Neither journey was for the faint-hearted; both involved a considerable distance by mail coach – more than 300 miles for the first route, nearly 400 miles in the second route. At an average speed of not much more than five miles per hour, this would have translated to between 60 and 80 hours spent in very uncomfortable conditions. Travel to Gräfenberg from England took between ten and twelve days to complete. The route via Hamburg, involving a shorter distance by mail coach would have been quicker and somewhat less uncomfortable than the alternative. However a modest diversion from the Frankfurt am Main route allowed the traveller to visit Erlangen, just to the north of Nuremberg.

The interest of Erlangen to a British surgeon or apothecary, was revealed by a letter from 'Erlangensis' published in *The Lancet* in June 1841. The letter was headed:

Mode of Obtaining the Medical Diploma of the Erlangen University.

The author, who was a British graduate of the university, made the opportunity clear in the first paragraph:

Any British medical man who has testimonials of having passed through a regular course of medical

education, and of being of good moral character, may
be examined, and, if approved, will receive the diploma.

The Medical Diploma of the University of Erlangen conferred
the degree of MD, entitling the holder to be addressed as
'Doctor'.[6] The cost of the diploma and fees was £21 when
awarded in person. It could even be obtained by post,
although a thesis and testimonials were required. It is clear
that Smethurst visited Erlangen, probably after his visit to
Gräfenberg, and came away with his own medical diploma.
And not one to rest on his laurels, he was so impressed with
what he saw at Gräfenberg, that he too wrote a book about
his experiences and the methods used, dedicated it to Captain
Claridge, and signed himself 'Thomas Smethurst MD'. The book
was published in 1843. Furthermore, he established Spencer
House at Ramsgate as a Hydropathy centre, and started to
advertise in *The Times.*

Thomas Smethurst's book, *Hydrotherapia* or *The Water
Cure*, is interesting in a number of ways. It includes a full and
frank description and assessment of Priessnitz's sanatorium
and methods. The food was bad – greasy soup, bad beef and
lots of dumplings, sauerkraut, potatoes and gherkins. There
were 'disagreeable odours' from the kitchens and 'filthy smells
from the sweating-blankets and linen' that were hung up. It
was also cold – he was there in December. Being more tactful
than the editor of *The Lancet*, Smethurst described Priessnitz
as being '...deficient in the art of combining thoughts according
to the adopted rule' and '...wanting in the power of eloquence'.
Nevertheless, he was convinced that the Water Cure as
practised by him was not 'chance-work' without theory; he
acted on fixed principles.

---

6 Only the degree of MD, 'Doctor of Medicine', allowed the holder to be
addressed as 'Doctor'. The possessor of a Diploma in Medicine or Bachelor
of Medicine degree was still 'Mr'.

The book contained a substantial historical summary of attitudes to the health-giving properties of water, starting with the Egyptians and Persians, via the Greeks to the Romans. He quoted from Pindar in the original Greek. He then worked his way through the Arabs, medieval Europe, many examples from the sixteenth, seventeenth and eighteenth centuries and into the 'modern' period.

After descriptions of the various baths, showers and sweating regimes used at Gräfenberg, there was a substantial list of the various ailments that could be treated with the Water Cure. Smethurst conceded that not all diseases were treatable, including advanced cancer, heart disease and consumption. On syphilis he was ambiguous, implying that even secondary syphilis could be successfully treated. Otherwise, everything from mental disease to insect stings via epilepsy, St Vitus' dance, worms, gout, jaundice, cholera, constipation and piles would yield to the beneficial effects of the Water Cure.

Smethurst's new status as MD and published author may well have contributed to an honorary mention as 'Dr' Smethurst in *The Lancet* the following year. On 23rd January 1844, Sir Francis Burdett, a radical and sometime reformist politician had died. A few days later *The Times* printed a report on the causes of his death, an edited version of which was later reproduced in *The Lancet*. It was said that Sir Francis' daughter, Miss Burdett Coutts, was convinced that the course of hydropathy he had been following to cure his gout was responsible:

> [she asserted that] the cold water treatment had destroyed one of the noblest constitutions ever given to man...[and she determined to] resist the further use of such quackeries...

On 20th February, *The Times* printed a letter from Edward Johnson, MD, pointing out that Sir Francis was 75 years old and that his wife, to whom he was devoted, had died just a few days before his own death. He also stated that although thousands had undoubtedly benefited from hydropathic treatment, Sir Francis' treatment had been discontinued two months before his death, and he had subsequently not abstained from drinking beer and wine...

An editorial in *The Lancet* on 3rd February made it quite clear where its own opinion on hydropathy still lay. It started in whimsical mood:

> Sir Francis Burdett, after a lengthened career, has at last paid the final tribute to nature.

Then:

> ...it appears that this celebrated statesman has fallen a victim, not to disease alone, but partly, if not principally, to the "water-cure"...That hydropathy is not a science, but merely one of the numerous forms of quackery which are periodically foisted on the notice of the public, most of our readers will admit.

The editor sought to examine why

> many of the noble and learned...as well as the ignorant and lowly...[and] learned doctors should come forward as [hydropathy's] champions and disciples...

He was less than complimentary about Vincent Priessnitz, calling him an 'illiterate peasant', without the 'slightest knowledge of medical science'. He went on:

> The most palpable fallacies in religion, in philosophy, indeed in every branch of human learning, have found not only men of ordinary merit, but men of the greatest talent and learning, to embrace and defend them.

Two pages later, the editor concluded that the solution to the conundrum was a simple want of common sense.

Smethurst, now an active proponent of hydropathy at his establishment in Ramsgate, wrote to *The Lancet* in response. His letter was not published, but the editor was quite complimentary considering his previously withering attack on hydropathy:

> The letter we have received from Dr Smethurst on the death of Sir Francis Burdett is decidedly the most temperate and the most scientific communication that has been addressed to us since we editorially noticed the merits of hydropathy.

Whatever the medical establishment thought of hydropathy, and one assumes that the editor of *The Lancet* generally reflected those opinions, a number of clinics dedicated to it were established in England. Malvern in Worcestershire became a centre, and Tennyson, Dickens and Charles Darwin were patients at the establishment run there by Dr James Gully. No doubt the ascetic regime, accompanied by exercise and the consumption of pure water, really did cure many people of a mixture of some of the milder ailments. It would also have helped those ills brought on by the application of medicines of doubtful efficacy and purity, the drinking of less than clean water and the consumption of excessive rich food and alcohol.

Perhaps encouraged by the positive response to his latest communication by *The Lancet*, Smethurst was back in London in mid-1844, with a practice at 11 Beak Street, a turning off Regent Street. His advertisements now proclaimed an endorsement by Captain Claridge to the effect that:

> Your [book] contains everything that can possibly be said or desired on [the water cure], and only requires to be read to be appreciated by everyone.

By 1848, Smethurst had moved to Harrington Square, close to Regent's Park, and later on in the year he was appointed editor of the *Water Cure Journal*. The *Water Cure Journal and Hygienic Magazine* had been launched in August 1847, price sixpence. The journal was published monthly, and Smethurst contributed letters and articles to it. His editorship commenced with No 18, the January 1849 edition, where he ended an introductory essay on the benefits of hydropathy by announcing that the proprietor of the journal, Mr Gadsby, had agreed that any profits from the publication, 'when there shall be any', would be given to a proposed 'Benevolent Hydropathic Institution'. Apart from a monthly editorial, Smethurst continued to contribute articles to the journal including from time to time testimonials from grateful patients of his praising the benefits of hydropathy. However, in the December 1849 edition, he announced:

> Our professional engagements now preclude the possibility of our continuing any longer the responsibility of Editor...

Business in Regent's Park must have been good, and no doubt making the most of the publicity afforded by the journal, Smethurst felt able to invest in the purchase of the lease to a substantial estate. In 1850 he announced in *The Times* of 11th March, that his Hydropathy establishment was removing to Moor Park, Surrey, an estate boasting '...good trout streams, still water fishing, together with extensive shooting on the estate...' Terms were between £2 2s and £3 3s per week (two to three guineas).[7] Moor Park was a mansion set in its own grounds near Farnham in Surrey; it was there, one hundred and fifty years earlier, that Jonathan Swift had written *Tale of a Tub* while he was secretary to the then owner, Sir William Temple.

---

7   A guinea was £1 1s = 21 shillings, equal to £1.05 in decimal currency. With 20 shillings to the pound, a shilling was equivalent to 5 (new) pence.

By July 1850, Smethurst had increased his prices; terms were now two and a half to three and a half guineas per week although there was 'no charge for bath attendants [altered to "attendance" in a later advertisement]'. By February 1851 his book was in its fourth edition and business at Moor Park appeared to be booming. The journey time from Waterloo had dropped from an hour and a half to an hour and a quarter, and The Sanitary Commission had declared the water at Moor Park to be 'the purest water in the kingdom'. The 1851 census for Moor Park, carried out on Sunday 30th March, lists Thomas Smethurst and his wife, Mary, two housemaids, a footman and four visitors – a barrister, a woollen manufacturer and two annuitants.[8] If the visitors were paying an average of 3 guineas a week, that would have yielded a minimum revenue of £650 a year, remembering that occupation was likely to be low during weekends. This was more than the salary of the governor of the new prison at Wandsworth, and would have provided the Smethursts with a comfortable living, depending on the costs of running the establishment.

The following year, however, Smethurst's fortunes started to decline. In July of 1852, he announced that he was to be available for consultation at 80 Harley Street on Saturdays; possibly the revenue at Moor Park needed some boosting. By September, he was available for consultation every day in London, and had dropped the Harley Street address. He stated later that in 1852 he sold the lease of Moor Park to Dr Lane, although it continued to be advertised under his name until 1854; other evidence suggests that he was mistaken over the date. It may be that although the estate was ideal for the wealthy unwell, Smethurst's capital was insufficient to develop it to its full potential. This was certainly rectified by the new owner, Edward Wickstead Lane who numbered Charles Darwin among his celebrated patients. (Darwin stayed

---

8   An 'Annuitant' was a person living on an annuity, i.e. of independent means.

at Moor Park in 1859, the year that the *Origin of Species* was published.) In April 1854 Smethurst advertised a practice at Sloane Street, and shortly after that he moved into his own house in Thurlow Square, Brompton, giving up the running of a hydropathy establishment, and effectively retiring at the age of 49 or 50.

Notwithstanding the lack of success at Moor Park, Smethurst was not uncomfortable financially. His assets were in the region of £3,500, with some of this invested in property generating an annual income of around £270. He also had more than £500 in cash at several banks. He decided to undertake a 'grand tour'. He and Mary travelled in France and Germany. They stayed for some time in Paris and spent six months in Heidelberg. In 1857, they were back in England, and having moved out of the house in Brompton while they were travelling, they went to stay with Mr & Mrs Smith who ran a boarding house at 4 Rifle Terrace, Queen's Road, Bayswater. It was a boarding house in which they had stayed on a number of previous occasions.

Isabella Bankes

On 20th September 1858, five days after her forty-second birthday, Isabella Bankes came to stay at the boarding house in Rifle Terrace. The terrace was in Queen's Road (now Queensdale Road), not far from Holland Park in London. The Smethursts had been in residence there on and off for about eighteen months.

Isabella Bankes was the second of six children of George Bankes and Hannah Vernon. Isabella's grandfather, John Bankes, had made his fortune refining sugar, 'white gold', presiding over a ten-fold increase in consumption in Britain during his lifetime. He left well over £60,000 when he died in 1809, and Isabella's father, George Bankes, inherited the business along with £10,000 in cash. In fact, the business had been left jointly to George and his younger brother Charles, but the latter incurred his father's wrath by his intention to contract an 'inappropriate marriage'. As a consequence, a portion of Charles' share of the assets such as would not impede the proper conduct of the 'sugar baking business', was invested in government securities with only the interest paid to him. In a codicil to the will, John Bankes' trustees were charged to 'prevent any imprudent marriage connection by him', and were apparently empowered to continue the arrangement at their discretion. Consequently George Bankes took over the business and when he died he left it to his only son, George Vernon Bankes, Isabella's younger brother.

The Bankes family were not generally favoured with good health. Isabella's mother had died in 1826 at the age of 32 from 'a cold that turned to inflammation'. George Bankes died in 1843 aged 55. The official cause of death was stated to be typhus, although it was said that he suffered greatly from diarrhoea 'which they were unable to arrest'. The eldest daughter Anne, for whom George Bankes had made special provision in his will, must have been an invalid for some time; she died of consumption in 1844 aged 29. Isabella herself was subject to bilious attacks and flatulence, as were the whole family. She also suffered from travel sickness and was afflicted with a 'womb complaint' for which she used silver nitrate douches administered using a glass syringe. She had been under the care of several doctors for various complaints before she met Dr Smethurst. Mrs Smith at Rifle Terrace reported that she was sick twice in the house and always complained of nausea when eating. Mrs Smith considered Isabella to be very delicate; she ate very little.

Isabella had three sisters living, she being the eldest. In descending order of age they were Jane, who had married Alfred Haffenden, Louisa, unmarried, and Elizabeth the youngest; she was married to Friend Tomlin. The four sisters each inherited around £1,750 from their father, and this was lent on mortgage to Mr Tarte, a lead merchant, father of the deceased first wife of Isabella's brother George. The money was secured on property, and at 5% per annum yielded around £7 6s per month to each sister.

The sisters had an uncle, James Rhodes Bankes, their father's youngest brother, and he had been ill for some time. James Bankes had been diagnosed with cancer of the bladder in 1856 and by the time that Isabella arrived at Rifle Terrace, he must have been quite ill; he died a month later. James Bankes had been left £10,000 by his father in 1809. He seems not to have been involved in sugar refining, but when he died in 1858, not being married and having no children of his own, he left most of his £60,000 fortune for the benefit of his nephew and nieces. Isabella, Louisa and Elizabeth were each left the interest on £5,000 invested in 3% government stocks and securities. They had no access to the capital, which reverted to the other legatees on their deaths, but during their lifetimes they received the dividends of around £140 a year each. The other sister, Jane, was left nothing in the will, possibly because she was already quite well-off. She had married a widower, Alfred Haffenden, a landed proprietor, in 1851. Ten years later she was living with her husband, two step-daughters and eleven servants in a manor house in Nottinghamshire.

In September 1858, Isabella and Louisa were living with their sister Elizabeth, her husband Friend Tomlin, and their three-year-old daughter Mabel in Paddington. According to Tomlin, Isabella left because he was giving up the house and her medical man had suggested a change of air. She may have done this, deciding to live independently, in anticipation of the legacy from her uncle. However, since Elizabeth sued for divorce in 1861, and Friend Tomlin was bankrupt by 1867, it seems possible that Isabella might also have left to avoid an 'atmosphere' at the Tomlins'.

It was the habit of Mrs Smith's lodgers to eat together at one table and thus Isabella would soon have met and got to know the other occupants of the house including Dr and Mrs Smethurst. What happened next has been described by Mrs Smith, Mary Smethurst, and Thomas Smethurst himself. Isabella took a fancy to Thomas. Perhaps it was the fact that he was a doctor – and an MD addressed as "Doctor" – not just a surgeon-apothecary. Since Isabella's health was precarious he probably treated her in some way. Possibly he romanced her with stories of his times in France, Germany and Austria or tales of various well-known persons that he had treated at Moor Park. In any event, she took a shine to him, and he, perhaps flattered by the attentions of a younger woman (he was 53 years of age by this time, while his wife was 74) responded to her interest, possibly finding within himself something rekindled that he might have forgotten was there... According to Smethurst later, Isabella had proposed a secret marriage while they were out walking together in Kensington Gardens. She had said that both a cousin and a friend had been secretly married, and she mentioned the latter fact in the presence of Mrs Firth, another boarder at Rifle Terrace. Isabella insisted that Smethurst visit Doctors' Commons in order to read the will of her uncle James, and thus confirm the value of the income she was to receive under that will.[1]

Mrs Smith, the landlady, decided that Isabella's behaviour towards a fellow boarder and married man was incompatible with her sense of decency and gave her notice to leave. Smethurst tried to intercede on her behalf but Mrs Smith was adamant. Isabella had to go, and go she did, leaving on 29th November. She went to lodge with a Mrs Grabouska at Kildare Terrace, Bayswater, barely a mile away, where she stayed until 9th December. On that day, in the parish church of St Mary's at Battersea, Thomas Smethurst and Isabella Bankes were married by special licence. Witnesses were James Sprice, the parish clerk, and Lucy Ambrose. Whether 'the Smethursts' spent the next one or two nights together is not recorded, but Thomas Smethurst finally departed Rifle Terrace either on 11th or 12th December, telling his wife Mary that he was first visiting friends and then making a 'tour'. By way of a honeymoon, Thomas and Isabella spent two weeks in Tunbridge Wells and a week in Dorking, followed by three weeks in Surbiton. In January they were in Withyham in Sussex, from where Isabella wrote to her sister Louisa, telling her that she was 'quite well', albeit 'covered in "plaisters" and...obliged to wear flannel drawers'. She carried her pet bird, Bob, with her who '[sang] in the railway carriage'. In February 1859, Dr and Mrs Smethurst went to live at No 6, Old Palace Terrace, Richmond;

---

1   Doctors' Commons, was a society of ecclesiastical lawyers, already virtually obsolete in Smethurst's time. It was effectively abolished by the Court of Probate Act of 1857. Charles Dickens described it as 'the place where they grant marriage-licences to love-sick couples, and divorces to unfaithful ones...[and] register the wills of people who have any property to leave...'

the landlady was Mrs Robertson. Old Palace Terrace was at the corner of Richmond Green not far from the eighteenth-century stone bridge over the river, and effectively in the centre of the town.

After a month or so, Isabella began to suffer from sickness and diarrhoea. Initially, Smethurst treated her himself, but she did not improve so he decided to call in a second opinion. Mrs Robertson recommended a local doctor, Dr Julius. Dr Frederick Gilder Julius was the senior doctor in the area. He was a member of the Royal College of Surgeons, and had the degree of MD; following the Medical Act of the previous year, he was also registered with the new General Medical Council. He first visited Isabella on 3rd April 1859. After questioning her as to her state of health, he prescribed a mixture of chalk and catechu which was made up by his assistant Mr Caudle and sent up to the house. He visited Isabella the next day to find her no better. Smethurst had also given her some medicine, castor oil and some laudanum – the latter probably as an enema since it was described subsequently as 'an injection'.[2] Dr Julius visited again on 5th April to find still no improvement. This time he prescribed pills containing *Grey powder* and *Dover's powder*, again with no effect on Isabella's state of health. *Grey powder*, containing metallic mercury, was a laxative and *Dover's powder* was either a laxative or emetic depending on the dose. Dr Julius commented later, '[his prescribed medicine] seemed to have no effect [on Isabella] whatever...'

Smethurst suggested a mixture of quinine, gentian, ether, dilute sulphuric acid and hydrocyanic acid (hydrogen cyanide) to give Isabella an appetite. Dr Julius thought it was not the correct medicine, but reluctantly agreed to provide

---

2 Hypodermic injection, as understood today, only commenced in 1853, being first reported two years later by Dr Alexander Wood in Edinburgh. It is clear from evidence given in court and subsequent statements by Smethurst that an 'injection', as administered to Isabella Bankes, referred to a douche or an enema.

it since Smethurst would be present to observe any adverse symptoms and stop the treatment if necessary. In the event, although it had no negative effects, the treatment produced no improvement either. Dr Julius continued to visit Isabella trying other medicines but her condition deteriorated. Mrs Robertson reported hearing her retching in the early mornings. She reported 'green and yellow vomit', and evacuations that were 'just like coloured water'. Isabella had virtually no appetite.

At this point Mrs Robertson decided to increase the rent from eighteen to twenty-five shillings a week; it may have been because of the extra and unpleasant work she was having to do in relation to Isabella's illness. Smethurst refused to pay any more, and on 15th April, he and Isabella moved. They went to 10 Alma Villas, now Rosemont Road, about a mile away at the eastern end of Richmond. Alma Villas was a row of semidetached houses on Richmond Hill surrounded by fields and orchards, with the Wesleyan College and chapel to the south, and plenty of open ground to the north. The rent there was only fifteen shillings a week, probably because the situation was less convenient than the town centre with further to walk to the shops. Smethurst said later that they moved to Alma Villas because the air was healthier on the hill. The landlady there, Mrs Wheatley, recalled that by the time Isabella arrived in a cab she was so weak that she could hardly walk, and did not leave the house the entire time she was there. Dr Julius continued to attend her most days, but was starting to wonder why his medicines were having no effect on the patient who was becoming weaker. He asked his partner Mr Bird to examine Isabella. Mr Bird had had considerable experience dealing with dysentery in the Crimea. He carried on with the hydrogen cyanide mixture, agreeing with Smethurst that the enemas of laudanum which he had been giving Isabella should also continue. He also recommended enemas of beef tea and the use of ice to cool the liquids Isabella was drinking. None of the medicines seemed to have any effect. After consultation with Smethurst, he prescribed lead acetate with opium. They decided that the opium was having 'too much effect on the patient' and used instead pills of silver nitrate which caused 'violent burning' and increased the diarrhoea.

On 18th April, Smethurst wrote to Isabella's sister Louisa, who now lived at Maida Hill near Ladbroke Grove, asking her to visit them in Richmond as Isabella was very ill. He told her to ask for 'Dr and Mrs Smethurst', cautioning her to relate the contents of the letter to no-one. She arrived on the 19th and spent some hours with her sister before leaving. While she was there Isabella was sick twice, once after being given some milk to drink. There was some discussion about the possibility of consulting an uncle of theirs, Mr Lane, who was a surgeon at St George's Hospital. Isabella said she preferred not to involve him. The next day Louisa wrote to her sister commenting on her 'tender and kind nurse' (Smethurst) and his 'commendable patience...and...amiability of disposition'. On the 21st Smethurst replied, saying that Isabella had passed a very bad night with 'vomiting and purging...at a fearful rate'. Louisa made her a jelly which she despatched to Richmond via the omnibus. She also wrote saying that she would visit again the following weekend. Smethurst replied on 23rd saying that she should delay her visit as Isabella was very weak and her doctors had '... prohibited everything of a nature that might try her very weak powers...' He wrote again on 27th April saying that Isabella had eaten some of the jelly, managing to keep some of it down. He also mentioned that he 'insisted' on having a consultation with Dr Robert Bentley Todd of King's College Hospital, one of the most celebrated physicians of the day. In fact, it seems that Dr Julius had suggested Dr Todd.

Dr Todd, who was a very busy man, arrived around 10 o'clock at night on Thursday 28th April, accompanied by Dr Julius who had met him at the station and briefed him on Isabella's symptoms and the treatments used. Dr Todd examined Isabella by candlelight in the presence of Dr

Julius and Smethurst, and commented on the rigidity of her abdominal muscles. He prescribed pills of copper sulphate and opium. According to Smethurst later, the pills thus prescribed produced a burning sensation all through Isabella's body.

On the 29th April, Smethurst wrote to Louisa again. He told her that Dr Todd 'entertains favourable hopes' of Isabella's improvement. The sickness at least had stopped, although she was still retching and having large numbers of bowel movements and she was too ill for a visit from Louisa. On 30th he wrote once more. Isabella was worse, and he had 'a great dread for the result...' He now asked Louisa to come as soon as she could. He also went to see a solicitor in Richmond, Frederick Senior, and asked him to come to the house on the following day (Sunday) to make Isabella's will. A draft will had been prepared for him by an old friend, James Mellor Smethurst.[3] He was a barrister entirely unrelated to Smethurst – someone he had successfully treated at Moor Park. James Mellor Smethurst had written to say that the will ought to be properly drawn up by a solicitor. Mr Senior said he would come on Sunday if it was absolutely necessary. Smethurst called on him again on the Sunday morning asking him to come immediately and Mr Senior reluctantly agreed to attend. The will left everything except a brooch to Isabella's 'sincere and beloved *friend*, Thomas Smethurst...', and was signed Isabella *Bankes*, 1st May 1859. (Author's italics). It was witnessed by Mr Senior and Susannah Wheatley, the landlady's daughter.

Meanwhile, on 30th April, Dr Julius had obtained a sample of one of Isabella's evacuations from Smethurst, ostensibly to examine it for evidence of ulceration of the bowels. Mr Bird had obtained another sample. They were sealed in two bottles and sent to Dr Thomas Buzzard in London. Dr Buzzard was a friend of Mr Bird; they had practised medicine together in

---

3   In fact, the draft will was in Thomas Smethurst's handwriting. James Mellor Smethurst had just modified it.

the Crimea. On Sunday 1st May, Dr Buzzard took the samples to Dr Alfred Taylor, a professor of chemistry at Guy's Hospital. Dr Taylor made an initial examination and thought he could detect metal, but it being Sunday, he was reluctant to proceed without a magistrate's order. In the evening, Dr Buzzard brought him an authority from Edward Penrhyn, the chairman of the Surrey Magistrates, to finish the analysis. This he duly completed by the Monday morning, 2nd May, concluding that arsenic was definitely present in one of the samples tested. He immediately wrote to Dr Julius telling him of the result and commented that considering Isabella's symptoms, he was of the opinion that she was being slowly poisoned with arsenic and recommended immediate use of magnesium hydrate, the antidote for that poison. He advised that her life depended upon her being immediately placed 'under the care of some trustworthy person...' who should, henceforth, administer all of her food and medicines. Dr Julius then went to see Edward Penrhyn.

Louisa had arrived at Richmond at around 2 o'clock the previous day. She brought some soup with her that Smethurst diluted with warm water. Smethurst gave it to Isabella but she brought it up immediately. He advised Louisa not to stay in the room as Isabella was so ill. Louisa wanted to stay all night with her sister, but Smethurst said it would be better if she didn't and she took lodgings nearby. She came back on Monday morning around half past nine. Smethurst and Dr Julius were in conference about another medicine. After Dr Julius had left, Smethurst sent Louisa to London to have a prescription made up. She was away about three hours. When she returned, Smethurst told her that Isabella was too ill to see her.

Around five o'clock in the evening, Inspector Robert McIntyre of the Richmond Police arrived accompanied by constable John Jukes. Inspector McIntyre lived a few doors away from the Smethursts, at No 7 Alma Villas, but this was no social call. He had a warrant for the arrest of Thomas

Smethurst. Leaving Constable Jukes at the house, Inspector McIntyre took Smethurst to appear before Mr Penrhyn, the magistrate who had authorized the analysis of Isabella's stools. Shortly afterwards Dr Julius' assistant, Mr Caudle, arrived at Alma Villas with a nurse, Jemima Chetwood, who was to look after Isabella from now on.

No doubt Mr Penrhyn called upon Smethurst to account for the arsenic found in the stools of his wife. Exactly what was said has not, unfortunately, been recorded. However Smethurst convinced the magistrate that his wife was dying – at this point, no-one else was aware that they were living bigamously – and that he should be with her. Since there was now a constable at the house, all Smethurst's medicines had been impounded by Inspector McIntyre and there was a nurse to look after Isabella, Mr Penrhyn concluded that even if he had been poisoning her, Smethurst could not now continue to do so. He was released on his own recognizance. When he arrived back at Alma Villas at around 9 o'clock in the evening, he told Louisa in a very excited state that Dr Julius had charged him with poisoning her sister, but that it was he, Dr Julius, who was killing her.

Louisa Bankes and Jemima Chetwood stayed with Isabella all night and through to the next day, Tuesday 3rd May. Isabella took some arrowroot, tea and brandy during the night without retching, but she sank steadily, and at five past eleven in the morning she died. Inspector McIntyre immediately rearrested Smethurst on a charge of murder.

Gathering the Evidence

The coroner for Surrey, Mr William Carter, ordered a post-mortem on Isabella's body, and Dr Julius instructed Mr Richard Barwell, FRCS, Assistant Surgeon and Lecturer at Charing Cross Hospital, and Mr Palmer, a surgeon from Mortlake, to conduct the examination. This was done at 9:30 am on Wednesday 4th May, 22 hours after Isabella's death, in the presence of Dr Julius who wrote down the notes dictated by Mr Barwell. The liver, stomach, spleen, intestines, uterus 'and appendages' were removed and sealed in a jar which was delivered as evidence to Inspector McIntyre. Examination of the uterus revealed the presence of a foetus, of age between five and seven weeks.

That afternoon, Smethurst was called to appear before the Surrey magistrates. Already, barely 24 hours since Isabella's death, word had got around Richmond and the case was causing 'considerable excitement'. Smethurst was described variously as 'gentlemanly-looking' and 'rather stout, [with a] swarthy complexion [and] dark moustaches'. The press reports stated that he was 'charged with causing the death of a woman with whom he was living...', and that 'He is a married man, but has parted from his wife...', so the pretence of him and Isabella being married was already out in the open. However, at this stage the only evidence against him, apart from the suspicions of Dr Julius and Mr Bird, was the small amount of arsenic found by Dr Taylor in one sample of Isabella's stools. Smethurst was remanded in custody to allow Dr Taylor time to 'examine the contents of the stomach', and was sent to the Surrey County Gaol at Horsemonger Lane. The magistrates' hearing was due to be resumed on Saturday 7th May, but was adjourned since Taylor had not yet completed his analyses, disappointing the hundreds of people who had assembled to try and get into the hearing. However the Monday newspapers, in the absence of court proceedings to report, took the opportunity to summarize the facts of the case as known, reporting with some relish the fact that Smethurst and Isabella had been living together unmarried, and publishing the text of Dr Taylor's letter to Dr Julius after he had discovered arsenic in Isabella's stool. The *Daily Chronicle* reported that interest in the case was such that tickets for the next court session were being applied for in Richmond.

On Wednesday 11th May, the case was reconvened before Edward Penrhyn and a bench of seven other magistrates. It was to be a heavyweight session, with Serjeant-at-Law William Ballantine prosecuting and Mr Hardinge Giffard defending. Ballantine opened for the prosecution. Since the last hearing, he said, 'circumstances had transpired which gave a very different aspect to the whole affair...' Consequently he decided to ignore previous depositions and start the case again from the beginning. He would charge the prisoner with the wilful murder of a very respectable and financially independent lady.

Serjeant Ballantine then summarized the facts of the case. Smethurst had been living at Rifle Terrace with a lady much older than himself, 'whom he called his wife'. He met the deceased there and shortly afterwards they left together, married, and went to live in Richmond, where she started to suffer from sickness and diarrhoea. Two local doctors, Dr Julius and Mr Bird, failed to cure her, and eventually called in the 'highest medical assistance in the kingdom', Dr Todd. He too could not account for the symptoms. However, 'secretions' from the deceased were found to contain arsenic. Since none was present in any of the medicines prescribed by Dr Julius and Mr Bird, and Smethurst had the 'entire management and control of the sickroom', if there was poison administered, it must have been by the prisoner. Following the post-mortem, it could now be proved that the deceased had had poison administered to her rendering death, 'slow, though perfectly certain'. Regarding motive, the deceased was possessed of around £1,700 and had made her will, drafted by Smethurst, only two days before she died. The will left virtually everything to him. Furthermore a letter had been found on the prisoner, ready to post, when he was arrested. It was addressed to his first wife Mary and was read out in court:

Monday, May 2, 1859

My dear Mary, I have not been able to leave town, as I expected, in consequence of my medical aid being required in a case of illness. I shall, however, see you as soon as possible. Should anything unforeseen prevent my leaving for town before the 11th I will send you a check for Smith's money and extras. I will send you £5. I am quite well, and hope you are the same, and that I shall find you so when I see you, which I trust will not be long...With best love, believe me, yours affectionately,

Thomas Smethurst

Much was to be made of the fact that Smethurst used the phrase 'should anything unforeseen prevent my leaving for town before the 11th...'

Louisa Bankes was called and confirmed that the deceased was her sister Isabella who was 43 and unmarried (she was actually 42). She said that she (Louisa) had been introduced to Dr Smethurst when she visited Isabella at Bayswater, at which time Isabella had been in very good health. She read out the correspondence she had exchanged with Smethurst when he and Isabella were in Richmond. She described visiting her sister there and finding her very ill and much changed from the last time she had seen her. She visited again on Sunday 1ˢᵗ May, and was with her sister when she died on the Tuesday.

Other witnesses confirmed the marriage between Smethurst and Isabella, and their subsequently living together as man and wife. Mr Senior, the Richmond solicitor, confirmed the making of Isabella's will. His evidence added to the public perception of Smethurst as being a scoundrel. He described making the will, almost entirely in Smethurst's favour, just two days before she died, telling the court that Smethurst had not wanted the other doctors present as he and 'Miss Bankes' were not married.

Serjeant Ballantine now told the bench that he had gone as far as he could without the full medical evidence; Dr Taylor had still not finished his analyses and he requested a further adjournment. As Smethurst was being taken down, the police were obliged to suppress an 'expression of feeling' towards him from the residents of Richmond. The next day, Thursday 12ᵗʰ May, Isabella's remains, those that had not been sent to London in jars, were laid to their final rest in Norwood cemetery.

The first full session of the inquest was held on the following day, 13ᵗʰ May. There had been a preliminary hearing, not reported in the press, in which some evidence was given, but in this hearing, following an application made to the Home Secretary, Smethurst himself would be present. Not only that, he would be allowed to question the witnesses personally since he was not otherwise represented. Serjeant Ballantine was also present to 'watch the proceedings on behalf of the friends of the deceased'. The coroner told Smethurst that the purpose of the inquest, unlike the magistrates' hearing, was to establish whether anyone was accountable for the death of the deceased. He was not charged with anything at present.

After the evidence taken at the previous hearing was read, witnesses were called. The first of these was Mrs Wheatley, the landlady at Alma Villas. She described how medicines for Isabella were brought to the house by Dr Julius' boy, and how she prepared Isabella's food which was taken to her in the bedroom. She never saw Isabella eat, other than the first Sunday she was there, when they all had tea downstairs. She said that the Smethursts' bedroom door was generally kept open day and night and that she, and her husband, son and daughter, all had access to it. She also told the hearing that 'discharges from the night commode' were always put out on the landing for her to dispose of; Smethurst never took them down himself. Mrs Wheatley considered Smethurst's conduct always to be gentlemanly and he was always kind to the deceased.

Dr Julius' boy, William Marchant, was called and confirmed that he had delivered the medicines to "Mrs Smethurst". The pill boxes were sealed and the bottles covered and labelled. He had never left the wrong medicine, and had never had to change any. Following a question from Serjeant Ballantine, the coroner stated that it was not for them to 'entertain an assumption of wrong' until the medical testimony had been considered.

Mrs Ann Robertson of Old Palace Terrace, the Smethursts' previous Richmond lodgings, was called. Isabella was quite well when they had arrived. After the illness started, about three weeks before they left, Mrs Robertson had purchased rhubarb and laudanum and she had seen castor oil in a glass in their room. She said that the diarrhoea started first, followed shortly by the vomiting – the results of which were always disposed of either by herself or her daughter. She also noted that Smethurst was very kind and she never heard one word of discord. Serjeant Ballantine now questioned her, attempting to establish what Isabella had eaten and who had prepared and given it to her. After the diarrhoea had started, she had no appetite, and only took a little arrowroot in milk or water or beef tea. Again Ballantine received a mild rebuke from the coroner who commented that once more he was assuming wrongdoing in his questioning. At this point, and following a question from Smethurst, Mrs Robertson confirmed that on several occasions Isabella was left in the charge of herself and her daughter for a whole day when Smethurst was away. During those days, and in Smethurst's absence, the vomiting continued.

After Mrs Wheatley had been recalled and questioned about Isabella's leftover food and what became of it, Louisa Bankes was called and questioned by Smethurst on Isabella's previous state of health. Having started by saying that Isabella had not complained of vomiting or diarrhoea in previous years, she conceded that Isabella had suffered sickness and biliousness for which she was treated by Dr Barker of Notting Hill. She could not ride in a coach without being sick. She had also been treated by Dr Thompson of Eastbourne for an unknown illness. Louisa considered that her sister had a 'fragile constitution' and all the family suffered from bilious attacks. Isabella had vomited in the carriage on the way to Dr Jackson's surgery, and had been treated by Dr Hoffman of Margate, again for an unknown complaint. She said that she was unaware that Isabella suffered from a 'womb complaint', but on being pressed by Smethurst, she admitted that she had 'used a syringe for her sister at her request'. She went on to describe her various visits to Alma Villas. She said that her sister never complained of any pain during her illness.

The coroner now announced that he had received a letter from 'Professor' Taylor saying that he had still not completed analysis of the various samples sent to him. Since he wished to be present at the enquiry during the presentation of the medical evidence, the coroner adjourned the enquiry until 25th May.

The next day, 14th May, *The Lancet* commented on the 'horrible offence' of the alleged poisoning at Richmond. Seeking to distance itself and the medical profession from the affair, it commented that neither "Dr Thomas Smethurst", nor "Mr Thomas Smethurst, Surgeon", appeared in any of the medical directories of England, Ireland and Scotland. However, not long after that, it was discovered that *The Lancet* itself had published a number of letters from Dr Smethurst...

The inquest and magistrates' hearings were being conducted in parallel and inevitably were covering identical ground which would again be analysed in detail in the Old Bailey trial. Detailed reportage of those facts will be deferred until the main trial.

The magistrates' hearing was reconvened a week later on Friday 20th May. Serjeant Ballantine told a 'densely crowded' court that he had medical evidence of 'an extraordinary nature' to present. Dr Taylor had not only completed the analysis of the organs removed post-mortem, but he had also analysed the contents of many bottles and packets of medicine removed from Smethurst when he was first arrested. Furthermore, the evidence to be presented contained 'a development of medical science of a novel description...' The 'development' related to one of the bottles removed from Smethurst, which Dr Taylor found to contain 'chloride of potass'.

At this point it is necessary to introduce some clarification; 'Potass' referred to a compound containing the element *potass*ium. 'Chloride of potass', also known as 'chloride of pota*sh*', chemical formula KCl, was a compound of potassium and chlorine, a chemical known in modern parlance as potassium chloride. In fact, either Ballantine or the press report got it wrong, since it is clear from the context that he meant Chlor*ate* of Potash, potassium chlorate, $KClO_3$. Ballantine went on to say that it was a 'most destructive salt of a highly inflammable nature' used in the manufacture of lucifer matches and percussion caps[1]. The Serjeant produced a bottle originally containing a quinine mixture that had been prescribed by Dr Julius; it now contained a colourless liquid

---

1 Lucifer was the old name for a match.

which on analysis by Dr Taylor produced a 'fearful result'. As well as 'chloride' of potash it had arsenic in it. According to Ballantine:

> ...[The liquid] would be pleasant to the taste, and appear similar to a saline mixture, but the effect would be to lodge the arsenic most certainly and fatally upon the coats of the stomach, and the poison would the more quickly become introduced into the system.[2]

He went on to say that Dr Taylor had examined the organs removed from Isabella Bankes but found no arsenic 'nor did he expect to find any...' after finding the mixture of arsenic and 'chloride' of potash. It would be Dr Taylor's opinion that the effect of this mixture on the system would produce 'sickness, irritation, inflammation and ultimate mortification and death'.

Dr Julius was called. He described his puzzlement as to the 'obstinacy' of Isabella's disease considering the medicines he prescribed, and called in his assistant, Mr Bird, to view the patient. Eventually Dr Todd was called and he prescribed further medicines at which point the 'symptoms became exaggerated'. Evacuations were procured which were analysed by Dr Taylor, the result of which was that Dr Smethurst was apprehended.

In response to questions from Serjeant Ballantine, Julius said that Isabella had told him that she was 'always in good health...' and habitually walked seven or eight miles a day. Initially he thought her condition was bilious diarrhoea but his remedies failed to alleviate the condition; she was intensely thirsty. As her condition worsened, he found blood in her motions. Laudanum was administered to try and control the diarrhoea. Dr Todd was called in. He considered that Isabella was dying from irritation of the bowels. He prescribed pills of opium and copper sulphate, but according to Smethurst

---

2   Saline mixture – lightly salted water.

these caused an intense burning in the throat accompanied by vomiting and 'fifteen motions...' Dr Julius suspected metallic poisoning. The patient died on the Tuesday morning from exhaustion.

Dr Julius' partner, Mr Bird, was called next. He had had considerable experience of the treatment of bowel complaints. He said that Isabella's condition could not arise from natural causes. He thought that arsenic or antimony would produce the effects seen.

Mr Frederick Caudle was called. He was a medical student and assistant to Dr Julius and Mr Bird. He confirmed that the medicines had been made up exactly as prescribed, but none of them contained arsenic, antimony or chlorate of potash. He confirmed that the bottle now containing chlorate of potash was one that he had supplied containing quinine and ether.

Thomas Buzzard, a surgeon of 41 Marlborough Street London, confirmed that he had taken the two bottles containing Isabella's stools to Dr Taylor for analysis.

Now it was the turn of Serjeant Ballantine's star witness, Dr Alfred Taylor. Alfred Swaine Taylor was one of the most experienced 'medical jurists' and toxicologists in the country. He was a Professor of Chemistry at Guy's Hospital, Fellow of the Royal College of Surgeons and Fellow of the Royal Society. Born in 1806, he was apprenticed at the age of sixteen to a medical man, and became a Licentiate of the Society of Apothecaries in 1828. He was a student of Sir Astley Cooper at Guy's Hospital, and in 1831 he was appointed to the new lectureship in Medical Jurisprudence at Guy's. He produced his first book *Elements of Medical Jurisprudence* in 1836, but it was his third publication, *On Poisons in relation to Medical Jurisprudence and Medicine*, 1848, that was relevant to the Smethurst case. In the book Taylor described his preferred method for detecting arsenic post-mortem. There were several methods available at the time, and practitioners disputed the relative merits of each. Taylor favoured the so-called Reinsch test. In 1841 Hugo

Reinsch had described a rapid and relatively simple procedure for detecting arsenic in organic matter. The material under test was first boiled with water and hydrochloric acid after which a copper foil was introduced into the solution. Any arsenic present would be deposited as a metallic film on the copper. Taylor claimed, in his 1848 book, that a quantity of arsenic equal to one three-thousandth of a grain in thirty drops of water was detectable using this process – one part in 90,000. By substituting copper gauze for foil, the increased surface area of the copper speeded up the process.

Subsequently, Dr Taylor's evidence was to prove highly controversial so it is appropriate to report it in detail. He confirmed that bottle No 2 (the sample of Isabella's stool) contained arsenic, although bottle No 1, sent with it and containing another sample of stool, contained no arsenic. He then analysed some 37 other bottles and packets confiscated from Smethurst by Inspector McIntyre. Of these only two were of interest to the investigation. Bottle No 5 contained 355 grains (about 0.7 ounce) of chlorate of potass (potassium chlorate), a diuretic. He commented:

> If poison were given in a small dose in company with
> it, it would be rapidly carried off in urine...[purifying]
> the system from all noxious matter.

Bottle No 21 was analysed.[3] It was half full of a watery liquid, pleasant to taste. He then tested it for arsenic, however:

3   In the report in *The Times*, Taylor said: 'I found no arsenic or antimony in any one of them except one and the homeopathic medicine. That one was the bottle marked 21'. Inspector McIntyre, in his evidence, had mentioned fining 'homeopathic medicine' among Smethurst's possessions when he was arrested. Clearly then, Smethurst believed in homeopathic medicines in line with his belief in the principles of the Water Cure. He had previously railed against conventional medicines, 'poisonous drugs' he called them, in an editorial in the Water Cure Journal.

> ...every [Reinsch] test I tried was destroyed, and failed to show the existence of arsenic, owing, as I supposed, to there being something in it...very peculiar...that I had never met before...it dissolved the copper gauze as soon as I put it into the liquid...

He determined to 'exhaust this noxious agent' and continued putting copper gauze in until it no longer dissolved:

> I then put in a piece of copper, which at once received the arsenic

He was able to determine that the mixture in bottle No 21 contained between one and two percent potassium chlorate and about two tenths of a percent of arsenic:

> The taste [of the liquid in bottle No 21]...was such that no one would...suspect that the mixture contained arsenic...[it] might be mixed with any kind of food... without the person being aware of it...I believe the effect of giving small doses...would be to produce nausea, vomiting, pain in the bowels with purging... chronic inflammation and ulceration of the bowels and stomach...[leading] to death by exhaustion.

Thus not only had Taylor identified arsenic in an evacuation taken from Isabella while she was still alive, but he had identified the method by which it was administered to her in small, undetectable doses.

Next on the stand was Dr Robert Bentley Todd of King's College Hospital. He described his visit to 'Mrs Smethurst' at 10 o'clock at night:

> I found her apparently suffering from a great deal of pain....looking with a terrified look...as if she were under some strong influence, and...very greatly emaciated.

He then described her other symptoms; however:

> When I retired from the bedroom I told Dr Julius, without hearing his suspicions, that it was a case of arsenical or some mineral poison given in small doses.

It was his view that there was an 'irritant' introduced into Isabella's system that prevented the various remedies tried from curing her diarrhoea. He prescribed copper sulphate and opium, a remedy he had used thousands of times, but he never knew it to cause a burning in the throat. He said that he had not examined the viscera removed post-mortem,

> ...nor do I wish to do so, as I desire not to be brought into this trial any more than I can possibly help.

He did agree though to listen to Mr Barwell (who had performed the post-mortem) read the report of his examination.

Dr Taylor, who was present during the reading, agreed with the findings. He then told the court that he had found:

> ...antimony in one of the kidneys, in the smaller intestines, in some blood taken from the heart and in some blood from the jar in which the viscera was contained.

No antimony was found in the stomach, large intestines, liver or spleen. No arsenic was found in any of the viscera. Nevertheless, he said that he had no doubt that death was caused by inflammation, as a result of antimony and arsenic given, at intervals, in small doses. Dr Odling of Guy's Hospital, who had assisted Dr Taylor, agreed with his opinion.

Serjeant Ballantine said that that closed the case for the prosecution, and he asked that the prisoner be committed for trial. Mr Penrhyn asked Smethurst if he had anything to say; he didn't, and he was committed for trial at the Old Bailey on a charge of wilful murder.

Five days later the inquest resumed. Since Smethurst was now awaiting trial on a charge of murder he could not be present, and given the outcome of the magistrates' hearing, the result of the inquest was a foregone conclusion. Nevertheless, the evidence from Dr Julius, Mr Bird, Dr Todd and Dr Taylor was heard and the inquest was adjourned yet again until 31st May. On that day evidence from Dr Odling and the results of the post-mortem were given, together with testimony from Smethurst's and Isabella's various landladies. The bigamous marriage and Smethurst's previous marriage to Mary Durham was proved, and testimony from the solicitor who had made Isabella's will was given. Louisa Bankes' evidence was also read over again. The coroner, Mr Carter, summed up and the jury, after half-an-hour's absence, solemnly recorded a verdict of wilful murder against Thomas Smethurst.

The following day, 1st June 1859, Smethurst wrote to *The Lancet* from prison outlining Isabella's symptoms in life and the post-mortem findings. He was at pains to present a full report of her condition to his peers in the medical profession; this was done in order to counter the position taken by Dr Julius and others who were convinced that Isabella Bankes had been poisoned. The journal declined to publish the letter at the time, although it was printed in September after the murder trial was concluded. Since the communication was written by Smethurst himself its objectivity could obviously be challenged, although a number of the facts were later confirmed. The post-mortem results were a matter of public record. One thing though is quite clear from the letter, Isabella had a number of pre-existing medical conditions relevant to the case and Smethurst named the doctors who had previously treated her. Louisa Bankes had also named several doctors who had treated her sister in the evidence she gave. If Smethurst's letter had been published at the time, these doctors could have come forward and given evidence in support of Isabella's delicate state of health. When the letter was finally published, the editor of *The Lancet* stated that publication had been delayed until after the trial because it had been sent by Smethurst rather than his 'legal advisors'. For the most part the account is written in sober and objective medical phraseology. However, in referring to the medicines prescribed by Dr Julius and others, Smethurst calls them 'mineral poisons'.[4] It may be that the editor of *The Lancet* was concerned about libel. In other respects the letter is interesting in that it represents Smethurst's evidence on his own behalf which could not be heard in court; the rules of evidence at the time forbade the defendant from giving testimony. It is a moot point as to whether the letter could have influenced the court proceedings had it been published at the time it was written. The letter is reproduced in Appendix 3.

The various hearings of the inquest and magistrates' court had been copiously reported in the newspapers. Some of the witnesses' names were incorrectly given and the press had difficulty with the names of the chemicals, nevertheless, what emerged was a perfect storm of evidence against Smethurst. He had deserted his wife of thirty years and bigamously married a younger woman while still on affectionate terms with his proper wife. He had caused his bigamous wife to make a will on her death-bed almost entirely in his favour, while trying to misrepresent to one of the witnesses the nature of the document she was signing, the press reports adding that Isabella had a fortune of £1,700 or £1,800. He had impregnated his new wife while slowly dosing her with either arsenic or antimony or both to induce her death. As proof of the latter, arsenic was found in her stools, with antimony in some of her viscera, and arsenic was found in one of Smethurst's bottles. Finding an unbiased jury for his forthcoming trial was likely to be difficult.

---

4 He had used similar terms to describe conventional medicines in an editorial in the *Water Cure Journal*.

Thomas Smethurst was to be tried for murder and the outcome could well be his death, but that was not the only thing on his mind. Under the laws of England a felon convicted of murder forfeited his property to the Crown.[5] Smethurst was worth around £3,500 in cash and property at the time and if he were to be convicted, whether hanged or not, all of it would be confiscated by the State. If that were to happen, his wife Mary and his disabled brother William would be deprived of the financial support his assets would provide. In such a situation it was not against the law to transfer one's possessions to someone else before the trial, usually a member of the family or trusted friend. If the defendant were then found guilty, the goods would not be forfeit. However the transfer, in order to be legal, had to be for a 'valid consideration' – a payment of some sort, and that was the catch; the consideration, if it had value, would itself be subject to confiscation. One way of avoiding this difficulty was to effect the transfer to settle an outstanding 'debt', and no doubt clever and enterprising lawyers had worked out other ways of protecting their clients' assets. Smethurst may have been so advised, because on 13th June 1859, two days before his trial started, he transferred all of his money and land to his brother James, *in trust for his disabled brother William*. In this way he seems to have avoided having to receive a consideration. It must be said that the legal language of the transaction is opaque (and this writer may have misunderstood what was done). What was not in doubt though was that Thomas Smethurst's assets *were* transferred to his brother James, and the transfer was legal, as was clear from some subsequent Home Office correspondence.

Two days later, on 15th June, Smethurst was placed at the bar at the Old Court of the Old Bailey, before Judges Mr Justice

---

5   This law dated from the 12th Century. According to Kesselring, the original
     law applied to 'Land, Goods and Chattels'. From 1814, only those convicted
     of murder or treason forfeited land. The confiscation of goods and chattels
     from convicted felons continued until 1870 when the law was repealed.

Crompton and Baron Bramwell. But rather than present the case for the prosecution, Serjeant Ballantine applied to the court to postpone the trial until the next session, on the grounds that the evidence was of great length and more time was needed to prepare. Mr Giffard, who was appearing for Smethurst, pointed out that a very full investigation had already taken place, both before magistrates and the coroner, and Serjeant Ballantine had been present at these. Three weeks had elapsed since Smethurst's committal, and Mr Giffard was anxious that the trial should take place without delay. Justice Crompton requested that Serjeant Ballantine draw up an affidavit setting out the precise reasons for the delay, then the proceedings were postponed and Smethurst was returned to Newgate.

The following day he was again placed at the bar, and pleaded not guilty both to the indictment from the magistrates' court and the verdict of the coroner's court. Serjeant Ballantine repeated the application he had made the previous day to delay the trial, referring to his affidavit. Serjeant Parry, appearing for Smethurst, opposed the delay. He pointed out that there had been ample time to prepare the defence since the committal on 20th May.

Ballantine urged a delay of two weeks saying that such a delay could not prejudice the prisoner, and that if the trial took place immediately there might be a 'failure of justice'. After consultation the judges agreed that the trial would be postponed until the next session in July. Serjeant Ballantine undertook to acquaint the prisoner and his team with full details of the evidence to be presented against him.

It might be wondered, given the wealth of evidence presented against Smethurst both at the magistrates' hearing and the inquest, why Serjeant Ballantine was requesting a further two weeks on top of the three he had already had to prepare his case. What he did not tell the court was that Dr Taylor had discovered a fatal flaw in the chemical analysis that he had used to detect arsenic. Serjeant Ballantine's prosecution case, once apparently unassailable, was in serious danger of unravelling. He needed the extra time to assemble a panel of expert scientific and medical witnesses prepared to give testimony on that part of the evidence that was still valid. In the event Serjeant Parry, after having been apprised of what had happened, started to assemble *his* panel of expert witnesses for the defence case...

The trial started three weeks later, on Thursday, 7th July 1859. The press reports stated that the 'avenues of the court were filled at an early hour by persons...anxious to obtain admission'. The bench was also fairly crowded since the Lord Mayor and his aldermen (there were four aldermen present) had the right to sit with the judge. They took little part in the formal legal proceedings.[6] The judge was Sir Frederick Pollock, the Lord Chief Baron. He was 76 years old and was described as 'indefatigable if sometimes sleepy', one of his shortcomings being a 'tendency to make his mind up early in a case...' He had been Attorney General twice in Sir Robert Peel's administrations; he was a very senior trial judge, although his main experience was in civil rather than criminal law. He had also been a Fellow of the Royal Society since 1816 and had contributed papers to it on mathematics.[7]

The clerk of the court read out the indictment from the magistrates' court as well as the coroner's inquisition, to which Smethurst pleaded 'Not Guilty'. Smethurst's counsel was Serjeant John Humffreys Parry, assisted by Mr Hardinge Giffard. Serjeant Parry objected to a number of the jury, but when he was satisfied and the trial was about to start, Smethurst said that he wished to address the court. Although

---

6   Exactly what part, if any, aldermen took in the trial is unclear. The Act of Parliament which constituted the Old Bailey required two 'commissioners' to be present on the bench, although it was the judge who tried the case. Aldermen, who were magistrates, performed the role of commissioners.

7   ODNB

the rules forbade the defendant from giving evidence, the judge allowed him to speak. Smethurst said he understood the judge to be a personal friend of Dr Taylor, 'an important witness for the prosecution' (the key witness as it was to turn out), and he objected 'upon that ground' being tried by him. The problem with Dr Taylor's analyses had been imparted to the defence, and Smethurst wished to make sure that whatever evidence was presented, there would be no bias on the part of the judge. Serjeant Parry, as Smethurst's chief counsel, should have raised the objection; perhaps he felt that etiquette (or self-preservation) prevented him from doing so. The judge acknowledged that he was acquainted with Dr Taylor (both were fellows of the Royal Society), but said that probably so were all of the judges on the bench.[8] Sir Frederick added that he had not seen Dr Taylor 'for a considerable time' until a few days previously at a party at his (the judge's) house. Mr Justice Wightman was consulted for his view and was in agreement that the trial should proceed with Sir Frederick Pollock as judge when another objection was raised. This time it was one of the jurymen who said firstly that he was strongly prejudiced against the prisoner, and asked to be excused because of his bias. When this was refused, he said that 'it would cause [him] great inconvenience in his business...' to continue. This request was also refused and at last Serjeant Ballantine was able to make his opening statement for the prosecution.

William Ballantine had been admitted to Inner Temple in 1829, called to the bar in 1834 and appointed Serjeant-at-Law in 1856.[9] He was thus a very experienced barrister and used his considerable rhetorical skill in his address to the jury:[10]

---

8   Dr Taylor was a prolific expert medical witness, being consulted in 20 to 25 cases a year. He was likely to have appeared in front of practically every sitting judge between 1831 and 1859.

9   ODNB

10   Ballantine's words have been have been changed into the first person.

It is my duty to lay before you the evidence in this painful enquiry and I am sure you will give your most serious attention to it...I should feel my task a very heavy one if I did not know that I will have your full attention and impartial consideration directed to this important case; but, as I am sure that you will give all your consideration to the evidence to be brought forward, I feel my duties will be comparatively light...

And so on. He outlined the facts of the case, saying that the prisoner was a 'man of information and learning' who had taken every means to 'shroud the whole affair in the deepest mystery'. Since every one of the previous court hearings had been reported in the newspapers in the minutest detail, there can have been very few people in court who were unaware of the facts. Nevertheless Serjeant Ballantine went over all of the evidence, even reading out the various letters Smethurst had sent to Louisa Bankes. He then handed over to Mr Bodkin to examine the first witness, Mary Smith, the landlady at 4 Rifle Terrace, where Isabella Bankes had met the Smethursts.

Mrs Smith described the 'improper familiarity' between Smethurst and Isabella Bankes, and related how Isabella had told Smethurst in her presence that she had been given notice to leave and why. Isabella had left on 29th November, 1858, followed by Smethurst on 12th December, although he did come back to visit his wife once or twice afterwards. Mrs Smith observed that Isabella 'never had good health' and appeared to be delicate, constantly complaining of a bad appetite. She said she felt nausea when attempting to eat and left the table more than once through sickness. She ate very little. On the question of Smethurst's marriage status, everyone in the house, including Isabella Bankes, knew that 'Mr and Mrs Smethurst' were man and wife. Mrs Smith also confirmed that after he had left, the prisoner arranged to pay her money for his wife's lodging.

Mrs Marian Grabouska, the landlady at 37 Kildare Terrace, Bayswater, was called next. She was the landlady at the lodging house where Isabella Bankes resided after she left Rifle Terrace. Mrs Grabouska confirmed that Isabella had arrived on 29th November and departed on 9th December. Although Isabella never complained to her of any illness, she 'appeared to be very delicate...'

The parish clerk of Battersea now produced the marriage register containing the entry of 'a marriage between the prisoner and a person named Isabella Bankes on 9th December'. He confirmed that the prisoner was the person who was married and Louisa Bankes identified her sister's signature in the register.

Mrs Ann Robertson was called next; she was the landlady at 27 Old Palace Terrace, Richmond. She confirmed that the prisoner and 'Mrs Smethurst' hired an apartment at her house on 4th February 1859. Mrs Smethurst appeared to be quite well; she walked for three hours every day and took her meals regularly. Her illness came on about three weeks before they left and Mrs Robertson recommended that they call in Dr Julius to see her. He prescribed medicine but Isabella did not improve; she was living on 'arrowroot and slops'. Mrs Robertson said that Dr Smethurst was particularly kind to Isabella. She also remembered that while they were there, Smethurst had had a severe attack of toothache and had gone to London to see a dentist. They left her house on 15th April.

Mrs Susannah Wheatley was called; she let a bedroom and sitting room at 10 Alma Villas, Richmond, to the Smethursts who arrived by cab on 15th April from Mrs Robertson's establishment. Isabella appeared to be very ill and went to bed almost immediately. She only came down a few times while she was there and ate nothing but arrowroot, tapioca and rice which Mrs Wheatley prepared. Smethurst was kind and affectionate to Isabella. Mrs Wheatley had suggested to Smethurst that he should employ a nurse, but he replied that he could not afford it. Mrs Wheatley recalled that on one occasion Smethurst had asked her to preserve a 'portion of the evacuation' for Dr Julius to see. In the event he did not see it because he was late arriving and Smethurst told her to throw it away. This had happened on 2nd May by which time Dr Julius had already contrived to get the sample that was being analysed by Dr Taylor...

Louisa Bankes was now called. She repeated her evidence given at both the magistrates' hearing and the inquest. Under cross-examination she conceded that Isabella had been seen by a number of doctors. She said:

> ...a good many members of my family have suffered from repeated bilious attacks.

Next on the stand was Mr Senior, the solicitor who had drawn up Isabella's will. He said that Smethurst had called on him on the Sunday morning, 1st May, asking him to come and make the will as Isabella had had a very bad night. Mr Senior requested that a doctor be present as she was so ill, but Smethurst had told him that she was only suffering from diarrhoea and was 'quite right in her mind'. Smethurst also told him that although they were living together they were not man and wife, and this was another reason why he did not want a medical man to be present. He said that Smethurst proposed to misrepresent the will to the landlady's daughter, who was to witness it, as 'some Chancery paper'. Mr Senior said that that would not do; she had to be informed that it was a will. The will was duly made and witnessed by Mr Senior and Miss Wheatley, the deceased describing herself as a 'spinster' and the prisoner as her 'sincere and beloved friend'.

Louisa was briefly recalled and stated that nothing had been said to her about her sister making a will.

Mr Tarte was then called; he was the father of Isabella's brother's first wife, now deceased. Isabella's £1,740 was lent to him on mortgage. His evidence was that he had known Isabella for twenty-five years and her health was 'generally very good'.

It was now the turn of Dr Julius who had treated Isabella for a month before she died. Much of his evidence has already been covered in the magistrates' and inquest hearings but some new facts emerged. When Smethurst had suggested medicine for Isabella containing prussic acid (cyanide), Dr Julius had objected on the grounds of safety. Smethurst had replied that he was conversant with its use and used to test it by putting the preparation on breadcrumbs which he threw out for the sparrows to eat... The medicine was duly prescribed to Isabella, but Smethurst complained to Dr Julius that it had affected Isabella very painfully, and questioned whether a mistake in the preparation had been made.

Dr Julius described how the two samples of Isabella's evacuations sent to Dr Taylor for analysis had been obtained on separate occasions by himself and Mr Bird. Following the finding of arsenic he (Dr Julius) had communicated the information to the magistrate, Mr Penrhyn. Dr Julius also stated that from what Smethurst had told him, Isabella could not have been pregnant. However if he had known her to be pregnant, it would not have altered the medicines he prescribed. He said that in his opinion the symptoms shown by the deceased could be explained by the administering of small amounts of an irritant poison like arsenic or antimony. His evidence ended day one of the trial, and the jury were taken to the 'London Coffee House' in the charge of officers of the court.

The court reconvened at 10 o'clock the next day, Friday 8th July, the jury having returned from the coffee house after an 'airing in Temple Gardens'. First on the stand was Mr Easton, the clerk of St Mary's Church, Kennington. He showed the entry of the marriage between Thomas Smethurst and Mary Durham in 1828. A clerk at Smethurst's bank identified the signature on the register as that of the prisoner.

Mr Bird, Dr Julius' partner, was called next. He agreed with his partner that Isabella's symptoms could be accounted for by small doses of arsenic or antimony, and that neither arsenic nor antimony was present in any of the medicines prescribed to her. He had no previous experience of arsenic or antimony poisoning and he went on to say:

> I had not formed any decided opinion as to the nature of the case until Dr Julius spoke to me on the subject...

At this point a juryman was taken ill and removed from the court. He was seen by Mr Gibson, the surgeon of Newgate (the prison was next door to the Old Bailey), and also by Drs Copland and Todd who were in court. Dr Todd then told the judge that the juryman, Thomas Instone, was seriously ill (he died a few months later). The judge had a conference with Serjeants Ballantine and Parry. Then, after Dr Todd and Mr Gibson had sworn that not only would it be dangerous to the life of the juryman for him to continue, but that he would be unlikely to recover in the short term, the judge discharged the other eleven members of the jury and the trial was abandoned. It would be a brand new trial that would commence at the next session. Smethurst was most unhappy with this, but given the circumstances he had no alternative other than to acquiesce and return to Newgate and wait.

Capital Charge

Thomas Smethurst had to cool his heels for several weeks in Newgate, but finally, at 11 o'clock on Monday 15th August, 1859, his trial started for the second time. And somehow, even though it was not his turn, the Lord Chief Baron, Sir Frederick Pollock, was again the trial judge. Once more the bench as well as the court was crowded, with the Lord Mayor and seven Aldermen or Sheriffs, as well as Sir John Lawrence (recently returned Chief Commissioner for the Punjab during the Indian Mutiny) and General Sir George Pollock (Sir Frederick's brother) attending. Sir George Pollock was a career soldier, a commandant of the Royal Horse Artillery.

Smethurst was dressed in a morning suit and following the reading of the indictment he pleaded 'Not Guilty' in a firm voice. He then proceeded to object, via Serjeant Parry, to a number of the jury as they were called. A jury satisfactory to all was finally agreed and once more Serjeant Ballantine prepared to make his opening address. He was accompanied on the prosecution bench, as before, by Mr Bodkin, Mr Clerk and Mr Merewether. Serjeant Parry had just one deputy to assist him, Mr Giffard. Once more, Ballantine went over the facts of the case and the prosecution evidence. Since it had been repeated several times now, even some of the newspapers declined to print the details.

Serjeant Ballantine's first witness was Mrs Mary Smith, the landlady at Rifle Terrace. Mrs Smith repeated her view of Isabella's fragile state of health; she had been sick twice while in the house, and had told Mrs Smith that she could never ride in a carriage or omnibus without being sick. Following a question from the judge, Mrs Smith confirmed that no-one in the house or at the dinner table could doubt that Dr and Mrs Smethurst were man and wife.

Mrs Marian Grabouska, who was Isabella's landlady at Kildare Terrace (after she left the Smiths' establishment), said that Isabella appeared to her to be very fragile; she had said that she needed a change of air and was leaving for Clifton.

Next were the parish clerks of Kennington and Battersea who verified Smethurst's two marriages, first to Mary Durham, then to Isabella Bankes; Mr McCrosty, a clerk from the London and Westminster Bank, identified the signature on the parish registers as that of the prisoner. The judge asked Serjeant Ballantine whether he intended to prove

> that Mary Durham was the old lady...known as Mrs Smethurst.

Serjeant Ballantine:

> I do not propose to carry the matter further. I do not think we shall be able to identify her.

The parish clerk from Kennington stated that there was nothing in the register about the age of the signatories.

Ann Robertson, the Smethurst's first landlady in Richmond, was called next. Her testimony was as before, although a few new points emerged. After Isabella fell sick, and on the occasions when Smethurst went up to London, Isabella always had a basin by her side. When Mrs Robertson went up to see how she was, there was always vomit of a blue-green colour in the basin. Mrs Smethurst would take arrowroot, beef tea and food made with cornflour. Mrs Robertson also had to clear away the 'evacuations' which she described as just like coloured water. She also reported hearing the deceased retching in the mornings. Mrs Robertson described how she, or her daughter, removed the remains of Isabella's meals from the room as well as the vomit and evacuations. Mrs Robertson's daughter, Elizabeth, confirmed her mother's evidence and commented that Smethurst

> appeared to be particularly kind and attentive [to Isabella] during her illness.

She added that Isabella was sick whether Smethurst was away in London or not.

Susannah Wheatley, the landlady of Alma Villas, now gave evidence. The Smethursts had come to her house after leaving Mrs Robertson's, and it was at her house that Isabella had died. Mrs Wheatley was examined at length on the question of who prepared Isabella's food, what she ate, who gave it to her, and who removed the leftovers and slops.[1] Mrs Wheatley prepared the food and took it either to their dining room, or to the Smethursts' bedroom door. In each case, Smethurst then took the food to Isabella. Leftovers were put on a box in the passageway. When there were evacuations to dispose of Smethurst left them on the landing. There were three 'chambers' and a 'pan' in their room, as well as two basins.[2] The court was quite exercised about what was in what; Mr Clerk asked:

> When the pan or the chamber were placed outside on the landing, do you recall whether different things were poured into the pan together, or whether you had the evacuation there by itself?

Mrs Wheatley:

> It appeared altogether, sometimes quite full...

---

1 Here, 'slops' appeared to mean evacuations and vomit.
2 From the context this probably refers to 'chamber' pots and a bed 'pan'.

The judge wanted still further clarification:

> That is, all the slops of every kind appeared to be together in the same vessel?

Mrs Wheatley confirmed that was the case repeating: 'Yes; and sometimes that was full.' She added later that there was never any concealment of the evacuations.

Mr Clerk now asked her whether she had recommended a nurse for Mrs Smethurst. She replied that Smethurst had said that he could not afford it and declined Mrs Wheatley's offer to sit up with his wife at night, saying that she had her work to do. She remembered Dr Julius coming to the house when Smethurst was away, and taking a motion away with him. There was a cupboard on the landing that Mrs Wheatley called an old-fashioned secretary with two keys, one for the drawers and one for the top. Smethurst had both keys and it was kept locked. She did not know what was kept in it; she did not interfere with her lodgers.

She was now asked about the tapioca she made twice a day for Mrs Smethurst. Initially Isabella said how nice it was, but on one occasion she complained about the taste. Smethurst told her that it was the bitterness of the medicines she was taking that had made it taste bad.

Next on the stand was Louisa Bankes, Isabella's sister. Much of her testimony was identical to that given to the magistrates' and inquest hearings. She described visiting her sister in Richmond, and read out the letters she had sent to her and the answers received which were always written by Smethurst. Serjeant Parry asked her whether her father's death was due to diarrhoea. She said:[3]

---

3 Smethurst claimed later that Isabella had thought herself to be suffering from the same complaint that was responsible for the death of her father, hence Serjeant Parry's line of questioning.

> ...he died of a complication of diseases; I never heard
> it called diarrhoea...the climax was purging that could
> not be stopped...

In fact, George Bankes' death certificate stated that he died of typhus.

Parry went on to ask her about a visit to Mr Tarte's, when Isabella was obliged to stay there a whole day 'sick and purged'. She said she did not remember it. She was aware that her sister suffered from some sort of discharge which she treated with 'injections'.

Jemima Chetwood was called. She was the nurse engaged by Mr Caudle, Dr Julius' assistant, to attend Isabella after Smethurst's initial arrest. She arrived on the Monday evening (2nd May) at between 6 and 7 o'clock. She administered some medicine that had been given to her by Mr Caudle, and together with Louisa Bankes gave Isabella some food. Isabella vomited twice on being given the medicine, but managed to keep down some beef tea fortified with brandy. The vomit was placed in a container, sealed and given to the police constable, apparently at the request of Smethurst. Isabella got weaker and weaker and died at five past eleven the following morning.

Mr Frederick Senior, the solicitor who had drawn up Isabella's will, now gave evidence. He repeated the details of how he drew up the will on a Sunday, how Smethurst did not want Isabella's doctors to be present, and had suggested representing to the landlady's daughter that the document was a 'Chancery paper'. He read out the will:

> *This is the last will and testament of me, Isabella*
> *Bankes, now residing at No 10, Alma-villas, Richmond*
> *in the county of Surrey, spinster: I give and bequeath to*
> *my beloved friend, Miss Jenkins, of Walthamstow, Essex,*
> *my brooch set with brilliants and pearls, and containing*
> *the hair of my late father; and as to all my real and*

personal property, estate, and effects whatsoever and [wheresoever], and of what nature or kind soever the same may be, I give, devise, and bequeath the same unto my sincere and beloved friend, Thomas Smethurst, doctor of medicine, now also of No 10, Alma-Villas, Richmond, aforesaid, for his own use absolutely and for ever. And I hereby appoint the said Thomas Smethurst sole executor of this my will; and hereby revoke all former wills or testamentary dispositions at any time heretofore made by me, do declare this only to be my last will and testament. As witness the hand of the said Isabella Bankes, the 1st day of May, 1859.

Signed by the testatrix, Isabella Bankes, and declared as her last will and testament in the presence of us present at the same time, who at her request, in her presence, and in the presence of each other, have hereunto subscribed our names as witnesses—FREDERICK B. SENIOR, Solicitor, Richmond, Surrey; SUSANNAH WHEATLEY, 10, Alma-Villas, Richmond, Surrey.

ISABELLA BANKES.

The draft will given to Mr Senior to copy was produced and shown to have been in Smethurst's handwriting. Serjeant Parry then asked Mr Senior whether Isabella understood what she was doing when she made the will. He said that '...she was perfectly sound as I believe...' He slowly and distinctly read the will over to her; she '...did not make the slightest objection, but nodded assent...' not making the slightest observation on the words: 'Isabella Bankes spinster'. She was not excited or agitated. Mr Senior reported that Smethurst told him that although they were living together as man and wife, they were not married, but that as soon as some Chancery affairs were settled they would leave Richmond, get privately married, and then return to settle in Richmond.

The last witness of the day was William Tarte. He saw Isabella several times a year when she collected the interest on his loan. He had known her for a long time and said she had never complained of sickness or vomiting. The court then adjourned until 9 o'clock the following day.

First on the stand on Tuesday 16th August was Dr Julius. Once more he related how he was first called to Isabella and the events leading up to her death a month later. He was asked whether he had enquired if Isabella was pregnant. He said that Smethurst had told him that 'her usual periods were on her.' From around 8th April, she was getting blood in her stools. By 18th April, after the Smethursts had removed to Alma Villas, Dr Julius said he had formed the opinion that something was being administered to Isabella that was irritating the stomach and bowels. He asked his partner Mr Bird to visit Isabella, not telling him his suspicions, and leaving him to form 'an unbiased opinion'. He next saw Isabella a few days later by which time she was much weaker and looking very ill. He then had a conference with Smethurst about getting a third medical opinion. Since Dr Julius was the senior medical practitioner in Richmond, he proposed a London doctor and Dr Todd visited Isabella on 28th April. Dr Julius said he purposely did not communicate his suspicions to Dr Todd. Todd prescribed pills of copper sulphate and powdered opium which, according to Smethurst, when taken had produced intense burning in the mouth, throat and throughout the bowels and intestines, as well as vomiting and fifteen bloody motions. Following a discussion with Dr Todd, Dr Julius had obtained a sample, previously referred to, of Isabella's evacuations. He then communicated his suspicions to the magistrate. He repeated his view that small 'irritant doses...administered from time to time' would account for Isabella's symptoms.

In response to a question from Serjeant Ballantine, Dr Julius stated that no arsenic, antimony or potassium chlorate had been administered to Isabella as part of his treatments.

He went on to describe some correspondence he had had with Smethurst from prison, where he had been asked to detail the various medicines that had been supplied to Isabella from Dr Julius' practice, and also to declare whether arsenic was kept. He was not asked about antimony. Arsenic was present in Dr Julius' surgery only in *Donovan's* and *Fowler's* solutions. *Donovan's* solution, arsenic triiodide, was used to treat rheumatism, and Serjeant Parry had asked Louisa Bankes whether her sister ever suffered from rheumatism – perhaps prompted by Smethurst seeking to establish alternative means by which Isabella might have had arsenic administered.

Dr Julius was cross-examined by Serjeant Parry. He repeated that he did not communicate his suspicions of poisoning to Mr Bird when he asked him to examine Isabella. He was asked whether he had heard Mr Bird's examination at the previous trial, and emphatically denied that he had heard him say that Dr Julius had mentioned to him his 'unfavourable impression'. He also denied repeating his suspicions to Dr Todd, telling him only of Isabella's symptoms, the medicines prescribed, and her failure to respond positively to those medicines. He said he did not recall Smethurst saying that he would have preferred soothing remedies, '...an occasional emetic with calomel and opium and no irritants', for Isabella if she had been his patient.

Dr Julius was then called upon to comment on the prescription containing prussic acid that Smethurst had suggested. He said that it was used to check vomiting in early pregnancy.[4] Mr Caudle had thought the dose too strong, and had reduced the strength by a third on his own responsibility. Once more Dr Julius was asked about Isabella's pregnancy. He had not known of it until the post-mortem, but even if he had done so, it would not have changed his treatment of Isabella.

---

4   Later on there was much speculation by the judge and others as to whether Smethurst was aware that Isabella was pregnant. No one ever referred to this evidence from Dr Julius that might have pointed to Smethurst suspecting her pregnancy...

He added that the cause of vomiting or retching in the morning by a pregnant woman was likely to be the pregnancy itself.

Responding to further questions from Serjeant Parry, Dr Julius denied knowledge of any instance where a pregnant woman suffering from severe vomiting and diarrhoea had not yielded to treatment. He was unaware of a case, reported by Dr Barker of Bedford, where the life of a woman of between 40 and 45, thus afflicted, was saved only by aborting the foetus. He had heard of cases of vomiting only where the patient's life was only saved by abortion.

Dr Julius was asked about his qualifications. He was a member of the 'Company' of Apothecaries, as well as a Fellow of the Royal College of Surgeons. To Serjeant Parry's surprised amusement, Julius told him that he had had the degree of MD bestowed upon him by the Archbishop of Canterbury.[5] The judge said that the Archbishop of Canterbury could also bestow the degree of MA.

Serjeant Ballantine now resumed his examination. On the question of the burning sensation in Isabella's throat, Dr Julius said that it was not a symptom of pregnancy. The judge asked whether it was caused by the vomiting that is associated with early pregnancy. He said that it was not in his experience. Vomiting was, he said, almost the first symptom of pregnancy but not in combination with diarrhoea. Isabella had suffered from violent retching. He said that in general sickness from pregnancy was rejection of food, 'unaccompanied with any violent exertion', and followed by a good appetite. It was not a difficult symptom to manage. After a few remarks concerning the unusual 'shreddy' appearance of Isabella's stools, he repeated his assertion that 'irritative' substances were being given to Isabella during her illness. In response to a question from the judge, he said that he could account for her symptoms

---

5 Dr Julius father, George Charles Julius, MD, had been a physician to George IV. His connections may have assisted in his son being granted the Archbishop of Canterbury's degree.

in no other way. He had not made a post-mortem examination on anyone who had died of arsenic poisoning.

Dr Julius' partner Mr Bird now took the stand. Samuel Dougan Bird was a registered surgeon, a one time pupil of Dr Todd, who had joined Dr Julius from the Crimea where he had 'many opportunities...of seeing...cases of bowel complaint and dysentery'. He had trained at the Hospital for Consumption at Brompton where he was a clinical assistant. He took his diploma and passed for the College of Surgeons in 1854 after which he went to the Crimea. He said that Dr Julius had not mentioned his suspicions to him when he requested him to see Isabella. As her condition deteriorated, he said that her bowel movements were bloody and shredded. The medicines prescribed did not check the vomiting and diarrhoea; the beef tea enema seemed to increase the diarrhoea and the effervescing mixture and ice failed to check the vomiting. Having discussed various alternatives with Smethurst, Mr Bird prescribed bismuth, lead acetate and opium and silver nitrate. The opium was discontinued after it was found to have 'too much effect on the patient'. The silver nitrate too was discontinued after Smethurst reported that it caused burning in the intestines and the diarrhoea increased and contained more blood. Mr Bird commented:

In my opinion the nitrate of silver was decidedly not calculated to produce the symptoms he described...

Mr Bird was asked for his view on the continuance of the symptoms despite the medication being prescribed, and replied that he thought that some 'irritant was being administered' which counteracted the effects of the medicines. He claimed that his opinion was formed several days after his first visit to Isabella, and that he formed it independently of Dr Julius. He said that Isabella had mentioned more than once, in his and the prisoner's hearing, that she would like the opinion of another medical man. Following Dr Todd's visit and Isabella's bad reaction to the opium and copper sulphate which gave her violent palpitations of the heart, Mr Bird recommended no further medicines should be taken by mouth. Dr Todd had also prescribed an injection (enema) of catechu and starch which should have had an astringent effect, but this also increased irritation to the bowels. Mr Bird said that he recommended the continuation of injections of laudanum with small amounts of brandy by mouth. Isabella's mouth was sore and had apthous spots (mouth ulcers) and she drank large quantities of cold water.

On 30th April, Mr Bird requested a sample of one of Isabella's evacuations which Smethurst provided. This was sealed in a bottle, bottle No 1, and sent with bottle No 2, which contained the evacuation that Dr Julius had obtained, to Mr Buzzard. Mr Bird described a visit to Isabella on the Sunday before her death. She was very weak with a pulse rate of 130 and her tongue was bright red and covered with white fur. He then described a conference between himself, Dr Julius and Mr Buzzard after which he and Dr Julius visited Mr Penhryn and made a statement. When Smethurst was arrested for the first time and then released, Mr Bird returned to the house with him and together they handed the various 'bottles and pill-boxes' to Inspector McIntyre.

Mr Bird was called to the house on 3rd May. He said that Isabella was sinking; there was no vomiting or diarrhoea and she was 'perfectly conscious, though evidently dying'. Although he saw her every few minutes or so on that morning, he was not actually with her when she died. Mr Bodkin asked him:

...to what do you attribute the symptoms that she was labouring under?

Mr Bird:

> I attribute them to some mineral irritant poison, administered in frequent small doses...arsenic would produce those symptoms...antimony would also produce [them]...I was not then aware that she was in a state of incipient pregnancy; that fact would not alter my judgment in the matter in the least...

Being asked about antimony, he said that it would definitely not be a suitable drug to give to Miss Bankes, and as far as he was aware it had not been administered. Having seen many cases of dysentery, he said that Isabella's symptoms were not compatible with such a diagnosis 'or [with] any other natural form of disease'. On being cross-examined by Serjeant Parry, he said that he had never attended a patient dying from slow poisoning by arsenic, nor had he carried out a post-mortem on such a patient.

At this point Serjeant Ballantine successfully objected to Serjeant Parry asking Mr Bird whether it was not until after Dr Julius had suggested slow arsenic poisoning that he had formed the opinion. The judge clarified what he thought had been said:

> What you stated was that you attributed the symptoms you witnessed to some irritant mineral poison, administered in small doses, and that arsenic or antimony would do; for anything you know, perhaps many other things would do as well?

Mr Bird agreed, saying that 'any of the mineral irritant poisons' would produce the same symptoms. Serjeant Parry tried again:

> Then have you never formed an opinion that this lady was the subject of slow arsenical poisoning?

To which Mr Bird replied: 'I have.' The judge intervened again:

> What is your opinion then about her being the subject of arsenical poisoning?

Mr Bird:

> I have formed the opinion that she was the subject of slow arsenical poisoning.

Serjeant Parry:

> Did you ever form that opinion before Dr. Julius suggested it to you?

Mr Bird:

> I did not...he first suggested it to me, and then I agreed with him...other mineral poisons might have caused the same effect...what I am now speaking of is a matter of opinion founded on my experience and reading...

Serjeant Parry had finally received the answer he had been looking for. Mr Bird went on to say that mercury bichloride, known as corrosive sublimate, might also have been used. He went on to detail the various medicines he had prescribed to Isabella.

The judge then asked him whether the symptoms he observed in Isabella differed in any way from those as described by Smethurst:

> Not in the least...the lady told me herself of her symptoms...the account that she gave of herself completely agreed with that Dr. Smethurst told me, and with what I observed...

That completed the examination of Mr Bird. In most respects there was nothing very new, although from the point of view of the defence Serjeant Parry had at least established two important points: Mr Bird only came to the conclusion that arsenic or something similar was being administered *after* Dr Julius spoke to him about it, and he had no experience of anyone dying of arsenic poisoning.

Next on the stand was Mr William Caudle, Dr Julius' assistant and the person responsible for filling out the prescriptions and manufacturing the various medicines. The exact formulations used, and when they were prepared, were listed in great detail. He did say that Smethurst had been present when he prepared the silver nitrate pills and was very particular about their preparation. Asked whether he kept any arsenic or antimony in the surgery, he reported that they had *Donovan's* and *Fowler's* solutions, both containing arsenic, kept separately in a poisons cupboard. Tartarised antimony (tartar emetic) and antimonial wine were kept on a high shelf. He categorically denied that any arsenic, antimony or mercury bichloride had been included in any of the preparations made up for Isabella. Following Isabella's death, he had provided Inspector McIntyre with samples of the bismuth, copper sulphate, silver nitrate and lead acetate that had been used for Isabella's prescriptions.

Dr Julius' son George was called and stated that he had taken the two sealed bottles containing Isabella's evacuations and delivered them to Catherine Murray, Mr Buzzard's servant, who was also called. Two of Dr Julius' servants were called and confirmed safe delivery of the various prescriptions from Dr Julius' surgery to 'Mrs Smethurst'.

Thomas Buzzard was now called, and confirmed that the two bottles had been delivered to Dr Taylor for examination. He also described how he had then visited Richmond and carried the letter from the magistrate back to Dr Taylor instructing him to complete the analysis of the bottles.

Next on the stand was Richard Barwell, Fellow of the Royal College of Surgeons, who described in detail the post-mortem he had carried out on Isabella Bankes. Inflammation appeared to be limited to the intestines with ulceration of the caecum. Having seen a great many bodies, Mr Barwell declared that the symptoms were not consistent with any natural disease with which he was acquainted. He concluded that the symptoms in life, combined with the appearance of the body after death, resulted from the administration of an irritant poison. Unfortunately the graphic description of the post-mortem caused the foreman of the jury to become unwell; a glass of water had been sent for when he was seen to become pale and put his hands to his head. The judge advised:

Let him stand up and have some air...

At which the juryman promptly fainted. Sir Frederick handed down a 'scent' bottle which brought him round such that he could walk out of the court with some assistance, being attended outside by some of the many medical men who were on hand. The judge told Serjeant Ballantine that it was unnecessary to go into so much detail about the post-mortem, particularly as the jury would fail to understand most of it. Serjeant Ballantine promised to avoid the painful details as far as possible. After a few minutes, the foreman recovered and was able to take his seat.

There followed questioning both from Ballantine and Parry concerning the appearance of the liver. Mr Barwell initially considered that having a fatty appearance, it might be in the first stage of cirrhosis but upon further examination he decided that it was normal. The judge asked him whether it was connected in any way with the diarrhoea and vomiting, to which he said that it was not.

Dr Samuel Wilks, Fellow of the Royal College of Surgeons was called. He had accompanied Dr Taylor in the examination of the intestines that took place at Guy's Hospital and concurred with the findings of Mr Barwell who performed the post-mortem examination. Dr Wilks said that he thought death was due to an irritant; he was unfamiliar with any natural disease that would account for the symptoms in life and appearance post-mortem. Asked whether severe dysentery would have produced the inflammation described he said he thought so, but that acute dysentery was a rare disease in Britain. He was then asked whether any other disease could account for Isabella's symptoms and stated that there was no other natural form of disease that could account for them. Dr Wilks added that acute dysentery, sometimes called Eastern dysentery was considered to arise from a specific poison acting on the system:

> ...I have seen...two cases in which we have not been able to arrive at any conclusion as to the cause, and we have been obliged to call them by that name...in those cases we only had the post-mortem appearances to assist us...and after a strict investigation as to the cause of it...they were put down as natural disease.

Dr Robert Bentley Todd was called to give evidence. He had attended Isabella just once, a few days before her death. Dr Todd was a very eminent physician but was criticised in some quarters for his habit of prescribing alcohol for a variety of disorders, in some cases up to 30 ounces a day. When he died a few months later he was found to have advanced cirrhosis of the liver.[6]

Dr Julius had not told him beforehand of his suspicions of poison. He saw Isabella in the presence of Drs Julius and Smethurst. He examined her abdomen which was hard and rigid, but was concerned with the look on her face:

> ...a very peculiar expression of countenance, a peculiar terrified look, as if she was under the influence of fear or terror...

---

6   ODNB

Serjeant Ballantine asked him what he thought Isabella was suffering from:

> I was very strongly impressed with the opinion that she was suffering from the influence of some irritant poison.

He suggested that Dr Julius should obtain a sample of a motion for analysis. Dr Todd had never known such a reaction to his prescribed copper sulphate and opium pills as was described by Smethurst, with increased diarrhoea and burning throughout the body. The medicines prescribed by Dr Julius were correct treatments for the symptoms displayed. In Dr Todd's view, Isabella had died from the administration of an irritant poison, possibly arsenic, antimony or corrosive sublimate.

Serjeant Parry now examined the witness. In response to questioning Dr Todd admitted that he did not examine the deceased's intestines himself as he did not have the time, but that they were examined by 'two competent men'. Nor had he ever conducted a post-mortem on someone who had died from any of the three poisons he had mentioned. He was unaware of anyone of Isabella's age, pregnant, and suffering from severe vomiting and diarrhoea whose life had been saved by an abortion. He said that sickness and diarrhoea could accompany pregnancy, but they would not lead to intense ulceration of the bowels such as had been seen on Isabella's body. Serjeant Parry pressed him on his experience of dysentery:

> Have you...ever come across cases of dysentery, from which the patient has died, which you have been unable to refer to any cause?

He said that he had great experience of chronic dysentery caused by exposure to miasmata; he had never seen an isolated case of very acute dysentery.[7] Serjeant Parry suggested that there were constantly cases of rapid and acute dysentery breaking out in the country. Dr Todd said the term 'dysentery' was used frequently for ordinary diarrhoea. He went on:

> ...the fact that this lady had been the subject of bilious sickness, and occasionally of bilious purging...would not at all alter or modify the opinion I have expressed.

Serjeant Parry was not satisfied:

> Supposing an early stage of pregnancy, in which you admit it is possible that violent diarrhoea and violent vomiting might occur, would not the fact that the patient had suffered from bilious sickness and bilious purging form any element at all in your consideration?

Dr Todd:

> It would during the life of the patient, but it does not affect my opinion in this particular case.

Serjeant Parry:

> Would it produce inflammation and ulceration?

Dr Todd said that it would not. Serjeant Parry pressed Dr Todd on his experience of vomiting in pregnancy:

> You must have read...of cases of very violent vomiting from early pregnancy...where, in order to save the life of the mother, the foetus has been aborted?

Dr Todd:

> It is quite possible...

---

7   Certain infectious diseases were supposed to have been carried by 'miasma' or 'miasmata' – bad air – before the germ theory became established.

Dr Julius did not say anything to him about irritant poison just that the diarrhoea and vomiting had failed to yield to any of the medicines he had applied.

Dr Todd:

> I at once formed a strong suspicion of the existence of irritant poison...I think I said arsenic, or some other irritant; I think those were my words.

He went on to say that he was aware that Isabella complained about a ball in her throat and a burning sensation, but he commented again on the expression of terror on her face.

Harry Smith Palmer, the surgeon who had assisted Richard Barwell in the post-mortem, deposed that he had given the various organs removed from Isabella's body to Inspector McIntyre to pass on to Dr Taylor for analysis.

Inspector Robert Graham McIntyre himself was called next. He had first arrested Smethurst when Isabella was still alive, and had taken him before the magistrate. Smethurst was released on his own recognizance the same day. Upon returning to the house with Smethurst and Mr Bird, Inspector McIntyre took possession of a number of bottles and pill-boxes which were passed on to Dr Taylor. McIntyre again took Smethurst into custody after Isabella had died. He then went to see Mary Smethurst at Rifle Terrace and having interviewed her, he went to Kennington Church to find the record of her marriage to Thomas Smethurst.

Serjeant Parry now asked for a letter from Isabella to her sister Louisa to be read in court. The letter is poignant, given that Isabella had only a few months to live, because it portrays a bright and happy personality; it is the only insight we have into the character and demeanour of Isabella Bankes:

> *The Grubs, Withyham, Sussex, 18th Jan 1859. My dearest Loo, In reply to your very kind note, I am happy to inform*

you that I am now quite well, and take my rambles in the country, as usual, and with no inconvenience, and with a deal of pleasure, for I am in a very pretty part. Since seeing you, I may say I have truly enjoyed the change, having had every happiness and comfort, and remain in the same fortunate condition; I am much obliged to all kind friends for their kind inquiries and good wishes. I shall write to Mrs. Williamson. Tarte has annoyed me much by his delay in paying the balance of the last quarter, as I paid Miss—her account, which has left me without cash; you will, therefore, greatly oblige me, dearest, by having the £11 15s made up in a small parcel, and written "Cash" on the outside, and directed to me in the care of Messrs. Marshall and Snellgrove, until I send a note for it to them, for I shall have an opportunity of getting it so without charge. Please, dear, to leave it on receipt of this. Give my affectionate love to dear Tiny and darling child. I grieve to have so bad an account of darling Jane Haffenden. If writing, give my fondest love to her; and, with many thanks, believe me your affectionate Isabella. Pray write soon, and all news. My sweet little Bob is well; he sings in the railway carriage. I am covered with plaisters, and am obliged to have flannel drawers. I send you twelve stamps for the shoes, with thanks.

Serjeant Parry's reason for having this letter entered as evidence is clear from the first sentence; Isabella had been ill. But what is also clear is that she was enjoying life as Mrs Smethurst: 'I have truly enjoyed the change, having had every happiness and comfort'. She sends her love to 'Tiny and darling child' – probably a reference to her youngest sister, Elizabeth, and her three-year-old daughter Mabel. She also sends love to Jane Haffenden, her other sister who was clearly not very well.

Alexander McCrosty of the London and Westminster Bank was now called. He proved that Smethurst paid £71 5s into his account on 16th April 1859 (that was one shilling less than Isabella had received as her interest under the will of James Rhodes Bankes). He had a balance of between £100 and £150 at the bank.

Thomas Buzzard was re-examined. He was a personal friend of Mr Bird – they had practised medicine together in The Crimea. He had acted as messenger between Dr Julius and Dr Taylor. He also expressed the view that Isabella's condition was incompatible with any natural complaint; it could result from an irritant substance taken by mouth or injected into the bowels – possibly both. He was present when Dr Taylor analysed the content of bottle No 2 using Reinsch's Test and found arsenic, following which he went to Richmond with a letter for Dr Julius.

Serjeant Ballantine now called Dr Charles Metcalfe Babington. He was a Fellow of the Royal College of Physicians, and physician at Queen Charlotte's Lying-in Hospital. He had seen some cases of acute dysentery, but considering Isabella's symptoms, the treatments applied and the appearance of her body, he thought she died from the effect of irritant poisons. Having delivered over 2,000 women, he did not consider Isabella's death in any way attributable to her pregnancy. He was cross-examined by Serjeant Parry and asked whether he was familiar with cases of severe vomiting and diarrhoea in early pregnancy; he responded:

...I don't remember any of so severe a character as to endanger life; I do not know of any case in which the life of the mother has been saved under such circumstances by procuring abortion...

He went on to say that the post-mortem results of the dysentery cases with which he was familiar were quite different from

93

those on Isabella's body; the burning sensation in the throat was not a symptom of dysentery, and in his opinion was the result of irritant poison.

Serjeant Ballantine now called two medical witnesses who did have experience of acute dysentery. First was Dr Lewis Squire Bowerbank. He had practised medicine for 23 years in Jamaica where dysentery was a common disease. Although he admitted that he had no practical experience of 'slow poisoning' he said that he thought the symptoms were of irritant poisoning. Isabella's symptoms in life, and the post-mortem results were not consistent with acute dysentery.

Dr James Copland was called next. Dr Copland was a very experienced physician, Fellow of the Royal Society and author of the *Dictionary of Practical Medicine*. He had seen many cases of acute dysentery in Africa as well as in France and Germany in 1815 'after the peace'.[8] In his view, considering the symptoms, the medicines prescribed and the post-mortem results, Isabella was poisoned by irritants administered either by mouth or injection (anally). Dr Copland was cross-examined by Serjeant Parry; he did have some first-hand experience of poisoning by arsenic. Serjeant Parry asked him whether he had conducted a post-mortem on 'any animal body, human or otherwise' killed by slow arsenic poisoning:

> I have seen...two cases of poisoning by arsenic...they produced very severe symptoms of vomiting and purging; those two cases recovered...they produced burning pain in the oesophagus, down the gullet into the stomach...

He described the post-mortem symptoms he would expect:

---

8 Dr Copland was 68 years old in 1859; he was referring to the peace in Europe following the defeat of Napoleon.

...in a case of slow arsenical poisoning I should look for inflammation of the oesophagus, but I should not be disappointed in not finding it...I might expect to find traces of the poison in...the liver...I should consider a considerable portion of the poison would be eliminated from the system...purging and vomiting do accompany slow irritant poison...

Asked by Serjeant Parry whether he would expect to find arsenic in the body of someone who had died of arsenic poisoning, he said that he had never done such an examination. The judge asked him the same question, considering his knowledge and what he had read. He said that he would expect to find poison in the liver. Serjeant Parry pressed him on the point; Dr Copland:

I should expect to find traces...more especially in the liver, but I should scarcely expect to find much where there is much sickness, vomiting, and purging...the other vital function of absorption scarcely takes place...

Serjeant Ballantine asked him whether the inflammation would depend on what the arsenic was mixed with if taken orally. Dr Copland replied:

...to a certain extent at least; if no arsenic or antimony was found [in the body], but some small quantity in an evacuation, I should still entertain the opinion that the death was occasioned by an irritant poison...it may be combined...with other substances which may mask their detection...

It was now a quarter to five in the evening. The judge wanted to continue but following representations of exhaustion from the jury, he agreed to adjourn until the next day.

Day three of the trial, Wednesday 17th August, opened with the judge asking Mr Bird, who was called briefly, to confirm that he had told Smethurst that since Isabella had been excited by the visit of her sister on 9th April, he (Mr Bird) had suggested that she had better not come again. Mr Bird said that he believed that was so.

Now it was the turn of Dr Alfred Swaine Taylor. He had been Serjeant Ballantine's star witness, although his brightness had subsequently waned considerably. Dr Taylor described how he became involved in the Smethurst case. Mr Buzzard called on him at home at one o'clock in the afternoon of Sunday 1st May with two bottles containing material that he wanted tested for arsenic. Mr Buzzard having explained the circumstances, Dr Taylor consented to test one of them even though it was a Sunday. The analysis used was the Reinsch process. Dr Taylor first tested his apparatus and chemicals to ascertain that they were clean and free of arsenic, and then analyzed a sample taken from bottle No 2. He found that a 'metallic deposit of a greyish steel colour had become attached to the [copper] wire'. He said that the deposit indicated the presence of arsenic, antimony or even mercury. He went on:

> ...I desired to have the authority of a magistrate to proceed further...after [Mr Buzzard] had left, I proceeded further with my process...the application had been made to me to do something to save the life of this lady; and though I do not make analyses on a Sunday, I thought it proper to come to a conclusion as soon as I could...

He boiled some copper gauze in the remainder of the liquid and examining the copper under the microscope, saw what closely resembled metallic arsenic which he then heated in a tube and obtained crystals of arsenic which he held up in court:

> I have no doubt that these are crystals of arsenic; not the slightest.

Later on the same Sunday, Mr Buzzard had come back with an order from Mr Penrhyn, the magistrate, to continue with the examination. On the Monday morning he analysed the contents of both bottles, repeating the analysis of bottle No 2 on a larger sample of its contents and finding the same result. He found arsenic in the blood which was in the bottle. He also found a trace of copper but no antimony, mercury or bismuth. Having examined portions of the evacuation under the microscope, he came to the conclusion that it was typical of that from someone suffering from arsenic poisoning. He immediately advised the use of the antidote for arsenic, magnesium hydrate.

He then examined the contents of bottle No 1 and found no arsenic or any other metallic matter at all. Subsequently he received jars containing the organs removed from Isabella's body, as well as a number of bottles, packages, parcels, pill-boxes, and a other articles removed from Alma Villas as well as samples from Dr Julius' surgery. He described his examination of the viscera. After looking at the uterus, he concurred with Mr Barwell's estimation that the foetus was between five and seven weeks old. He then analysed the other viscera for poisons. There was no arsenic or antimony in the gullet, stomach, liver or spleen. He did find a very small amount of antimony in one kidney (the second kidney was not examined), in the small intestines in two distinct places and in the blood from the heart. Dr Odling assisted him in the analysis, and they calculated that the whole quantity of antimony found did not exceed between one quarter and one half of a grain. He agreed with Mr Barwell's comments regarding the extensive ulceration in the intestines and elsewhere, and that there was no appearance of disease in the other organs to account for death.

He described his analysis of the contents of certain pill-boxes, and found 'that they were what they were represented to be', variously containing mercury, silver and copper corresponding with the various prescriptions. He examined an 'Indian rubber' enema bottle and a glass syringe. In the wadding of the glass syringe, he removed traces of some white metal:

> ...it was neither mercury, bismuth, or silver, but what I cannot say; it was a mere trace of white metal...

He examined the bottles and packets of powders delivered to him; again they corresponded to the prescriptions. Also examined were some samples of sugar and tapioca; nothing suspicious was found in any of them.

He now came to the bottles numbered 5 and 21. Bottle No 5 was unlabelled and was found to contain 355 grains of pure potassium chlorate. Bottle No 21, 'about which an error arose', was labelled as containing a quinine mixture, but actually contained a clear watery liquid of a 'cooling' saline taste. He gave an ounce and a half of it to his assistant to boil for testing by Reinsch's process, but on putting the copper wire or gauze into it found that the copper was completely dissolved. He said:

> ...that seemed rather a remarkable circumstance; at any rate, it had never occurred to me in my experience before...I then plunged a portion of copper gauze into it for a very short time; removed the copper gauze, examined it, and obtained crystals of arsenic...I then put this bottle aside...thinking there was something remarkable about it, and wishing to have the assistance of another chemist in the matter...

The Judge:

> Did that lead you to suppose that there was arsenic in it?

Dr Taylor:

> It did; Dr. Odling assisted me in a further examination, and we both came to that conclusion; [but] it turned out ultimately that there was no arsenic or antimony in the fluid; the arsenic was found, by subsequent research, to come from the copper gauze we had used...

Mr Bodkin:

> The copper gauze being dissolved, set free any arsenic that was in it?

Dr Taylor:

> Yes.

This was a major blunder and must have seriously embarrassed Dr Taylor, not to mention Serjeant Ballantine. In the magistrates' hearing in May, Ballantine had made much of Taylor's evidence of 'an extraordinary nature' and 'a development of medical science of a novel description'. More than anything else, that evidence would have established extreme prejudice against Smethurst in the minds of anyone with knowledge of the case. Now it transpired that Dr Taylor had made an elementary error. He was apparently unaware that a simple solution of dilute hydrochloric acid (used for the Reinsch test) and potassium chlorate was known in the engraving business as *Dutch Mordant*, and used for etching, that is, dissolving copper. Rembrandt, for example, had used it for his etchings. But it was worse than that; in his evidence given in the magistrates' court, Professor Taylor had stated that potassium chlorate was a diuretic:

> If poison were given in a small dose in company with it, it would be rapidly carried off in urine...[purifying] the system from all noxious matter...

Serjeant Ballantine had emphasized that comment when he said that no arsenic had been found by Dr Taylor in Isabella's organs, '*nor did he expect to find any*', since the diuretic action of the potassium chlorate would have rapidly removed the poison. Now it emerged that not only was no arsenic found in Isabella's body, but the supposed vehicle for dosing her with the arsenic was perfectly innocent, Dr Taylor having made a serious error in his analysis of the potassium chlorate solution. If that analysis had been faulty, what credence could be given to his insistence on having found arsenic in the motion contained in bottle No 2 not to mention antimony elsewhere in Isabella's body?

In fact Dr Taylor's use of the Reinsch test had already been severely criticised in *The Lancet*. Taylor first described his findings during the last session of the magistrates' hearing on Friday 20th May. The proceedings were published in the newspapers the following day. On Tuesday, 24th May, Henry Letheby, medical officer for London and Professor of Chemistry and Toxicology at the London Hospital, had written to *The Lancet* on the subject of '...Tests for Arsenic in Chlorate of Potash'. The letter was published on Saturday 28th May. No mention was made of the Smethurst case or Dr Taylor, but the allusion was clear from the first sentence:

> The recognition of arsenic in a solution of chlorate of potash is a matter of so much ease and certainty that it ought not to fail in the hands of anyone, nor should it be a subject of the least embarrassment or difficulty.

He went on to detail several tests so 'delicate in their reactions' that they would detect the smallest levels of arsenic, and showed how having detected the presence of the metal, the exact quantity could be determined. There was, he said, one test

...altogether unsuited for the recognition of arsenic in chlorate of potash...Reinsch's test.

In Reinsch's test, he said, the action of hydrochloric acid on potassium chlorate releases 'chlorine [and] chloric oxide', which proceed to dissolve the copper; if arsenic is present, the mixture also produces 'chloride of arsenicum', a volatile gas which would escape. Thus there was the danger of 'losing the arsenic which ought to be found', as well as contaminating the solution under test with arsenic from the copper and the hydrochloric acid, which could also contain arsenic as an impurity. He said that the process was incapable of determining the amount of arsenic present, which could only be guessed at.

Finally, he referred to Dr Fresenius' 1844 proposal for the use of potassium chlorate and hydrochloric acid in the analysis of organic matter for arsenic, which was objected to for the very reasons he had just stated:[9]

> The process, therefore, never came into use; and the objection to it shows its inapplicability to the present case.

Dr Letheby appeared to have demolished any justification for the use of Reinsch's test in the presence of potassium chlorate.

Three months later, and Dr Taylor had to concede that he had not tested his copper for arsenic content; it was the chlorine in the potassium chlorate, he said, that had 'destroyed' the copper:

> ...it is never necessary to dissolve the copper; as a general rule, in applying the [Reinsch] test we never dissolve the copper...

But he insisted that his general diagnosis of the cause of Isabella's death was correct:

---

9   This was an article in *The Lancet* of which more later.

I have heard the evidence of the symptoms under which this lady laboured, the remedies applied, and the post-mortem appearances; taking all the circumstances into consideration, I can ascribe the death to nothing but the action of irritant poison.

Dr Taylor was now cross-examined by Serjeant Parry and asked about the arsenic he found in bottle No 2. He said there was about one sixth of a grain of arsenic in the entire evacuation, and he had used the same copper gauze in that analysis as he had used in the analysis of bottle No 21. He tested his copper gauze to see whether it contained arsenic by boiling it. He repeated that it was the action of the potassium chlorate 'which destroyed the action of the [Reinsch] test'. Dr Odling had then made an independent test of the mixture, and came to the same conclusion, i.e. that arsenic was present in bottle No 21. Dr Taylor:

...in that respect he was wrong, as I was wrong...

He applied another test for arsenic, 'March's test', to the liquid in bottle 21.[10] The implication from the transcript of Taylor's evidence was that it was also positive:

I did not know fully then, when I was making this examination, that the chlorate of potass was present...I had to find that out...we found, ultimately, that we had deposited arsenic, but our belief at the time was that the arsenic was in the liquid...

Now he seemed to be saying that he was unaware that bottle 21 contained potassium chlorate before he tested it for arsenic.

---

10 This refers to 'Marsh's' test, a more sensitive but also more time-consuming method for the detection of arsenic. Appendix 4 contains a description of Marsh's test.

Dr Taylor went on to confirm that he had sworn on oath both to the magistrates and the coroner that bottle No 21 contained arsenic. He said that he 'discovered the mistake' on the afternoon of Friday 20th May (he had given evidence to the magistrates' hearing that morning, at the end of which Smethurst had been committed for trial on a charge of murder), and told Serjeant Ballantine the following morning. The Serjeant, he said, recognized the importance of the new finding saying that it ought not to be concealed. (But who was told what and when? When the inquest was reconvened firstly on 25th May and then on 31st May, nothing was said about Dr Taylor's mistake. Indeed on 25th May, Dr Taylor maintained that arsenic had been found in bottle No 21, and the effect of the potassium chlorate would be 'to carry the metal [arsenic] quickly through the stomach'.)

Serjeant Parry proceeded with the cross-examination. Dr Taylor admitted that he had sworn before the Magistrate and the Coroner, more than once, that he had discovered arsenic in the bottle. Serjeant Parry quoted his words to the magistrate:

...Understand, Sir; I tested all my tests before I made this discovery of arsenic...

Dr Taylor responding to Serjeant Parry:

...we tested them in the usual way in which they are tested for the application of this process...I have used the copper gauze for fourteen years, and I never found a trace of arsenic in it until this...I have given evidence before on the faith of this copper gauze, and shall do so again; but I shall take care not to put chlorate of potass in my liquid.

He went on to say that he had conducted seventy-seven analyses for the Smethurst case, but found arsenic only once (in bottle No 2).

Dr Taylor's mistaken evidence that bottle No 21 contained arsenic was first presented during the magistrates' hearing on Friday 20th May, and his deposition on that occasion was read out from the record. Serjeant Parry:

> At the time you delivered that evidence before the Magistrate and Coroner you firmly believed, did you not, that you had made a correct analysis of this bottle, and had discovered arsenic in it?

Dr Taylor:

> Yes...and I firmly believed...that arsenic had been placed there at that time, not by my tests, but by somebody else...

His evidence then became confused as he attempted to say what he had meant; possibly the court reporter was confused, or was Dr Taylor trying to sow a little confusion to cover his embarrassment? He went on to say that he had told the magistrate and coroner that Isabella's symptoms were 'more referable to antimony than to arsenic...' In fact he had said 'antimony *and* arsenic' in the magistrates' court. Dr Taylor continued:

> I had not made the analysis at the time of the deposition which has just been read; therefore, I could give no opinion of the cause of death...I formed no judgment about the administration of this liquid [in bottle No 21] to the deceased at all...

He went on to describe a series of tests conducted in conjunction with Dr Odling and 'Professor' Brande after which they finally concluded around 7th June that the arsenic was in the copper. He went on:

...my tests have been contested; they have been disputed sometimes [but] I never remember an occasion when I conscientiously believed my tests were correct, and they were found not to be correct upon further examination...

He denied having knowledge of his being mistaken in a case involving a Professor Rodgers.[11] Serjeant Parry continued with his examination and on the question of Dr Taylor's assertion that potassium chlorate, used as a diuretic, could carry off the arsenic in the urine, Serjeant Parry asked:

Supposing no foreign agent of that kind to be used in cases of slow poisoning by arsenic or antimony, would you not expect to find traces or deposits in small quantities, more or less, of antimony or arsenic, in the tissues of the body?

Dr Taylor:

That would depend upon several circumstances...in cases of slow arsenical poisoning, I look... for arsenic in the tissues, and expect to find it...

He said he wrote a letter to either Dr Julius or Mr Penrhyn saying that

...supposing there is no disturbing influence, we expect, as a general rule, in cases of slow arsenical poisoning, to find the actual metal in the tissues...

He said that he was asked whether potassium chlorate would have any particular effect; he said that it would act as a diuretic, and carry off the arsenic or any mineral matter that might have been administered. But now he said that before he

---

11 He may have been referring to Dr Julian Rogers, one of the witnesses for the defence.

analysed the bottle he had never had any 'actual experience of the effects of 'chlorate of potass' in carrying off any mineral poison'. He then said:

> ...I did not form this as a theory...to account for the absence of arsenic in the body [but] it acts generally as a diuretic...

He went on to cite another poisoning case in which he had given evidence. In 1855, Joseph Wooler was tried for the poisoning of his wife Jane Wooler in Durham (he was subsequently found not guilty). Dr Taylor found a grain of arsenic in the body of Jane Wooler:

> I did not examine the stomach; it was examined by Dr. Richardson of Durham...I did not see it at all, and know nothing of the state of it from my own knowledge...I heard the evidence of some other gentleman about it...

Dr Taylor described some of the symptoms of arsenic poisoning:

> inflammation of...the eye...there is an eruption known to science called the *eczema arsenicale*...excoriation of the anus...great redness of the nostrils, and even ulceration...sometimes the mouth and the lips are excoriated...a hacking cough...where there is irritation in the throat...a mucous discharge...always increased by the action of arsenic...

He was not familiar with dysentery, but in cases of poisoning by antimony:

> a clammy sweating is chiefly observed...where there is not diarrhoea...in all cases of antimonial poisoning there is not invariably vomiting; it depends upon the dose...the administration of small doses of antimony

would have a tendency to enlarge the liver, and to cause a deposit of fat, and sometimes to soften it...

Mr Bodkin then brought the questioning back to the error with bottle No 21 and the judge asked what must have been on the minds of many in the court:

Does the blunder that was made about the bottle and the mixture in it at all affect what you said in your examination-in-chief about the arsenic you found in No. 2?

Dr Taylor:

...it does not in the slightest degree affect the inference I have drawn, or the application of the test in the usual way...I have made other experiments since to verify and prove that; and sent some of the copper to professors in Scotland and Ireland to have it tested...

Mr Bodkin then asked an interesting question:

If half a grain of copper had been administered to this lady during life, would that not at all by any action of any acid in the stomach, account for the quantity of arsenic found in the evacuation?

Dr Taylor:

Certainly not...I examined two of the copper pills, and could detect no arsenic in them.

And then Serjeant Ballantine:

Did you examine the four specimens of medicine that you received from Dr. Julius' surgery?

Dr Taylor:

> Bismuth, silver, and copper; they were all examined;
> the acetate of lead also...in ten grains of the sulphate
> of copper we found distinct traces of arsenic, in two
> of the pills, separately examined, as representing half
> a grain of the sulphate of copper, and two of the pills
> have been examined by Professor Brande, and Dr.
> Odling, with, I believe, the same result; there was not
> a quantity to be seen...I apprehend that the ten grains
> would contain a quantity we could speak to, but the
> two grains and the half-grain did not...there was none
> in the bismuth...there was no antimony in any of the
> medicines.[12]

Serjeant Parry:

> How did you examine the bismuth?

Dr Taylor:

> By Marsh's process only...there was not the slightest
> indication of arsenic...

And that, no doubt to his extreme relief, ended Dr Taylor's
examination.

Harry Palmer was recalled – he had assisted at the post-
mortem examination. He was asked about the appearance of
the liver:

> ...we found the liver enlarged, hardened, and in, I
> believe, an incipient condition of fatty degeneration...I
> noticed that it was very much hardened in the left

---

12 Dr Taylor says they found traces of arsenic in 10 grains of copper sulphate,
but none at all in two half-grain pills of copper (sulphate). If there was
arsenic present in the latter case, the amount was too small to detect.

lobe...that might be the effect of continuous bilious irritation...

Dr William Odling was called. He was a physician, Fellow of the Royal Society and Professor of Practical Chemistry at Guy's Hospital. He had assisted Dr Taylor in the analyses he had made of the intestines and bottles Nos 2 and 21. He had been a student of Dr Taylor. Dr Odling stated:

> I am satisfied that there was antimony present in the body...I also assisted in the analysis of bottle No. 21 with Dr. Taylor's gauze, and came to the same conclusion with him...I also partly assisted in testing a portion of evacuation [in bottle] No. 2 for antimony, but none was found...the result of my examination of the contents of the bottle does not in any way alter the opinion I then formed of the existence of arsenic in the tissues...

The Judge:

> You fell into the same mistake...as Dr. Taylor did?

Dr Odling:

> Yes; that mistake did not relate to antimony at all... it would leave the results of the probabilities about antimony just where they were.

The Judge:

> Does the blunder you made about the bottle that contained the fluid at all break in upon the conclusion that a chemist would form of [there] being arsenic in any fluid that did not contain the chlorate of potass?

Dr Odling:

> In a case where the copper is not dissolved there is no
> fallacy whatever in Reinsch's test...unless the copper
> is dissolved the test is as good notwithstanding; it is
> the best.

Serjeant Ballantine asked him what his view was of the cause
of death:

> I believe that the death was caused by irritant poison...
> there is not, to my knowledge, any form of natural
> disease to which I am able to attribute it.

Following a question from Mr Giffard, Dr Odling confirmed
that he no longer attended patients.

Finally, William Brande was called. He was a retired
Professor of Chemistry at the Royal Institution and Fellow of
the Royal Society, with fifty years of practical experience in
chemistry. He had replaced Sir Humphrey Davy at the Royal
Institution, and was assisted for a while by Michael Faraday...
He had been called in to check Dr Taylor's findings. He tested
the liquid in bottle No 21 using Reinsch's test as well as Marsh's
test. He concluded that no arsenic was present. He said:

> Reinsch's test is in all cases an admirable one; in my
> opinion and judgment it was properly applied to test
> the intestines and evacuations; and in my opinion the
> result obtained was a correct one, one upon which I
> would act.

He went on to say that he would have come to the same
conclusion as Drs Taylor and Odling did, had he carried out
Reinsch's test on bottle No 21:

> ...the matter that has appeared since, is to a certain
> extent new to the chemical world...we have always

been aware of the presence of very minute quantities of arsenic in copper, but we have never considered it as interfering in any way, until this particular case...

Nevertheless, here was another professor of chemistry with very considerable experience, apparently unaware of the simple property of potassium chlorate and dilute hydrochloric acid to dissolve copper... He had acquired the copper he used in the laboratory by having it

...rolled down from a piece of coin; from a halfpenny, which I considered to be pure enough for the purpose...

Several of the previous witnesses were recalled in order to check various dates. Dr Julius recalled Smethurst's statement to the magistrates the first time he was arrested:

...his statement was that it was very necessary that he should go back to his wife; that her death might be occasioned by his absence, and that it was imperative that he should go...everything that had been administered to her had been administered by himself, both of medicine and of food...if any metallic substance had been administered, it must have come from my [Dr Julius'] surgery.

And that was the case for the prosecution. Serjeant Parry requested a short recess for refreshment before the presentation of the case for the defence, and this was granted by the judge.

The Case for the Defence

Serjeant Parry had requested a break because he wanted everyone to be alert for his substantial opening speech, and he spoke for three hours. John Humffreys Parry, like Ballantine, was a master of rhetoric and it is sufficient to summarize what he said. His case was that Isabella Bankes had died of natural causes not poison. No deception had been practised on her since she knew that Smethurst was already married; the letter to her sister in January 1859 made it clear that she was perfectly happy as a 'married' woman. And rather than keeping Isabella 'entirely under his control' when she was ill, Smethurst had visited London regularly, being absent on a number of occasions for several hours.

The will provided no motive since the deceased had a life interest in a much greater sum of money than she was able to bequeath. Smethurst was very kind to Isabella, and was the first to propose extra medical attention as her condition deteriorated. No poison was found in the body of the deceased and the prisoner had no poison 'within reach or under his control', and since he was arrested suddenly, he had no opportunity of disposing of any in his possession. The letter to Mary Smethurst was merely a practical note detailing how he would settle her rent, not an intent to return.

Finally, the theory of the potassium chlorate 'carrying off the poison' would be exploded, and Serjeant Parry reminded the jury of Dr Taylor's blunder in believing to have found arsenic in bottle No 21. He also criticised Dr Julius; Julius had said that he came to suspect that Isabella was being poisoned on 18th April, and yet it was twelve days before any action was taken.

The first witness for the defence was Dr Benjamin (afterwards, Sir Benjamin) Ward Richardson. He was a Licentiate of the Royal College of Physicians (appointed Fellow in 1865), and Professor of Physiological and Pathological Anatomy at the Grosvenor Place School of Medicine. He had been awarded the degree of MD by St Andrews University, and had won the Astley Cooper prize of 300 guineas for an essay on blood coagulation.[1] He was the author of published works on toxicology and medical jurisprudence (Dr Taylor's speciality).

Dr Richardson's affiliation, the Grosvenor Place School of Medicine, which was also that of several of the other defence witnesses, was to become an issue during the trial and afterwards. There was a whiff of establishment disapproval of the Grosvenor Place Medical School, which may have had its roots in an unseemly quarrel that was publicly fought out in the press some twenty-five years previously. St George's Hospital had been founded in 1733 at Hyde Park Corner, on the corner of Knightsbridge and Grosvenor Place, and work started on rebuilding the hospital in 1827. The governors had decided that anatomy could not be taught on the premises, so a private medical school for that purpose was started in 1830, next door at No 1 Grosvenor Place, by Samuel Armstrong Lane. The school was known variously as 'The Grosvenor Place School of Anatomy and Medicine' and the 'Old St George's School of Medicine'. Lane had had his initial training in anatomy at William Hunter's School of Anatomy at Great Windmill Street where he met James Arthur Wilson, six years his senior. Wilson's father, another James Wilson, was lecturing and demonstrating at the school, and he was joined there by an ex-pupil, Benjamin Brodie. Subsequently, Brodie and Wilson junior were appointed surgeon and physician

---

1   ODNB

respectively to St George's Hospital. It was said that they fell out with each other over a financial dispute between Brodie and James Wilson senior, who died in 1820. The antipathy between the two may have been aggravated by their very different educational backgrounds. James Wilson was educated at Westminster School, Christ Church, Oxford, and Edinburgh. He was awarded MD at Oxford, and then travelled in France, Switzerland and Italy as physician to Earl Spencer and his wife. Brodie was educated at home by his father, rector of Winterslow in Wiltshire. In London he learned pharmacy in an apothecary's shop, and attended lectures at St Bartholomew's Hospital and the Great Windmill Street school. Brodie became house surgeon at St George's in 1808, then senior surgeon in 1822. Wilson became a physician to St George's in 1829.[2] Thus Wilson was an Oxford-educated physician, whereas Brodie was a surgeon, home-educated, who had learned part of his craft in a shop. Nevertheless, Brodie worked hard and proved himself to be very able. He was elected to the Royal Society in 1811, and was appointed personal surgeon to George IV in 1828.

Samuel Lane, who had started the Grosvenor Place School, aspired to a post at St George's Hospital and in 1834 a position for a second assistant surgeon became available. The establishment of the position itself was a matter of controversy, some of the hospital governors saying that it was unnecessary and simply the result of Benjamin Brodie seeking an assistant for himself which would be filled by one of his acolytes. Samuel Lane was a very suitable and well-qualified candidate for the post, and he was supported by James Wilson. Brodie, who supported Edward Cutler, a 'less experienced man than Lane', led a vicious campaign of vilification against Lane. There were letters and editorials in *The Lancet* and the *Morning Chronicle* (in favour of Lane), and the *London Medical*

---

2   Information on Brodie and Wilson from ODNB.

Gazette (supporting Brodie and his candidate). Some of the language used was decidedly intemperate and bordering on libel. Lane was defeated in the election, Cutler receiving nearly twice as many votes. Lane's reputation, and by association his medical school, was inevitably damaged. The dispute broke out again the following year when Brodie publicly accused Lane of leaking information about St George's governors' meetings to the Press. *The Lancet* published a letter Lane had written to Brodie, declaring his complete innocence in the affair, together with a response from Brodie who apparently accepted his word. But Brodie was not finished; in 1836 he purchased a house in nearby Kinnerton Street which he let to the hospital for £275 a year rent, in order to set up a rival medical school to that of Lane. Lane appears to have behaved with commendable forbearance during the affair, but it was clear that he could have no future at St George's. Eventually he became the principal founding-father of St Mary's Hospital in Paddington, which opened in 1851. Brodie's machinations backfired on him in 1843, when the hospital governors ignored his proposed candidate for assistant surgeon and elected another less suitable man, 'for fear of being accused of being under Brodie's thumb'. With Samuel Lane on the senior staff at St Mary's, and the rival medical school at Kinnerton Street diluting the number of students available, the Grosvenor Place School's days were numbered and it finally closed in 1863.

It was a sordid and discreditable affair, and sullied Brodie's reputation even though he had been made a baronet in 1835; *The Lancet* had contemptuously described him as a 'little eminence' (he was small of stature). As will be seen, Sir Benjamin Brodie was to have a key role to play in the Smethurst case. Samuel Lane's obituary in 1890 commented on his failure in the election 55 years earlier:

Lane was...as he thought, unjustly and hardly treated. Bitter feelings arose during the contest, which lasted for many years...

At the time of the Smethurst trial, Brodie was one of the most eminent surgeons in the land, president of the new General Medical Council, and the first surgeon to be elected President of the Royal Society.[3] But few members of the medical profession over the age of 45 could have been unaware of the bad blood that existed between Samuel Lane and his Grosvenor Place School and Sir Benjamin Brodie. Six of the prosecution medical witnesses came into that category, including Drs Julius, Todd and Taylor. There can be little doubt that Serjeant Ballantine had been briefed on the 'reputation' of the Grosvenor Place School, particularly since four of the medical witnesses for the defence were either current or former employees of that establishment. Furthermore, two of them had appeared, unsuccessfully, for the defence in the trial of Dr William Palmer – of whom more soon – and Sir Benjamin Brodie had appeared for the prosecution in that case...

Back to the Smethurst trial and Dr Richardson started giving his evidence:

...the symptoms under which Isabella Bankes, laboured...in my judgment, are not reconcilable with slow arsenical poisoning...

To which the judge added:

Or, I suppose, with slow antimonial poisoning?

Dr Richardson:

No...nor with both together...

3 ODNB

He went on to detail the specific symptoms of arsenic poisoning which were virtually identical with what Dr Taylor had already told the court.

The judge asked another question; he had intervened very little during the prosecution evidence, but was to have much to say during the defence case:

> You say the result of the post-mortem examination... is not, in your judgment, consistent with arsenical poisoning?

Dr Richardson:

> No...the inflammation which would establish arsenical poisoning was most demonstrated in [that part of the alimentary canal] which is [ordinarily] most free in arsenical poisoning...

Mr Giffard:

> In your judgment is it possible for a person to be poisoned by slow arsenical poisoning without arsenic being afterwards found in the tissues?

Dr Richardson:

> ..it is quite impossible...

Dr Richardson then reported the results of some experiments he had carried out. Following Dr Taylor's claim that potassium chlorate would carry arsenic out of the body by diuretic action, Richardson had performed some tests on a dog:

> ...my experiments were made after reading Dr Taylor's account in the newspaper...I took a large dog, and gave it daily, arsenious acid and chlorate of potass...I then killed the animal and made a post-mortem and chemical analysis in conjunction with Dr Thudichum

and Dr Webb...I found arsenic in the liver, in the lungs, in the heart, a trace in the spleen and in the kidneys, but by far the greater part in the liver.

The judge wanted to know how much arsenic he had found in the dog's body. Dr Richardson thought it was between half a grain and a grain (he hadn't performed a quantitative analysis).

The Judge:

Out of the whole eighteen grains that you administered?

Dr Richardson:

Yes...the chief object of the experiment [was] to show that chlorate of potass does not eliminate it...I would add that there was intense inflammation in the stomach of that dog, and in the lower part of the alimentary canal intense ulceration; the alimentary canal of a dog generally resembles the human...

The Judge:

Give me leave to say the value of the experiment is nothing if you give a dog arsenic day by day for 16 days, and then it is killed, and some arsenic is found left in it; is that all it proves?

Dr Richardson:

No; it was done to prove whether after arsenic had been given in small quantities with an overwhelming portion of chlorate of potass, the chlorate would eliminate the arsenic as fast as it was introduced...if in the case of supposed death from arsenic I found as much arsenic as I found in the tissues of that animal, I should have no doubt about connecting the case with arsenical poisoning.

The Judge:

> All that the experiment proves is, that chlorate of potass does not eliminate the whole of the arsenic, because it eliminated all but half a grain?

Dr Richardson:

> But if there had been no chlorate of potass given, as I shall show by a future experiment, the result would have been the same; the chlorate made no difference...

He went on to describe an experiment carried out on two other dogs; both dosed with arsenic and antimony on alternate days one with and one without potassium chlorate as well. The post-mortem and results of the chemical analyses were the same.

Mr Giffard asked:

> In cases of arsenical poisoning does the arsenic always pass away to some extent by the urine?

Dr Richardson:

> Always...

So if arsenic was ruled out, what about antimony:

> ...the symptoms...are not altogether reconcilable with slow poisoning by antimony...sweating would be one of the symptoms in a case of slow antimonial poisoning, profuse sweating, especially in the early stage of the process...a kind of pustular eruption is also a symptom...I have seen it in one case, and it is frequent.

The Judge:

> You have seen it in one case?

Dr Richardson:

> Yes; where antimony was given in excess...I have seen no other case where the poison acted slowly, but I have seen two cases of acute poisoning by antimony, neither of them fatal...

Mr Giffard:

> As a matter of medical science and reading, would you expect to find those two symptoms, sweating and pustular eruption?

Dr Richardson:

> They have been very commonly noticed in cases of this kind...

And on the question of the post-mortem appearance of antimonial poisoning:

> I can only speak of the effects of antimony on the liver from experiments I made in 1856-7...a series of experiments that I performed on animals...there have been so few cases of chronic antimonial poisoning carefully recorded...in a case of slow antimonial poisoning I should expect an effect on the lungs, congestion possibly, from the great fluidity of the blood, which exists always in antimonial poisoning... if antimony were exhibited in small doses, I should expect to find it on analysis in the liver...the liver is the great depot both for arsenic and antimony.

Dr Richardson's experience of dysentery:

> I have not had very much experience of dysentery...I have seen a few cases...perhaps two or three in this country...my description of it would be a disease

marked by purging, the matters thrown off by the bowels being tinged with blood, or mucus, or bile... sometimes with shreds of membrane...attended not [in]frequently with vomiting, [and] intense thirst in proportion to the purging and vomiting...I have never in my own experience met with a case of dysentery in the early stage of pregnancy...I have seen diarrhoea and vomiting.

Mr Giffard:

Having heard the description of the liver, as examined after death, in your judgment would Isabella Bankes have been a likely subject for dysentery?

Dr Richardson:

I think so; dysentery sometimes comes on of its own accord.

Mr Giffard:

You tell me that, having heard the description of her liver, you think she would be a probable subject of dysentery... having heard that she was liable to nausea and frequent sickness...would [you] confirm or alter your view that she was a favourable subject for dysentery?

Dr Richardson:

So far, that it would point out that she was a favourable subject for disease of the liver...

On the question of Isabella's pregnancy, Dr Richardson:

I mentioned that I had seen one case of diarrhoea in early pregnancy...I have met with one instance of diarrhoea and vomiting as a consequence of pregnancy, arising from it...

He was now asked about bismuth:

...I have analysed the ordinary drug, trisnitrate of bismuth[4], which is the form of bismuth usually administered in medicine, and every specimen of bismuth in London that I have examined contained arsenic...the largest quantity that I am acquainted with is very nearly half a grain to the ounce [about 0.1%] the specimen that I examined came from Squire and McCulloch's...I have a patient to whom I have given bismuth as a medicine...I analysed the urine of that patient.

The Judge:

How much did you give?

Dr Richardson:

Five grains of bismuth three times a day [for] six days... the urine passed on the seventh morning was subjected to analysis...I did it with Dr. Thudichum and Dr. Webb, and found arsenic...it was [prescribed] for dyspepsia, a form of disease I frequently give bismuth for.

He told several of his fellow lecturers at the Grosvenor Place School about his experiments on dogs, but had no idea why Mr Humphreys (Smethurst's solicitor) called on him to give evidence in this case. However, it might have been because he had given evidence in another recent trial of a doctor for murder by poison. That had taken place three years previously, and several persons involved in the current case had also been

---

4   This was probably 'Subnitrate of Bismuth', BiO_3NO_5, as described in John Biddle's Materia Medica.

involved. Mr Bodkin was one of the prosecution barristers, and Drs Todd, Taylor, Richardson and Rogers and Mr Brande had all given evidence in the trial of William Palmer. There were a number of parallels between the Smethurst and Palmer cases, so a brief account of the latter is probably in order.

William Palmer, the so-called Rugeley Poisoner, was a doctor who deserted medicine for the turf but soon ran up substantial debts. His wife and brother, both of whose lives were heavily insured by Palmer, his mother-in-law, six children and a creditor who was staying with him, all died of various mysterious ailments. There were local rumours that he was a mass murderer, and he was also a womaniser who had produced a number of illegitimate children (two of whom were among those that had died). Finally, the death of another betting man, John Cook, who had won heavily at the races and with whom Palmer was staying at a hotel, led to his arrest on a charge of poisoning with strychnine. His trial was moved from Stafford to the Old Bailey in order to find an unprejudiced jury. After twelve days he was convicted of murder and hanged in public outside Stafford gaol, although protesting his innocence of Cook's murder to the very end. The subsequent view of Palmer's trial was that the medical evidence was weak, and the alleged motive 'flimsy'. His conviction was obtained by a combination of circumstantial evidence, together with a judge, Lord Chief Justice Campbell, who appeared to be heavily biased towards the prosecution.[5]

Serjeant Ballantine questioned Dr Richardson about his evidence in the Palmer case. As a defence witness, Richardson had supported the view that the victim had died from angina rather than strychnine, whereas Palmer was eventually convicted of murder by poisoning with strychnine.[6] Ballantine

5   Information from ODNB.

6   No strychnine was found in Palmer's alleged victim, and it was Dr Alfred Taylor who had tried, but failed to find it...

was evidently seeking to discredit Dr Richardson as having supported the losing side in that trial.

Now Serjeant Ballantine asked about an instance when Dr Richardson had reported nearly poisoning a patient with antimony. He had written a note entitled *On Antimonial Poisoning* and sent it to *The Lancet*; it was published on 12th April 1856. Antimony as a medicine was administered in two forms: *tartar emetic*[7] had the appearance of white crystals, 'tartarated' in order to make the preparation water-soluble. Alternatively *antimony wine* was tartar emetic dissolved in a 20% alcohol solution. Dr Richardson had described two cases where patients had had a violent reaction to antimony. In the first case, the person who made up the preparation had made a mistake; the tartar emetic crystals had stuck to the neck of the bottle, and the patient received the best part of nine doses in one go. In the second case, 15 minims of antimony wine – a very small dose – prescribed for taking at bedtime, also generated a violent reaction. Dr Richardson said in his note that the size of a lethal dose was unknown for a medicine that was prescribed to between 5,000 and 10,000 persons a week in London alone. He considered that there was a lack of knowledge of how antimony was eliminated from the body and criticised Dr Taylor's views on the subject:

> With every respect for Dr Taylor as our leading medical jurist, I think that most practitioners will hesitate in regard to his opinion as to the periods of time in which this substance is eliminated.

Considering the contents of the note, Serjeant Ballantine asked him if he could still comment with confidence on the effect of antimony. Dr Richardson said he could:

---

7   Tartar emetic was tartarated antimony, antimony potassium tartarate.

...frequently feeble persons bear it very well... sometimes it causes purging, and sometimes, in cases of antimonial poisoning, it causes costiveness [constipation]...there are not sufficient cases to prove that it more frequently causes purging...it causes sickness and heat in the throat...

He said that the effects of taking antimony would depend on the individual circumstances of each patient. However on other medicines generally:

...if immediately after taking medicine, heat is felt from the mouth, through the body, to the anus...that would be in accordance with a large dose of copper [as well as] other substances; but arsenic...does not produce pain, nor does antimony immediately afterwards...

But he did not think that a quarter of a grain of copper sulphate would produce a burning sensation (this was the apparent reaction of Isabella Bankes to the copper sulphate pills prescribed by Dr Todd):

...if the irritant poison had been administered from time to time, in small doses, for three or four weeks, and a larger dose than usual was administered, it would produce purging, and it might produce a burning sensation through the whole intestinal canal...I believe the whole class of metallic medicines would produce that effect.

And:

...I have never in my experience met with or heard of a case in which antimony and arsenic were used, each of them occasionally, on the human subject...

On the question of dysentery:

> ...dysentery...may occur...either from a specific poison,
> or from disease of the intestines...the form of dysentery
> which I should think a lady, with a liver like Miss
> Bankes, would be subject to, would be the form of sub
> acute dysentery; not dysentery arising from poison,
> but which is prolonged over a very considerable
> period...

It was now six o'clock in the evening, and the trial was
adjourned until the following morning.

The court had been very hot and uncomfortable during the
day, aggravated by the presence of large numbers of the public
and others who had assembled to observe this extraordinary
trial. Among those present, himself a barrister, was William
Frederick Pollock, son of the trial judge. In 1887, the year before
he died, he published his *Personal Remembrances,* one of which
was of the Smethurst trial. He described an incident that had
happened on 17th August, 'towards the end of the sitting', when
the court proceedings had descended into farce. The judge had
asked, repeatedly, for ventilation to be increased. Finally the
sheriffs told him that they had done all they could. In William
Pollock's words:

> "Then," said the judge, "open the windows." "The
> windows will not open, my lord," said the sheriff.
> "Then break them," said the judge. Upon which one of
> the ushers, armed with his long white wand, went into
> the jury-box and, mounted upon the back of another,
> began thrashing away at the panes of glass in the large
> window above the jury-box. Another usher, similarly
> provided, and leaning as far forward as he could from
> the gallery, while a second man held him to prevent
> him falling over, began to attack the upper part of
> the window, and the two men belaboured it as if they

were beating a walnut tree to bring down the walnuts. The effect was irresistibly droll, and for five minutes everyone in court, including the judge and prisoner at the bar, was convulsed with laughter. At last enough glass was smashed to let in the desired amount of fresh air, gravity was resumed, and the case was proceeded with as if nothing had happened.

Day four of the trial, Thursday 18th August, opened at 9 o'clock, although there was a short delay because 'no alderman was present to sit as second commissioner'. After Alderman Phillips had been found, the trial commenced. The press reports stated that Smethurst 'presented a careworn and anxious appearance'.

First on the stand, and continuing his evidence from the previous day, was Dr Richardson. After a question about muscle rigidity post-mortem, he commented on the appearance of the liver:

> ...the liver was hard and large...I assume that it was indurated [hardened] and speckled...a liver in health is never speckled, the fat on the liver forms a basis of my opinion that there had been a chronic disease of the liver...I do not think antimony would cause that...my experiments upon dogs teach me that it would not...

He was asked about his experience of obstetrics:

> ...I was an accoucheur [obstetrician], but ceased to practise as such in 1854...sickness, accompanied with dysenteric diarrhoea, in the early stage of pregnancy might have been the cause of all the appearances that were exhibited in this case...

Serjeant Parry now asked about the Palmer case:

> Did you give evidence in Palmer's case, at the request of Mr. Serjeant Shee [the principal defence barrister]?

Dr Richardson:

> I did [but] I [refused] any remuneration for the evidence I gave...I confined myself, at that trial, to a statement of the causes of angina pectoris, and the symptoms with which I was practically acquainted...

On Isabella Bankes:

> ...the burning sensation in the intestinal canal...violent diarrhoea, and violent vomiting, are symptoms of irritant poison [but] they are as well symptoms in cases of natural disease, such as violent dysentery...

And the effect of medicine:

> if a dose of a quarter of a grain of sulphate of copper were administered to a patient it would not produce either violent vomiting, or violent purging, or burning sensation in the intestinal canal, but if the patient had been suffering from violent irritation of the intestines, arising either from natural or mechanical causes, the administration of sulphate of copper would have a tendency to increase that irritation...

The effect of Isabella's pregnancy:

> I know of cases of diarrhoea, vomiting, and burning sensation from pregnancy...I am acquainted, by my reading, with cases in which, in the early stage of pregnancy, a woman of from 40 to 45 years of age has suffered from burning sensation in the intestinal canal, and where there has been ulceration of the fauces [the back of the mouth] and apthous spots on the tongue... it may occur during the early period; it may occur at any period...

His experiments on dogs:

> ...experiments on dogs and the lower animals have been made by the greatest toxicologists with reference to the effects of poison on the human frame...they form the great bulk of scientific knowledge in Europe upon the subject of poisons, and their operation on the human frame...the materials for forming a judgment of the effects of slow antimonial poisoning upon the human system are very [rare]...

Coming back to Isabella Bankes:

> I still adhere to my opinion that the deceased lady may have died from natural causes.

Benjamin Richardson was 31 years old, with barely ten years' experience but a rising reputation as his eventual knighthood would affirm. Ironically, it had been Dr Alfred Taylor who having been impressed with Richardson had arranged a partnership for him in Barnes in 1849.[8] Now though, they evidently disagreed on fundamentals and found themselves on opposite sides during the Palmer trial as well as the present case.

Next on the stand was Dr Julian Edward Rodgers, a registered doctor of medicine, and sometime Professor of Chemistry at the 'Old St George's School of Medicine'.[9] He too had been a defence witness at Palmer's trial and was frequently called by coroners to make analyses of the human body. He made a rather interesting point on the question of potassium chlorate:

> ...chlorate of potass is in itself a perfectly innocent salt...I do not think that, supposing small doses of

8   ODNB.
9   The Grosvenor Place School of Medicine.

> arsenic or of antimony were administered to the
> human subject, either in chlorate of potass, or chlorate
> of potass contemporaneously administered, the action
> of the chlorate of potass would have the slightest effect
> in eliminating the poison from the system; if it did so,
> you would have no poison...if chlorate of potass was
> removing poison from the system as it was given,
> the poison would not have time to act as such; and
> consequently, it would be a kind of antidote; it would
> be administering poison with an antidote at the same
> time...

So if Dr Taylor's original thesis – that arsenic or antimony
were administered with potassium chlorate – was correct, the
hypothesis that the diuretic action of the salt would remove
the poison, meant that it would never have had time to act as
a poison.

Dr Rogers:

> ...chlorate of potass is a perfectly harmless agent...
> largely prescribed by many practitioners, and used as
> a wash for sweetening the mouth...

And if arsenic or antimony were given to a human patient over
a period of four or five weeks:

> I should...expect to find arsenic in the tissues, and
> antimony also, particularly in the liver; the liver is the
> great criterion...the absence of the poison from the
> liver would cause me to doubt whether the allegation
> was correct...I should expect to find either arsenic or
> antimony under such circumstances in the kidneys and
> in the spleen as well; their absence would be a strong
> element in favour of that opinion [that the allegation

was incorrect]...if I found poison in the blood, I should expect to find it in the tissues and everywhere...

And then:

...I do not believe it is possible to find traces of antimony in the blood without also finding it deposited in the liver...the blood in the heart must be regarded as a sample of the whole 28 lbs or so that is circulating in the system: if you find it there in one small portion, you must find it wherever blood flows...in a case of alleged slow metallic poisoning, the absence of the poison from the tissues would raise the greatest doubt as to poison being the cause of death...

Although Dr Rogers was a surgeon and apothecary and had practised as such, his main experience was in chemistry. He was aware of the impurities in medicines:

I am acquainted with the fact that...bismuth generally... contains arsenic...I have in my pocket a quantity obtained from about six doses (*producing some*)...by another analysis I found upwards of half a grain in an ounce of bismuth...

He went on to criticize Dr Taylor for using Marsh's test for finding arsenic in bismuth as not being appropriate (this was the bismuth from Dr Julius' surgery, when they were trying to eliminate his bismuth as a source of arsenic).

The Judge asked:

Is half a grain the largest quantity [of arsenic] you ever found in an ounce [of bismuth]?

Dr Rodgers:

I have never made the estimation before as to quantity, but I have had specimens [where] the quantity I found was such as to make it improper to use [that] bismuth as a medicine...bismuth is frequently prescribed by physicians in cases where it would appear proper; and it has done injury instead of producing benefit; and I have very little doubt that that has been from arsenic there, and not from any fault in bismuth as a remedy.

Serjeant Parry then asked him whether he had analysed *Grey powder*:

No, but I am aware it is frequently impure; I know...that it frequently contains antimony...commercial mercury is used, and it is often impure...I should think more than the arsenic I found in the bismuth...this I know more from what I have heard...if any traces of antimony were found in a body...it is contained in a great many medicines that are innocently taken...

On the question of the effect of poisoning by arsenic and antimony, his view of the symptoms that should be seen was the same as given by previous witnesses.

Cross-examined by Serjeant Ballantine, Dr Rodgers said that he had appeared in the Palmer case for the defence. He established, using animal experiments, that if strychnine had been given, it would have been found in the body; Dr Taylor, he said (who appeared for the Prosecution in the Palmer case), had not found strychnine in the body. He was asked about the arsenic found in one of Isabella's evacuations:

...if it is well [established] that in an evacuation there is one-sixth of a grain of arsenic...I should be convinced that there was a large quantity remaining in the stomach somewhere or other...[otherwise] it would lead me to doubt whether the experiment had been correct or not...

And coming back to the Palmer trial again:

> ...at the trial of Palmer, and with reference to strychnia, I confined my evidence to the statement of what I believed to be a chemical fact, viz., that if strychnia had been administered while living, and had caused death, it ought to have been found in the body; that is still my opinion...

References to the Palmer trial kept coming up, and it was mainly the prosecution that were mentioning them because the parallels were clear. Dr Todd, Dr Taylor and Mr Brande had appeared for the prosecution in that trial, and Drs Richardson and Rogers for the defence; the identical distribution as for the current trial. But reference had also been made to their affiliations: Drs Todd and Taylor were associated with large London teaching hospitals – King's College and Guy's respectively – whereas Dr Richardson was a lecturer at the (private) Grosvenor Place School of Medicine, a medical school not affiliated with a hospital, and Dr Rodgers had also lectured there until two years previously. In the case of the Palmer trial, the defence case had failed and Palmer was convicted of murdering Cook by the administration of strychnine. And although no strychnine was found in Cook's body, Dr Taylor did find a number of traces of antimony... History was repeating itself and Serjeant Ballantine seemed to be determined to keep reminding the jury that 'the team' from the Grosvenor Place School had been on the losing side last time round.

Next on the stand was Dr John Lewis William Thudichum. He was a doctor of medicine and a lecturer on Practical and Experimental Chemistry also at the Grosvenor Place School of Medicine. As Ludwig Johann Wilhelm Thudichum he had trained under Professor Liebig at Giessen. Having been a supporter of the Republicans in the 1848 Revolution, he was unable to get a university post in Germany and had come to London to seek employment.[10]

Dr Thudichum had collaborated with Dr Richardson in the experiments on dogs to establish the effect of potassium chlorate administered with poison. On Isabella Bankes:

> ...in my judgment her death is compatible with natural causes...in addition to the circumstance of pregnancy I should attribute the death of Isabella Bankes to diptheretic dysentery...the symptoms...are incompatible with slow arsenical poisoning [and] antimonial poisoning...in cases of slow arsenical poisoning I should expect to find the stomach ulcerated...in either case I should expect to find the arsenic or the antimony, as the case might be, in the tissues after death.

Serjeant Ballantine wanted to know what Dr Thudichum meant by diptheretic dysentery – was it the type prevalent in the East?

> No; I speak of dysentery occurring in Europe, and in this country...I speak of a specific form of dysentery called diptheretic dysentery...

Serjeant Ballantine:

> Have you ever seen the body opened of a person who died of it?

Dr Thudichum:

> [yes] I opened the body myself...I found that there was a false membrane[11].

---

10 ODNB
11 A 'false membrane' is a characteristic of diphtheria.

The Judge asked:

Was that throughout the intestines?

Dr Thudichum:

No; merely in the large intestines...that is why it is called diptheretic...there are several forms of dysentery, and that is one of them, well established in science...it is mentioned in Rokitansky's Morbid Anatomy, which is well known in this country...

In response to an unrecorded question:

I do not know Cooper's Medical Dictionary, or Copland's Medical Dictionary...I have not read Dr. Hooper's Vade Mecum; I do not read such books; they are merely compilations.

That was a snipe at Dr Copland, one of the prosecution witnesses. His three volume Dictionary of Practical Medicine had been completed the previous year and had earned him the title of 'The (Dr) Johnson of medicine'.[12]

The Judge:

Can you mention any book in which one is likely to meet with it in the library of a medical gentleman with a reasonable library?

Dr Thudichum:

I am sure that you would find it in Rokitansky's Morbid Anatomy, which would be found in the library of any gentleman of scientific acquirements...in the cases I have alluded to I had observed shreddy matters

12 ODNB

of membrane pass during life, and I found a false membrane...

Following some questions from Serjeant Ballantine and Mr Giffard regarding where he worked and his nationality, Dr Thudichum continued:

I am [German by birth]; I study my profession in almost all languages...I have heard the description of the intestines in this case...hearing that shreddy matters were found in the evacuations would confirm my view...

He went on to describe some chemical analyses that he had made:

I made an analysis of Grey powder...it consists of caustic, carbonate of lime [calcium oxide or quicklime], mercury partly oxidised, [silica], with phosphate of iron, arsenic, and antimony...I think there were ten materials in the Grey powder that I analysed... there was more arsenic than antimony...I have not weighed it...I have also analysed bismuth...obtained from Hearon, McCulloch and Squires...there was both arsenic and antimony in it...

The Judge:

Enough to be called a trace?

Considerably more than a trace, Dr Thudichum replied. He went on to describe some analyses he had made of bismuth used in medicine, which showed 'dangerous' levels of arsenic and antimony. He thought it improper to use as a medicine without purifying it.

He was asked about his analysis of *Grey powder* in which he had also found arsenic. Following a question from the judge he said that he had made a qualitative analysis only:

> ...the quantity is of importance, no doubt; but quantitative analyses are very laborious indeed...it could be done: I did not do it, because my occupation, and the time allowed, and all that, did not allow me to take the trouble...

Dr Thudichum was clarifying the difference between *qualitative* as opposed to *quantitative* chemical analysis. In the former, the purpose is to establish what elements or chemical compounds are detectably present in a sample. In quantitative analysis, which is much more difficult and time-consuming, the objective is to establish how much of each is present. He said he rarely prescribed *Grey powder* although it was a common medicine frequently given to children.

Serjeant Ballantine:

> Then do you think that the arsenic in the Grey powder poisoned Isabella Bankes?

Dr Thudichum reacted with some irritation to this question:

> I never said anything of the kind...the Grey powder might produce the apthous spots in consequence of the action of the mercury...it would not arise, either from the antimony or the arsenic...I do not think that the arsenic in the bismuth had any operation upon Miss Bankes...I have already stated to what I attribute the symptoms in Miss Bankes' case; neither the Grey powder [n]or the bismuth had anything to do with her death.

Serjeant Parry:

> Did you ever hear the absurd supposition that it had, until you heard it from my friend now?

Dr Thudichum:

> I never dreamt of so absurd a thing.

He went on to say that the arsenic found in the evacuation (in bottle No 2) could well have come from the bismuth Isabella Bankes was given as medicine, as could the antimony found in the intestines and elsewhere.

Following a question from the judge on the quantities involved, Dr Thudichum commented, perhaps with less tact than would have been appropriate, that since he had performed over 100 analyses for the case, he 'really could not give the time to...make a quantitative analysis'.

This was one of the most interesting exchanges in the trial so far. It is ironic that it took a German scientist to inject some precision into both the science and language in a British court, and get to the real and indisputable facts of the case. What is also clear is that what may have sounded arrogant: 'I do not read such books; they are merely compilations', and, '...did not allow me to take the trouble', not to mention some of the other comments clearly irritated the judge, since he commented later on his distrust of Dr Thudichum. Nevertheless, Dr Thudichum's evidence was clear, precise and entirely to the point. He provided credible scientific explanations for the arsenic in the evacuation as well as the antimony found in the intestines, and a diagnosis of Isabella Bankes' ailment based on his own personal experience.

The next witness for the defence was Dr Francis Cornelius Webb, MD from the University of Edinburgh, and a Licentiate of the Royal College of Surgeons. He was also a lecturer on Medical Jurisprudence and Toxicology at the Grosvenor Place School of Medicine and a physician to the Great Northern Hospital. He had collaborated with Drs Richardson and Thudichum on the experiments on dogs and analysis of medicines looking for poisonous impurities.

Dr Webb:

> ...from all that I have heard [in court], and from my experience as a medical man, I am of the opinion that the deceased died from natural causes...

The Judge:

> You say that the symptoms, and so on, are to be accounted for by natural causes?

Dr Webb:

> Yes and the post-mortem appearances also.

Serjeant Parry:

> We have heard that this lady was in from the fifth to the seventh week of pregnancy; is that a fact which, in your opinion, ought to be taken into consideration in judging of the cause of her death?

Dr Webb:

> Most decidedly...if I had been called in to attend her, as a married lady, and had been told she was subject to vomiting, I should, most decidedly have felt it my duty to ascertain whether she was pregnant or not.

The Judge:

> How would you have ascertained that?

Dr Webb:

> By a close examination of the symptoms; and by an
> examination of the mammae [breasts] and the uterus...
> if I found vomiting and purging going on, I should not
> have considered the fact that the catamenae [periods]
> had appeared once, of any importance, because it will
> frequently appear once after pregnancy; that would
> not have prevented my examining into the existence
> of pregnancy.

Serjeant Parry:

> We heard that this lady suffered from nausea and
> sickness, and vomiting; are you acquainted with cases
> of very severe vomiting from early pregnancy?

Dr Webb:

> I am; in very severe cases of vomiting I know that
> the only way of stopping it, and saving the life of the
> mother, is to procure the abortion of the foetus...if the
> pregnant woman...was also subject to bilious irritation,
> that would increase the symptoms...in all cases of
> severe vomiting and diarrhoea, where great acidity
> is generated in the system, there is always a burning
> sensation in the intestinal canal, from whatever cause
> it may arise...

On the question of the medicines prescribed to Isabella:

> ...I consider sulphate of copper, nitrate of silver, and
> acetate of lead, most incorrect medicines to prescribe
> in the case of early pregnancy...I consider that such
> medicines would have more tendency to increase
> irritation of the intestines, if it existed, than to allay it...

Serjeant Parry:

> Is the diagnosis of the body of Miss Bankes, taking the symptoms, the post-mortem appearances, and the whole together, consistent in your judgment with diarrhoea and vomiting, arising from early pregnancy?

Dr Webb:

> I consider that Miss Bankes died of dysentery, made worse by the condition of early pregnancy...all the symptoms that have been given in evidence, in relation to Miss. Bankes, might arise from the vomiting and diarrhoea of pregnancy...

He went on:

> I agree with Dr. Wilks, who was examined on the part of the prosecution, that cases of dysentery occur which it is impossible to refer to any particular cause...the two cases referred to by him in Guy's, which were styled dysentery, were in fact cases of idiopathic dysentery; a disease which is killing hundreds every year in this country.

The Judge:

> Does "idiopathic" mean that the disorder arises of its own accord?

Dr Webb:

> Yes; not from any poison or from any specific cause, as far as we know...

Serjeant Parry:

> In a case of chronic dysentery which might last for weeks, would the symptoms be great weakness and emaciation?

Dr Webb:

> No doubt: a rawness and tenderness of the mouth and fauces would exist, with apthae and minute ulcers; that is often accompanied with great tenderness in the oesophagus, and a burning sensation along the whole of the intestinal canal.

He went on:

> ...If there was a disease of the womb for which it was necessary to use an injection of nitrate of silver, that would probably indicate some ulceration of the *cervix uteri;* the neck of the womb...if there had been such a condition of the womb an appreciable time before pregnancy, I think it might add to the irritation of pregnancy...

(Isabella had such a condition, and it was being treated with 'injections' of silver nitrate...) Dr Webb:

> ...if I found a patient suffering from severe purging or diarrhoea, vomiting, burning sensation of the throat and of the intestinal canal, the sensation of a ball in the throat, accompanied by ulcerous appearances in parts of the body, that would not, in my judgment, necessarily lead to the conclusion that she must be the subject of arsenical or irritant poisoning, and that alone; unless I found other symptoms, it would never enter my head...

On poisoning with arsenic or antimony, he would expect to find traces in the liver:

> ...in cases of slow arsenical or antimonial poisoning, I should most decidedly expect, if death resulted, to find the poison in the tissues; as Dr Taylor has said, the finding poison in the liver is the great criterion...

Dr Webb went on to detail the appearance of the organs post-mortem, comparing them with what would be expected if poison had been used. He finished by saying:

> I am fortified in my opinion that she died from natural causes...

He then commented on Dr Taylor's analysis:

> ...if I am testing a liquid for the presence of arsenic or any other irritant poison, in arriving at a perfectly accurate judgment as to the quantity, I ought to make what is called a quantitative analysis; that is done by actually weighing the whole that I find...any other mode of proceeding is likely to lead to the most erroneous results, most certainly.

He thought Dr Taylor's assessment of the amount of arsenic found in the evacuation no better than a guess.

Serjeant Ballantine:

> ...supposing you were called in to attend the wife of a medical man, and he assured you she was not pregnant, and her courses were in order; do you mean that you would consider further investigation necessary?

Dr Webb:

> If I found her suffering from vomiting and purging, which went on in spite of all my remedies, I should

certainly...without pregnancy I should not have expected to find the vomiting so constant...the bowels would continue ulcerating, and would get worse and worse down to the death; the symptoms would become more aggravated, till exhaustion killed the patient; therefore I should not expect that any medicines given would check the disease...in such a state I think a quarter of a grain of sulphate of copper pill would produce the effect of irritation, and that it would increase the irritation...if I had been acquainted with all those symptoms I have heard described in court to-day I should not have dreamt of poison.

Serjeant Parry:

My friend asked you "Is dysentery common?" are you able to say how many cases of dysentery may have occurred in so many years?

Dr Webb:

From 1848 to 1854, more than 15,000 persons died in England of dysentery; from 1850 to 1854, in London alone, dysentery killed more persons than pericarditis, or inflammation of the covering of the heart, thrush, gout, syphilis, insanity, quinsy, or remittent fever, respectively...the disease which I have so described in its numerical effects, is what I call idiopathic dysentery, and is perfectly well known in the medical world and to scientific men.

Dr Webb's evidence hardly needs comment; he was critical of Isabella's care when she was alive and dismissive of Dr Taylor's analysis of the evacuation and the diagnosis of poisoning by the prosecution witnesses.

Dr Gilbert Finlay Girdwood was called next. His expertise was obstetrics, having delivered more than 3,000 women. He had experience of cases of vomiting in pregnancy combined both with diarrhoea and dysentery.

Serjeant Parry:

> In your judgment, if a person were pregnant, and suffering from dysenteric symptoms, such as you observed in that case, would it be proper to give mineral medicines?

Dr Girdwood:

> I should not give any in pregnancy, nor on any occasion whatever...unless I made out the reason why I should give it...in this country [dysentery] generally proceeds from a disease, which has been very well expressed by a celebrated man, Dr. Copland...it commences in that portion of the intestine called the caecum, extending thence to the anus, inflammation of that portion of the intestine, ending in ulceration and death if it is not stopped...

Serjeant Parry:

> In your judgment, was her death to be attributed to poison or to the effects of dysentery combined with pregnancy?

Dr Girdwood:

> I see the whole of the symptoms traceable to the dysentery, and to the consequent ulceration and exhaustion...pregnancy and dysentery would quite account, in my judgment, for the diarrhoea... this would be much aggravated by a bilious temperament and any affection of the liver.

The next witness volunteered himself to Serjeant Parry to give evidence. He had been in court on another case when he heard of the Smethurst trial and contacted Smethurst's solicitor, Mr Charles Humphreys, who was very interested in what he had to say.

Mr James Edmunds was a surgeon, general practitioner, member of the College of Surgeons in London and surgeon to the H division of police and the Royal Maternity Charity. He described a case of a woman in the seventh month of pregnancy with symptoms virtually identical to those of Isabella Bankes. He described two weeks spent treating the woman with a preparation of chalk, opium, and prussic acid or bismuth. Sulphate of zinc was also used as an injection. Sulphate of copper, recommended by the best authorities in the chronic stage of dysentery, was not used because of the vomiting. Large quantities of blood came away from ulceration of the lining of the bowels. After her death he

> examined the stomach and glands; the stomach was slightly injected, but not more than you find frequently in post-mortem examinations, but in the liver, the bowels, and the caecum there was the most frightful ulceration; the whole lining membrane seemed as if it had been swept away; that is a strong indication of dysentery...in the large bowels, from the caecum to the rectum, there were ulcers on which you could lay a shilling...

He went on:

> I am personally acquainted with the fact that diarrhoea, purging, and vomiting, and consequent exhaustion, exists in the early stages of pregnancy, but principally vomiting...

146

The last medical man on the stand was another obstetrician, Dr William Tyler Smith, lecturer in Obstetrics at Queen Mary Hospital, Fellow of the Royal College of Physicians, and author of a manual of obstetrics. He had more than fifteen years' experience of midwifery.

Dr Smith:

> ...excessive vomiting in the early part of pregnancy is often met with...[and can end] in death...If I were called in to a patient, a married woman, suffering from vomiting and intestinal disorder during the child-bearing period, I should certainly think of pregnancy amongst other causes, and should do my best to ascertain whether it existed or not...sometimes the periods go on after pregnancy has commenced; in some cases during the whole of pregnancy, but those are exceptional cases...they not unfrequently [sic] happen...

The Judge:

> You say "it not unfrequently happens;" do you mean that it happens to one woman in a hundred, or one in five hundred?

Dr Smith:

> ...one very often meets with cases in which patients are regular during the early months...it certainly happens as often as once in a hundred times...the cessation of the monthly periods is an ordinary normal natural symptom of pregnancy...women who have any uterine disorder are more likely to be unwell during pregnancy than other women...

And,

> ...I have been consulted in at least four cases of vomiting during pregnancy which ended in death, and a considerable number of other cases in which vomiting was excessive, and in which there was danger.

He continued:

> ...where women have been subject to bilious irritation and bilious attack; they are more affected by vomiting and intestinal irritation, including occasional purging, than others, during pregnancy...I have seen occasional purging as frequently as three or four times a day in connexion with vomiting...

Serjeant Parry:

> Have you known cases yourself where there has been excessive vomiting and general intestinal disturbance in the early stages of pregnancy, in which it has been necessary, to save the life of the mother, to abort the foetus and procure a miscarriage?

Dr Smith:

> That is a recognised practice in the vomiting of pregnancy which threatens life...nature generally does it herself, and this practice has arisen from an imitation of nature...if by an effort of nature the child is not got rid of, then the medical man intervenes and produces abortion.

Serjeant Parry:

> Have you known in your own practice cases of excessive vomiting, accompanied by purging or diarrhoea, with a burning sensation... erroneously attributed to poison?

Dr Smith:

> I have known one case in which there was a great
> amount of vomiting, and some amount of purging, in
> which the friends of the lady could not be brought
> to believe that her husband was not poisoning her...I
> have known evacuations examined by a chemist under
> that impression...an effervescing draught, composed
> of hydrocyanic acid (prussic acid) is one of the most
> valuable remedies in the vomitings of pregnancy...I
> have known this vomiting to cease a few days or a few
> hours before death...

Serjeant Parry:

> In cases of death occasioned by the natural causes you
> have described, and which are within your particular
> knowledge, have you noticed a peculiar expression of
> the face?

Dr Smith:

> The expression is that of death from starvation...it is
> recognised that there is a peculiar expression of the
> face in such cases...Dr. Paul Dubois, the first obstetrician
> in France at the present time, observed twenty cases
> of death by vomiting caused by pregnancy, in thirteen
> years, and he marks as one of the four or five distinct
> signs of danger, a peculiar expression of the face, "a
> painful expression of the face"...

Question from the jury:

> Could dysentery be kept up by the administration of
> medicine?

Dr Smith:

> If any irritating medicine were given, it would be kept
> up; any irritating medicine would tend to that...any
> medical or non-medical person could do that.

The last of the witnesses for the defence was Smethurst's dentist, Mr George Pedley. In response to a question from Serjeant Parry, he said:

> I have attended Mr. Smethurst as a dentist...I recollect his consulting me about his teeth, about the middle of last February...he complained of foulness of breath... in the course of conversation I mentioned to him a mixture which he might use for foulness of breath... chlorate of potass.

So that was the reason that Smethurst had potassium chlorate in his possession.

That completed the case for the defence. It is notable that Serjeant Parry called only medical witnesses with the intention of demonstrating that no poisoning had taken place and that Isabella's symptoms were entirely consistent with natural causes. He called no character witnesses, probably on the basis that since Smethurst was a self-confessed bigamist (and perjurer, having sworn an oath to obtain the marriage licence), witnesses to character would have been superfluous.

Also notable, is that the medical witnesses for the defence, although smaller in number than those for the prosecution, had given their testimony with precision, citing detailed evidence to support the positions they took. They described symptoms of arsenic and antimony poisoning that were absent from Isabella Bankes. They insisted that had she been poisoned with arsenic and/or antimony, those substances would have been found deposited in her organs, principally, her liver. They presented proper experimental evidence, dismissed by the judge, that Dr Taylor's thesis that potassium chlorate had been used in some way to mask the effects of those poisons, as having no foundation in fact. They also demonstrated, in the tests with dogs dosed with the two poisons, that arsenic and antimony were found in the bodies after death, particularly in the liver. They pointed out that both arsenic and antimony were frequent impurities in the medicines Isabella had been given. Several of them also presented evidence, apparently unknown by the twelve medical men of the prosecution, that severe vomiting and diarrhoea in pregnancy can lead to the death of the mother. Set against that, the prosecution medical witnesses had, for the most part, simply expressed opinions based on reports of Isabella's symptoms in life, and the post-mortem findings. And those who had treated Isabella, and who would be expected to be the best qualified to judge her condition, were criticised for failing to establish that she was pregnant, and prescribing inappropriate medicines.

Serjeant Ballantine now had the right of reply. After complimenting his learned friend, Serjeant Parry, on the conduct of the defence, he set out in his final address to the jury what he regarded as the critical points of the case. And having called twelve doctors and one chemist to provide evidence for the prosecution, he went on to warn against the verdict being decided on the medical evidence alone. He could not, he said,

> ...allow the fact of a swarm of medical men being called with a view to create doubt in your minds, and induce you to return a verdict that is not warranted by the real facts and circumstances that are before you.[13]

This was an odd position to take having called one medical expert after another who had declared that Isabella's symptoms and death could only be accounted for by irritant poisoning. He consolidated his argument:

> In all these charges of secret murder...nothing is more easy than for a medical man to come forward, and by a little alteration of the facts, make it appear that certain cases in which they were concerned resembled the

---

13 Serjeant Ballantine's words have been changed into the first person.

one under discussion, and this sometimes has an effect in opposition to positive facts...your duty...is not to be led away by evidence of this character, but to look at all the facts that are laid before you, and to say as men of common sense and acquainted with the ways of the world, whether the conduct of the prisoner could be fairly associated with the supposition of his innocence of the crime alleged against him.

So having gone to a great deal of trouble to establish a case based on hard medical evidence, Serjeant Ballantine was calling on the jury to ignore 'evidence of this character' and use their common sense and experience of the 'ways of the world' in their judgement. Perhaps he had realized the strength of the medical evidence called by the defence compared with that of the bungling Dr Taylor, and decided to concentrate instead on the apparently incriminating circumstantial evidence. He went on to question the prisoner's motives for the bigamous marriage pointing out that it could not have succeeded without Mary Smethurst's connivance, and suggesting that only Isabella's death could have released Smethurst from an untenable position. The letter to Mary Smethurst proved, he said, that Smethurst was not anticipating the connection to Isabella to be a long one. Ballantine went on to say that Smethurst had falsely stated to Dr Julius that Isabella was not 'in the family way'. (What Dr Julius had actually said, was that Smethurst had told him that Isabella's 'usual periods were on her...') He then sought to discredit the medical evidence for the defence:

> ...the evidence of Dr Julius, who saw the patient constantly, and who watched her day after day, [is] worth the evidence of twenty scientific men who merely came to state remarks and cases which they had read in books...

152

Serjeant Ballantine did not comment on the fact that with all of Dr Julius' experience and constant day after day attention, he had still failed to establish that Isabella might be pregnant. He summarized the other incriminating evidence – the apparent exclusion of Louisa Bankes from seeing her sister, and of course the will. He was interrupted by the foreman of the jury when he questioned why Smethurst had taken Louisa's soup outside the room 'if he did not intend to do something [to it]...' (Smethurst had taken it out of the room to cool it down.) The juryman said that that was only surmise. The Serjeant agreed but countered by saying that in cases of 'secret poisoning they could never get positive testimony...' but had to consider all of the facts and draw fair and reasonable inferences.

Ballantine then addressed the issue of Dr Taylor and his mistake, pointing out that the jury had been told of this at the outset. He reminded them of the finding of arsenic in one of Isabella's stools and commented on the failure to find arsenic in any of Dr Julius' medicines (that was not true; Dr Taylor *had* found traces of arsenic in some copper sulphate). Then, appearing to ignore the principle of 'beyond reasonable doubt', he said to the jury:

> If you entertain a fair and reasonable conviction, upon all the facts that are laid before you, that the prisoner is guilty of the crime of which he has been accused, your duty to the country and to your own consciences requires you to say so by your verdict.

Of all of Ballantine's thirteen medical and scientific witnesses, he only mentioned Drs Julius and Taylor, the latter almost apologetically.

This was now the fourth day of the trial. The prosecution and defence witnesses had been heard and it remained only to hear the judge's summing-up.

Verdict

Sir Frederick Pollock, the Lord Chief Baron and judge for the Queen vs Smethurst, began his summing-up in the early afternoon of the fourth day of the trial. It would be late afternoon of the fifth day before he had finished. Sir Frederick was 76 years old, and as trial judge one of his most important jobs was to keep notes of the evidence and summarize it for the jury before they retired to consider their verdict. It was a critical task, at least as important as the presentation of the evidence itself, particularly in a case like this where the pivotal evidence was provided by medical and scientific witnesses. They had given their testimony in esoteric technical language, including Latin medical terms. Sir Frederick was not a doctor or scientist (although he was a mathematician), but it was his responsibility to help the jury understand and weigh this evidence even though many of the details must have been unintelligible to them.

It is interesting to speculate exactly how the judge did keep notes of four days of complex witness statements and cross-examinations. There were comments in the press after the Smethurst trial that a case of the importance, complexity and length as that of Thomas Smethurst, ought to have had three judges presiding. Indeed on the fifth day of the trial, Sir Frederick was joined on the bench by Mr Justice Willes who read part of the evidence to the jury. For the examination of the witnesses, only Sir Frederick was present.

Evidence at the Old Bailey was recorded verbatim by a court official. Since this was taken down in shorthand, there would not have been time to write up a fair copy for the judge to use in his summing-up. The judge made his own notes as he went along – inevitably brief, condensed and limited only to what he thought to be relevant. In 1863, James Stephen, a barrister and judge, published his *General View of the Criminal Law of England*. He included a section on the Smethurst trial and commenting on the sources used, he said:

> This...[has been]...written comparing it with the notes of the Lord Chief Baron...I have compared the report [of the trial] in the 50th Volume of the Old Bailey Sessions Papers...the correspondence between the notes of the judge and those of the short-hand writer, is most remarkable. Allowing for a little compression by the judge, they are word for word the same...

That was an extraordinary feat for a 76 year-old who was also presiding over the trial. In fact Sir Frederick Pollock's notes of the trial consisted of 114 pages of foolscap in fairly legible handwriting.

Sir Frederick started by instructing the jury:

> ...if...you come to the conclusion, as sensible men, that the case for the prosecution [is proved], to the extent that in your important concerns in life, you would act on the persuasion that this evidence produces, then it [will] be your duty to find the prisoner guilty.

If not, then he was not guilty, since the prisoner was entitled to the benefit of 'all of the doubts, as far as they are grave, serious and solemn...', and he added that the prisoner was entitled to the 'benefit of the remark that no arsenic was found in his possession...' Sir Frederick said that the case was one of the most remarkable in all its circumstances that he ever remembered in his long experience. The jury had to decide, he said, whether a crime had been committed, and if so, by whom. He then proceeded to summarize in minute detail the circumstantial evidence against Smethurst, finishing by saying:

> ...it is not because he took [Isabella] to a church, and there went through a ceremony, which by the law of the land is a felony; it is not because he was guilty in respect of the will of a violation of what I think he owed to the unhappy woman, to her family and to society at large; it is not for that reason that you are to find him guilty of the present charge...

Although:

> Whatever belongs to his conduct, whatever blame may attach to him, whatever other matters may be against him, he is entitled to be relieved from the awful charge [if you think his guilt not proven]...

The judge then again went over the events from the time Isabella and Smethurst met, until her death. Again and again he stressed the sin, the crime, the immorality of their 'marriage' and the fact that they were living together. He suggested that Smethurst must have known Isabella was pregnant (since he was a medical man and one of the witnesses for the defence had indicated that there were ways of diagnosing pregnancy regardless of whether the periods had stopped). And coming back to the making of the will when Isabella was on her death-bed:

> Gentlemen, how to account for a sister being kept from the dying bed of her nearest relation, and an attorney being introduced at that moment...in these dying moments the attorney is brought in to make the will; and there is neither the consolation of a relative to smooth the pillow, [n]or the attendance of a clergyman to speak the whisper of peace to the tormented conscience...

He went on to say that the jury had to decide whether Isabella could be the 'willing partaker in all the crimes', implying that she was a victim in this also. He now defended Dr Julius' conduct in not acting immediately on his suspicions that Isabella was being poisoned; he spent some time over that, pointing out the seriousness of accusing someone of attempted murder. On the question of the financial motive, he claimed that the £1,700 or £1,800 lent on mortgage which would be immediately received would be equivalent to twelve years' worth of dividends on £5,000. That would be better than

> ...waiting for the doubtful chance of what Miss Bankes would say, when she found that she was burdened with a child, with no acceptance in society, with no friends... the scorn of one sex and the abhorrence of the other...

At this point Serjeant Parry challenged the judge over what he said that he (Parry) had said; he did not say that it was unparalleled to hear that a person was convicted when poison was not found in the body (this was the case in the Palmer trial), but that he challenged the prosecution to point to any case of a man convicted of poisoning, where no poison was traced to his possession. The judge dismissed the point as of no importance saying:

> It may be that no arsenic, no poison is traced to the possession of the accused, it may be that no poison is found in the body, and yet it may be the easiest thing in the world to put a case where no sensible man could doubt that the accused had possessed the poison, that he had used it, and that the deceased had died of it.

The judge then proceeded to instruct the jury on the principles of circumstantial evidence. The import of his thesis was that one small piece of evidence on its own may be insignificant, but add another and another and another and together they tip the balance. The court then adjourned until the morning.

Friday 19th August 1859, and the court was reconvened at 9 o'clock. The press reports said that the prisoner appeared 'very dejected'. However, Smethurst challenged the judge on a point of fact. Smethurst would have known that any communication should have been made via his barrister, Serjeant Parry, but he was determined to set the record straight:

> My Lord I wish to address a few words to your Lordship.

The Judge:

> I think you had better not do so at present.

Smethurst:

> ...your lordship made some observations which I wish to correct. It is simply in reference to this question: In addressing the jury last night with reference to myself, you spoke of me as a medical man in practice, and as one who intended to return to practice. For the last six years I have retired from the medical profession.

The Judge:

> I know nothing of that, and there is no evidence of it.

Smethurst:

> You spoke as if there was.

The judge addressed the jury:

> Gentlemen of the jury, if there is any mistake about that, the prisoner might have corrected it by giving some account of himself and his practice. I spoke of him as a medical man in practice, because on Monday

morning, the day after the will was executed, he wrote
to his wife to say that he should probably not return
before a certain time, his medical aid being required...
[the judge read out the letter]. In that letter he speaks
of himself as one of the three doctors, Dr Julius and Mr
Bird being the other two.

The judge dismissed any further debate on the subject,
including an intervention from Serjeant Parry.

Sir Frederick again went over the circumstances
surrounding the bigamy (even though the subject had been
covered at length on the previous day), observing that when
Isabella became ill in Richmond,

> ...[Smethurst] performed all the offices that were
> necessary in connection with the patient...

This, even though he had ample means to pay for a nurse:

> Did he refuse to have a nurse because he did not wish
> to have a witness in the bedroom?

And then:

> ...scarcely anyone was ever allowed to enter the [bed]
> room, and it was never cleaned out...

Serjeant Parry challenged this, pointing out that Mrs Wheatley,
the landlady, had said that she went in every morning and
evening to clean the room. The judge said that he had no note
of this evidence. He proceeded with his summing-up, and
again stressed Smethurst's unwillingness for Louisa Bankes to
visit her sister and the suspicious circumstances of the making
of the will, pointing out that the draft was in Smethurst's
handwriting even though he said it was drawn up by a London
barrister.

He mentioned Dr Julius' evidence, how none of his remedies worked, and only in the end was he forced to consider poison. He said that the magistrate who released Smethurst on the day before Isabella died could not be blamed for that action, out of 'motives of humanity', and he said that the prisoner having returned to his lodgings, the jury could not

> ...presume anything against him because he had an opportunity of destroying evidence.

Then:

> ...but if [the evidence] satisfied them that antimony or arsenic had been administered by him to the deceased, some light might be thrown on the circumstance that no poison was found by his returning to the house... and having access to the parlour and the bedroom...

After a break for lunch, the judge came to the medical evidence. He had spent the majority of his speech, around six hours, dealing with the non-medical and circumstantial evidence against Smethurst. This was evidence that had taken a day to hear. The medical evidence, from twenty doctors and scientists, had taken nearly three times as long to go through, but the judge spent barely two hours on it. It has already been noted that Serjeant Ballantine in his reply to the defence also seemed to place far less emphasis on the medical evidence than might have been expected given its critical importance to the case.

The judge came to Dr Taylor's testimony, saying that there could be no doubt that he had made a substantial blunder. But it was 'a new discovery in science' that potassium chlorate would dissolve copper, and the celebrated Dr Odling, said he would have made the same mistake. He went on:

> ...the learned counsel for the defence had no right to ask [you] to dismiss Dr Taylor's evidence altogether in consequence of this mistake.

Dr Thomas Smethurst (1805 – 1873),
from a sketch made at his trial.

Sir (Jonathan) Frederick Pollock (1783 – 1870), the Lord
Chief Baron and judge for both of Thomas Smethurst's trials
for murder. He entertained no doubts that Smethurst was
guilty.

Serjeant-at-Law John Humffreys Parry (1816 – 1880).
He defended Smethurst during the murder trial and later
charged Sir Frederick Pollock with misleading the jury.

Serjeant-at-Law William Ballantine (1812 – 1887). He prosecuted Smethurst for murder and bigamy, and remained convinced to the end of his life that Smethurst was a murderer.

Dr Frederick Gilder Julius (1811 – 1886). He was the first doctor, apart from Smethurst, to treat Isabella Bankes for sickness and diarrhoea. He suspected that she was being poisoned but failed to establish that she was pregnant.

Dr Robert Bentley Todd (1809 – 1860). He saw Isabella for a few minutes by candlelight. He commented on the look of terror on her face, and was convinced that she was being poisoned.

Dr Alfred Swaine Taylor (1806 – 1880). Initially Serjeant Ballantine's star witness, his bungling nearly wrecked the prosecution case.

Alfred Taylor with William Thomas Brande (1788 – 1866). Brande, a retired professor from the Royal Institution, had 50 years' experience in chemistry, yet he was unaware that a mixture of hydrochloric acid and potassium chlorate will dissolve copper.

Dr (later Sir) Benjamin Ward Richardson (1828 – 1896). He tested Dr Taylor's theories about potassium chlorate and arsenic on dogs, and showed them to be untrue. He was convinced that Isabella Bankes died of natural causes.

Sir George Cornewall Lewis (1806 – 1863). Home Secretary during Thomas Smethurst's trial for murder. He had to decide whether Smethurst should be reprieved and pardoned.

After briefly summarizing the points upon which the medical evidence for the prosecution relied, he came to the 'evidence for the prisoner'. The many witnesses called were of the opinion that the symptoms were not consistent with slow arsenical poisoning, and that such symptoms as were, were absent in Isabella Bankes. He said that 'a good deal of their testimony' was to show that potassium chlorate would have no effect in expelling arsenic from the body, but since the discovery that bottle No 21 contained no arsenic, this evidence was of no value whatsoever. He criticised one of them for performing only qualitative rather than quantitative analyses (probably Dr Thudichum), calling it neglect. He commented:

> I do not find in their [defence] testimony anything so distinct and positive as that contained in the testimony...called on behalf of the Crown...

He did make the point that a number of the defence witnesses were from the same institution (The Grosvenor Place School of Medicine), and the fact that they had been 'examined on a particular trial [the Palmer case]' was not of the slightest importance.

He said that he did not agree with the counsel for the prisoner that the real question for the jury 'was to consider which set of witnesses to believe...' They must consider the motive, and yet again he reminded them of Smethurst's desertion of his wife and his bigamous marriage to Isabella. After a few more remarks, he finished by wishing that 'the Almighty searcher of all hearts' would bring them to a 'just and safe conclusion'.

As the judge finished his speech, Smethurst asked leave to 'clear up some points'. The judge said that could only be done through his counsel, but nevertheless, Smethurst stated that he had informed Serjeant Ballantine as soon as he could about the details of the bigamous marriage. He further stated that he had no property motive; Isabella had a reversionary interest in a large sum of money, 'it is not a fair argument to use against a man'.

The jury were sent out to consider their verdict at ten minutes to four. They returned forty minutes later. The foreman seemed on the point of fainting (he had fainted during the post-mortem evidence). On being asked whether they found the prisoner guilty or not guilty he replied:

Guilty!

The deputy clerk of the arraigns then asked: 'And so say you all?', to which nearly every member of the jury replied 'Yes!' or 'We do!'

Sir Frederick Pollock donned the black cap, and the prisoner was asked whether he had anything to say. He pulled a sheaf of notes from his pocket, and proceeded to address Sir Frederick for a considerable time. It was his one chance – albeit too late – of relating his side of the story.

He admitted the bigamy, but said it was done at Isabella's request to 'protect her from reproach'. The £1,700 of Isabella's money was lent some 13 years previously, and secured after the event against some houses – the matter was in Chancery and after they were sold and expenses deducted, he doubted whether £600 would remain. He was writing to his wife (Mary) and visiting her fortnightly; they did not discuss 'Miss Bankes'. He talked at some length about Mr Caudle's surgery (Dr Julius' dispenser) commenting on his dissatisfaction with its arrangements. He claimed that neither Dr Julius, Mr Bird nor Dr Todd had told him Isabella's condition was likely to be fatal. He quoted some of Dr Julius' decidedly intemperate descriptions of local medical colleagues.[1] Isabella's expression

---

1 Smethurst had suggested consulting other local doctors; of Mr Hills, Dr Julius replied, 'It is no use to consult that fellow; he is such a knock-down fellow, he will bleed, and blister, and knock her off the hooks in no time; he will soon finish her.' Of Dr Hassell he had said, '...he is worse; he only attends tradespeople...he will murder her...'

of fear, reported by Dr Todd, was probably occasioned by having three strange men around her bed, in any case, Dr Todd was in the bedroom for no more than four minutes. He was critical of Dr Taylor's analyses, and made a good point on the arsenic detected in Isabella's stool. Taylor claimed to have detected a quarter of a grain of arsenic in one motion. Since Isabella passed fifteen motions on that day, if each one contained a similar amount she must have passed around four grains of arsenic, 'with none being absorbed or vomited...' (Smethurst could, with advantage, have developed this point. Four grains passed in a day equated to much more than that being administered – a considerable dose – and yet none was found in the body...) He commented on Mrs Wheatley's testimony (the landlady at Alma Villas). Here he became confused; he said she swore he kept her from the room. In fact she had said that she did not wait on Isabella, but she did say she made the bed up every night, and also that the bedroom door was frequently open. He then indulged in some gallows humour (he was, after all, about to be sentenced to death) referring to his 'wives' he said that the older one brought him no property, so,

> ...I am sure it is not likely I should have poisoned a younger one and kept the older...

Then he mentioned an incident at Moor Park where Dr Julius' brother, Reverend Henry Richard Julius, vicar of Wrecclesham in Surrey, had accused him of practising medicine without legal medical qualifications. The implication was that Dr Julius bore him a grudge, since according to Newton, Rev. Henry Julius was subsequently obliged to apologize. He commented on the various medicines prescribed to Isabella, saying that it was all recorded in a diary which was in the hands of the police. When he was arrested for the first time, he was away for three and a half hours. Isabella was very distressed when he returned.

It was a long and rambling address which made no difference to the sentence. After some preliminaries, the judge observed:

> I think it is difficult for anyone carefully to consider the evidence both against you and for you without coming to the same conclusion which the jury have pronounced...

The judge then responded to some of Smethurst's points. He commented briefly on the issue of Louisa being denied access to her sister, but his main concern was the will, and he had come back to this again and again in his summing-up. He said that it was incredible that Smethurst had introduced a strange attorney – to whom he made a false declaration – within two days of Isabella's death. He claimed that Smethurst 'insulted' Isabella by 'making her' sign the will in her maiden name, and he added that Smethurst's address to him was 'very unintelligible'. He then pronounced the sentence of death.

The prisoner was going to make some further comments, but he was led away from the dock. He did say though:

> I declare Dr Julius to be my murderer. I am innocent before God.

He was then removed to the Surrey County Prison at Horsemonger Lane to await his fate.

Storm in the Press...

Thomas Smethurst had been found guilty of murder on Friday 19th August 1859. The timing was perfect for the Saturday newspapers, and they had extensive coverage of the major part of the judge's summing-up, the guilty verdict, Smethurst's address to the court, the judge's reply and the sentence of death. Given the sensationalist nature of the trial, many of the newspapers also had editorials summarizing the facts of the case. The opinion of the process and outcome of the trial was not unanimous, and since the debate was to rumble on for some time, it is appropriate to gauge the significance of the opinions expressed by the circulations of the newspapers carrying them.

The fortunes of the daily newspapers varied considerably from 1855 when stamp duty was finally abolished. Until then, the publishers had been obliged to pay the Government one (old) penny per copy, although the newspaper was then delivered, post paid, to the purchaser's door by the Post Office.[1] From 30th June 1855, for papers of less than four ounces in weight, the penny stamp duty became optional but included the cost of postage. This disadvantaged *The Times*, which at 16 pages weighed more than the four ounce limit, and an extra halfpence postage was required for delivery; a move widely regarded as due to Government anger at the paper because of its highly critical reports from the front line in the Crimean War. The abolition of stamp duty stimulated the founding of the *Daily Telegraph*, initially costing two pence, but soon reduced

---

1   One old penny, '1d', where, 12 old pence = one shilling, and 240 old pence = £1.

to the extraordinarily low price of one penny (unstamped). By comparison, and after some shilly-shallying over its cover price following the change in stamp duty, *The Times* cost four pence exclusive of postage (five-and-a-half pence delivered). The outcome was inevitable; in 1856, circulation of the *Daily Telegraph* was 27,000 compared to 54,000 for *The Times*. By 1862, sales of the *Daily Telegraph* were 'in excess of 140,000', so considering that *The Times* circulation was only 65,000 in 1861, at the time of the Smethurst trial (1859) the *Daily Telegraph* must have already been outselling *The Times*. By 1876, the *Daily Telegraph* had the largest circulation of any newspaper in the world.

There were a number of other daily newspapers published in London at the time.[2] Circulation of the *Daily News*, price three pence, the *Morning Chronicle*, four pence and the *Morning Post*, four pence, all prices unstamped, were together considerably less than *The Times*. Two other newspapers are of note; the *Standard*, a four pence afternoon paper in 1857, reduced its price to two pence and then a penny and became a morning newspaper. By 1862 its circulation was around 50,000, stimulated by its support of The South in the American Civil War. The *Morning Star* had been started in 1856 by two Manchester Radicals, Richard Cobden and John Bright. Its tone of 'complaint and asperity' had given it the reputation of an 'anti-British' newspaper. Its circulation was modest – less than 12,000 in 1856, even though it was priced, like the *Daily Telegraph* and *Standard*, at only one penny (unstamped).

In the analysis that follows, only material from the seven newspapers mentioned will be considered, since they represented the majority of national press coverage. It is safe to assume that readers of the *Daily Telegraph*, *The Times* and the *Standard* constituted a fairly substantial majority of the newspaper-reading public, certainly in the London area, in

---

2   This survey is limited to the major 'nationals' published in London.

1859. All three newspapers had reported every detail of the Smethurst trial, and all three had editorials on Saturday 20th August, none of which was unequivocally in support of the outcome. Of the others, only the minority *Daily News* was satisfied with the verdict.

The Times pointed out that the case had been decided, unusually, on medical evidence, which was of 'debatable character', and 'not absolutely supported'. It did not argue with the verdict, but was clearly not completely at ease with the outcome. The *Standard*, while appreciating the onerous task of the jury and applauding the efforts of the defence advocates, was critical of the judge, accusing him of the same bias against the prisoner as the judge had shown in the Palmer case. It likened the circumstances of Smethurst and his wives to a French novel, but the medical evidence on which the conviction rested was 'sadly meagre'. It expressed unease with the fact that even young girls sat in the public gallery listening to evidence that made grown men sick. The case was a 'strange and deplorable episode' with a 'doubtful and unsatisfactory end'.

The *Daily Telegraph* was critical of almost every aspect of the trial. The members of the jury had spent just forty minutes 'to send a fellow creature to the gallows', having decided their verdict on two fallacious bases:

> ...the evidence of science, of which they were ignorant [and] the evidence of supposition, which it is contrary to all rules and maxims of England to use against the prisoner.

On the 'evidence of science', there were no hard facts, it was all supposition and probability. No arsenic was found in the body, the prosecution said it was 'some irritant poison', without declaring what it was. Mainly though, the newspaper was

167

exercised about the basis on which the jury considered their verdict:

> ...it is not, it should not, it must not, be a subject for the consideration of a common Middlesex jury to decide upon "conflicting medical testimony" when a man's life hangs in the balance.

After considering that the so-called financial motive for murder was trivial – the purchase of twelve years of Isabella's dividend, money Smethurst was already receiving – the editorial commented on the 'grievous error and blunder' committed by Dr Taylor when his copper gauze 'boiled away'. Then there was the question of Isabella's pregnancy, virtually ignored by the judge and prosecution in the context of the medical evidence. The newspaper reminded its readers:

> ...one of the most eminent of modern authoresses died of excessive vomiting during pregnancy...

That was Charlotte Brontë, who had died under circumstances similar to those of Isabella Bankes. Furthermore, the police surgeon, James Edmunds, had given evidence in his defence testimony of at least one other similar case. The editorial finished by saying that in future, in a trial for murder, 'confirmatory evidence of fact' should support scientific suppositions.

The *Morning Chronicle*, with perhaps a little exaggeration, '...remembered nothing like [the conduct of Smethurst] in the whole course of criminal history...'

However,

> ...the manner in which the scientific evidence was produced is a disgrace to justice, and even to the common sense, of the nation.

The way in which both the defence and prosecution medical evidence was dealt with was

> ...a spectacle to which we trust the honour and dignity of the country will never be again exposed.

The *Morning Star* provided the most hostile coverage. Professor Taylor's reputation was 'equivocal', the jury's decision was questionable and the judge's conduct 'merit[ed] the severest reprehension', following the 'evil example of Lord Campbell'.[3] The judge came in for extreme criticism. He browbeat the witnesses, constantly volunteered his own opinion, and his summing-up was

> ...an elaborate argument against the prisoner...the vehement partisanship of which he made scarcely an effort to conceal.

Thus the majority of the Saturday newspapers by circulation were, to a greater or lesser extent, unhappy with the process and outcome of the trial. The Sunday newspapers carried extensive reports and summaries of judicial proceedings (more than a page in the *Observer*), but it fell to the dailies to carry on the editorial comment, and this was recommenced on Monday 22nd August.

Several newspapers described how, after sentence of death had been passed, Smethurst was removed to Horsemonger Lane, avoiding the vast crowds of onlookers. A diversionary cab waited at the gate to Newgate Prison, while Smethurst was taken out from a side entrance to the court. They also carried a story that Smethurst had spent several days in Horsemonger Lane gaol in 1828, apparently for obtaining goods by fraud, after which he was freed by a magistrate. Since his age at the

---

3   He was the judge who had tried William Palmer, 'a ruthlessly tendentious judge' – ODNB.

time was given as 24, he must now (1859) be 55 and not 48 as given in his earlier court appearances.

There was a piece in *The Times* where it was stated that for many years executions in Surrey had been carried out on Mondays; but since this meant that the gallows had to be erected on a Sunday and 'remarks having been made upon the subject', the chosen day had been changed to Tuesday. It is an interesting comment on the social mores of the time, that while public hangings and all the ghastliness associated with them were perfectly acceptable, the thought of doing work on the Sabbath was entirely beyond the pale.

There was also a story to the effect that 'persons well qualified to form a judgment' were of the view that the capital sentence would be commuted to penal servitude. This was based on the words used by the Lord Chief Baron in passing sentence; he did not tell Smethurst that 'there was no hope' and that he should 'prepare to leave the world...' Little could have been further from the truth in the mind of the judge, but for the moment, the idea of a reprieve had started to gain ground.

An editorial in *The Times* started whimsically:

> Who can hope to penetrate the mysteries of this town?
> Who can tell what is passing in any one of the dull
> uniform rows of houses of which London is made up?

It went on to ponder the relative ease with which secret poisoning could be carried out, the likelihood of chemists to be mistaken in their analyses, as well as the difficulty of juries, 'notoriously deficient in special knowledge', to decide between 'professional witnesses' who disagreed. It called upon undertakers and life insurance underwriters to come forward when they suspected an unnatural death.

It was the *Daily Telegraph*, determined to maintain the momentum of its Saturday editorial, that pressed on with a sustained attack on the trial. Once more it criticized the jury for the short time they spent deliberating their decision and now censured the judge, Sir Frederick Pollock, for his lack of impartiality in the summing-up. And perhaps in an oblique reference to the majority circulation now enjoyed by the *Daily Telegraph* and the response it had had from its readership it said:

> ...we are not without authority when we state that, to a large portion of the public, the verdict was the very reverse of satisfactory.

The verdict should have been, it said, on the medical evidence or nothing at all; the other evidence was

> ...the merest inferences from...commonplace facts... loosely woven from circumstances that might, and do frequently occur, involving roguery, no doubt...but altogether inconclusive as proofs of murder.

Sergeant Ballantine understood this, it said, in his opening address to the jury, when he stressed the damning nature of the medical evidence, a position he had apparently abandoned when he made his reply to the defence evidence. The newspaper went on to examine and assess the prosecution and defence medical witnesses, commenting that Drs Julius, Bird and Todd were

> ...prescribing for a woman, believing her to be in one state, while she was actually in another...

Set against their opinions were a number of very eminent 'professors of medical science' who testified that Isabella Bankes' death was entirely reconcilable with natural causes:

Really, no man's life is safe when murder is demonstrated by witnesses such as these, and when the ablest men in the profession are heard with incredulity...

And heaping further opprobrium on the hapless Dr Taylor:

We do trust...Dr Alfred Taylor will not in future be called upon to follow the subtle tracks of poison; otherwise modern toxicology will eclipse middle-age witchcraft in the atrocity of its superstition and the ignorance of its cruelty.

The newspaper summarized its position:

...it would have been far more satisfactory, whatever the verdict recorded, had the judge been less hostile, and the jury more deliberate; and had the testimony for the defence been commented upon in a manner less superficial and flippant...

Then:

...a heavy doubt hangs over the result of this extraordinary trial...there is an uneasy feeling abroad lest medical dogmatism has prevailed over considerations of common sense and the spirit of impartiality which should distinguish an English Court of Justice.

The *Morning Star* continued its attack on Sir Frederick Pollock, citing instances of the 'reprehensible manner' in which he interfered during the presentation of the evidence. Following the fainting of the jury foreman, he had told Serjeant Ballantine that it was unnecessary to go into the details of the post-mortem, because 'the jury would understand very little of such a subject'. Effectively, the judge had said that they were

...utterly incompetent to form a judgment on the case
which they had been sworn to try.

The editorial was also critical of the judge's dismissal of the
significance of Dr Richardson's experiments on dogs, which
demonstrated that potassium chlorate had no effect on the rate
of excretion of arsenic. In addition to the editorials, five letters
were published in the *Daily Telegraph*, five in the *Morning Star*
and three in the *Standard* all critical of the verdict. One letter in
the *Daily News* declared that Smethurst was guilty.

Tuesday 23rd August, and the *Daily News* had an editorial,
hostile towards Smethurst, revealing the 'extraordinary idea'
in some quarters that he would be reprieved. It accused
many of those who had commented on the trial not to have
been present in court; no-one, it claimed, who was present
'entertained a doubt' on the subject. It contrasted the
appearance in the witness box of Drs Todd, Julius, Bird and
Copland, and their 'sober and disinterested truthfulness', with
that of the 'Professors of the Grosvenor School of Medicine'
who were rash in their speculations, and whose observations
were doubtful. On the question of a reprieve, it was

> ...not credible that any Secretary of State, unless
> some new and startling facts are discovered, [would]
> venture to disturb a verdict which deserves the praise
> of being not less honest than courageous.

The *Daily Telegraph* pressed the case that the verdict was a
miscarriage of justice, commenting on public anxiety that the
'great principles of English jurisprudence' had been violated.
'Old Bailey criminal justice' is deteriorating, it said; the term
"Old Bailey practitioner" had become one of contempt. It
questioned why 'Pollock', the 'intimate personal associate'
of Dr Alfred Taylor was on the bench instead of 'Erle' – Sir
William Erle, Lord Chief Justice of the Common Pleas, who was
on the rota for the Central Criminal Court for August, along

with judges Willes and Watson. The judge had 'acted as an advocate for the crown', he 'hinted at points which were not in the evidence'. 'It was not edifying', the newspaper went on, to see

> witnesses browbeaten, tripped up, and sneered at...
> while medical gentlemen of the highest reputation
> were snarled at from the bench...

And,

> ...In the midst of fainting, confusion, wrangling,
> recrimination, bluster, casuistry, jealousy, and
> empiricism, was this wretched trial dragged to an end.

The *Daily Telegraph* claimed that most of its contemporaries and influential classes of the public agreed that the verdict had been recorded upon

> ...insufficient evidence under the pressure of a partisan
> charge from the bench...[4]

Even so, it proceeded to take *The Times* to task for disingenuousness. For example it had said that Isabella Bankes' 'strange look of terror' could not be explained other than by the fact that she was being poisoned, but one of the defence witnesses, Dr Tyler Smith, had claimed that he had repeatedly seen just such a look on the faces of patients who were not being poisoned. And so on; the editorial ended after further criticism of the judge, Serjeant Ballantine, and Drs Todd, Julius and Bird.

The *Daily Telegraph* published five letters that day; there were also three in the *Standard* and two in the *Morning Chronicle*. All condemned the verdict. One of the letters in the *Morning Chronicle* is deserving of note, since it added a new layer of criticism to the process of the trial, and may have stimulated the following day's editorial. Previously,

---

4   Charge – the judge's summing-up and guidance to the jury.

the newspaper had accused the doctors in Smethurst's trial of using 'jargon' to puzzle the lawyers. Dr Charles Kidd, of Sackville Street in the West End, reacted to this, describing lawyers as,

> ...our guileless friends, the men in silk and horsehair... of purer eyes than to behold such iniquity without a shudder and a blush.

Jargon, he said, was the work of the lawyers not the doctors. One of the defence witnesses (it had been Dr Thudichum) was asked by the prosecution whether the fact he had just propounded was in Hooper's *Vade Mecum* or Copland's Medical Dictionary.[5] When told it was not,

> ...the barrister could not understand it...[showing] that his own medical knowledge was...culled out of these dust heaps of old blunders and jargon...

In fact, Dr Thudichum had said, 'I do not read such books, they are merely compilations...' But now Dr Kidd really laid into the lawyers, not sparing also some of the prosecution medical witnesses:

> We should not think of styling...their legal decisions "jargon" because we could not find [them] in Deuteronomy, the Brehon Laws, Lord Bacon, or Coke upon Littleton [which are to] serious lawyers what Drs Taylor, Hooper, and Copland are to serious doctors...[6]

---

5 The *Anatomist's Vade Mecum* and *Physician's Vade Mecum*, written by Robert Cooper, were published in 1798 and 1809 respectively. Hooper was a prolific writer on medicine (ODNB), but somewhat old hat by 1859. Copland's *Dictionary of Practical Medicine* was published in 1858, and Dr Copland was, of course, a prosecution witness in the Smethurst trial...

6 A collection of old law books: *Deuteronomy*, Moses' civil laws; the *Brehon Laws*, the ancient laws of Gaelic Ireland; Lord Bacon, Francis Bacon, Lord Chancellor at the time of James I & VI; *Coke upon Littleton*, written by Sir Edward Coke, a contemporary of Bacon, and published in 1628, was *A Commentarie upon Littleton*, (Littleton's Tenures, published in 1481).

After criticizing the newspapers for stressing the medical evidence against Smethurst, rather than seeking to correct public prejudice, he complained about Drs Taylor and Todd,

> ...and half a dozen old doctors from India [being paid the] most enormous sums of money to swear the sun is not the moon, or one kind of dysentery is not another...

And what was more unfair, he said, than to speak of the evidence of Dr Thudichum, who was 'Liebig's favourite pupil', as '...purely analytic, and valuable as it was...only "jargon"'.[7] But on the barristers, he was merciless; quoting from *Hudibras* (a satirical poem by Samuel Butler) they, like the Swiss, '...in court...had fiercer dudgeons than fighting Grecians or fighting Trojans',

> But out of foreign controversies,
> By aiding both sides, filled their purses

He then made an interesting point about the 'St George's School men';[8] why, it was asked, if they were right, were they not 'backed by the so-called great men of the profession?' To which he responded,

> ...Why, if Harvey was right about the circulation of the blood, or Jenner right about vaccination, were they not backed by the great men of their day?

Then,

> ...I know the decisions in the Palmer trial were the laughing-stock of all the medical journals of America and continental Europe.

---

7 Justus Liebig was a very eminent German chemist, a professor of chemistry at the University of Giessen, under whom Dr Thudichum had studied.

8 The Grosvenor Place School of Medicine, also called variously the 'Old St George's School of Medicine'.

(There were many uncomfortable parallels between the Palmer case and that of Smethurst), and,

> ...I see that the leading morning newspaper (so-called) will insert nothing but what tells against the unhappy prisoner.

He finished with another snipe at Dr Taylor, this time about the latter's interest in electricity as an anaesthetic, subsequently found to be nonsense.

Dr Kidd's letter was a rant, but he did make some useful points, and he obviously had some acquaintance with the law. From a letter of his published in *The Lancet*, it was clear that he was a surgeon working in one of the London hospitals, and he must have been familiar with the work of Dr Thudichum. What was most significant though, was that he highlighted what appeared to be the prejudice of the prosecution (and judge) against the medical men from the Grosvenor Place School of Medicine. But also of interest, was his view of the outcome of the Palmer trial, which may have been regarded then, and is definitely regarded now, as based on poor medical evidence and a biased judge.

The *Morning Star* had no editorial but a note to the effect that it had received more letters on the Smethurst case than any other matter of public interest since its establishment (three years previously), and needed some time to analyse these.

On Wednesday 24th, there were more editorials and 45 letters (31 in the *Morning Star*), 44 of which were highly critical of the trial. Of the letters in the *Morning Star* every aspect of the Smethurst case was condemned, from the conduct of the trial to the medicines prescribed to Isabella Bankes by Dr Julius, Mr Bird and Dr Todd. The editorial in the *Morning Chronicle* condemned the trial outcome. The verdict of the jury was, it said, 'nothing less than a public scandal'. The newspaper said it had had a 'host of complaints ...poured into our ears...', and went on to say that public confidence in the justice of the verdict would have been enormously greater, if the judge had been 'more guarded' and had exercised greater care. It was the process of the trial that was at fault.

Several newspapers had a piece on Smethurst's background. There was no attribution, and since much of what was reported was incorrect, it is impossible to place much credence on those facts not previously known. Smethurst was, it was said, the son of a schoolmaster, born near Coventry in 1804, but 'there is...no pretext for the allegation that his father was tutor to the Earl of Dysart'. He had a 'German degree (Giessen) of doubtful merit...', and apparently,

> ...[he] married his present wife [Mary] from feelings of gratitude for her attention to him when ill...

His interest in hydropathy was mentioned, together with his book, 'interlarded with quotations from Scripture, not very accurately rendered'. During his trial, Smethurst had objected, it was said, to any jurors connected with distillation, and this was explained by his advocacy in the book of 'Teetotalism'. The piece also says that while Smethurst was absent in Germany, his Ramsgate practice was taken over

> ...by a gentleman before whom he was eventually brought at Richmond on a charge for murder...

Some of this might have been very interesting, particularly the last item, were it not for the many errors of fact in the article. Smethurst was born in Budworth in Cheshire, as many census returns confirm. It was his grandfather who was tutor to the Earl of Dysart, his father was a warehouseman, and his German degree was from Erlangen not Giessen. There is one single quotation from Scripture in his book on hydropathy, 'Go and do thou likewise...', (Luke, 10, 37), perfectly reproduced from the Authorized Version, albeit with the comma after the 'Go' omitted. His book does not advocate 'Teetotalism', on the contrary, it says that beer and wine, in moderation, are perfectly good. It does, though, have strictures against distilled liquors. The article was a very shoddy piece of work.

The *Daily Telegraph* had no leader, but it prefixed a number of letters with the notice:

> From an enormous mass of correspondence which has [reached us] on the subject of this extraordinary trial and verdict, we select the following, as throwing the most light on the various features of the case...

And, as is likely to happen with a news story attracting so much publicity, people with first-hand knowledge of some of the facts started to come forward. 'G S' from Brighton wrote to say that Dr Taylor was well-known for his blunders in analytical research. A barrister wrote to say that Sir Frederick Pollock,

> ...I suppose on account of partiality arising from infirmity of temper, had more quarrels with members of the bar of the highest standing than all the other judges put together.

He commented that Dr Taylor,

> ...who is evidently, and has been long in intelligent circles considered no better than Titus Oates or a witch-finder [and] the witch-finding days have come back...when that so frequently confuted mountebank... boils up his copper and thus introduces the element he is seeking.[9]

---

9   Titus Oates, imprisoned and pilloried for anti-Catholic perjury in the time of Charles II.

He finished by saying that if Smethurst were to be hanged, he would be murdered, and his murderer would be the trial judge.

Many letters censured Sir Frederick Pollock, and in particular his treatment of witnesses from the Grosvenor Place School of Medicine, where his 'interruptions were almost insolent...' Dr Taylor also came in for much criticism. *The Times*, continuing to maintain neutrality (one letter to the *Daily Telegraph* had talked about 'your cowardly contemporary', *The Times*, still maintaining that the defence evidence amounted to nothing), published two letters central to the case. Dr Julian Rodgers, former lecturer on Chemistry at the Grosvenor Place School of Medicine, had given evidence for the defence in the Smethurst case. He had also spoken for the defence in the Palmer trial. He wrote to point out that the statement by 'Professor' Brande that the fact that a mixture of potassium chlorate and hydrochloric acid dissolves copper is a 'new fact in chymistry' was untrue. Since the judge had urged that this was a 'strong point on the consideration of the jury' it was important to set the record straight. Not only was the process not unknown, but it was actually used to separate copper from its ores. Furthermore, it could be used as an effective way of separating arsenic from body tissue. Dr Rodgers had used the process himself in cases he had been called upon by coroners to investigate. And Reinsch's process was not a test for arsenic, but a method by which it could be separated for analysis:

> ...[the Reinsch's test] is ill adapted where the blood organs and tissues form the subject of the analysis, and is totally inapplicable in all cases unless copper, perfectly free from arsenic, be employed.

He maintained, in reference to the post-mortem results on Isabella Bankes' body that

...in no other case has poison been found in the blood without, on examination, its presence being... demonstrated also in the various organs and tissues.

Thus the 'new finding in science', trumpeted by Serjeant Ballantine and repeated by the judge, was nothing of the sort.

The second letter was from a member of the jury on the Smethurst trial. It is worth reproducing in full:

Sir, in order to remove the impression that may exist in the minds of the public with respect of the summing up of the judge having a tendency to influence the minds of the jury, I beg to inform you that at the close of the defence, and before the judge commenced his summing-up, 11 of the jury were convinced upon the evidence adduced of the prisoner's guilt, and the remarks of the judge confirmed their opinions. I am, Sir, yours, One of the Jury.

So the jury had made up its mind on Smethurst's guilt before the summing-up speech and direction from the judge regarding what was and what was not significant.

On Thursday 25th August, there were four editorials and 26 letters. Of the letters, 22 were critical of the verdict, two were neutral and two were in favour. It was becoming clear that the correspondents were about ten to one in support of the opinion that the verdict in the trial of Thomas Smethurst was severely flawed. Many of the letters raked over various aspects of the evidence or commented on the judge's bias. Some announced the setting up of petitions to the Home Secretary for clemency. Some thought Smethurst guilty, but favoured a reprieve. The secretary of St George's Hospital wrote to make it clear that none of the witnesses for the defence were in any way connected with his institution...

One letter was from a doctor reporting on a case very similar to Isabella Bankes', where the unfortunate victim was shown, post-mortem, to have died of natural causes. Another was from a doctor reporting his treatment of a woman who apparently committed suicide by swallowing arsenic. The woman died eleven weeks after taking the poison, and the post-mortem examination showed arsenic in the liver, kidneys, spleen, stomach and intestines.

An editorial in the *Morning Chronicle* examined the medical evidence in the Palmer and Smethurst cases. It took its correspondent Dr Kidd to task for his comment about the decisions in the Palmer trial being the laughing-stock of medical journals in the USA and Europe. It was acquainted with someone who had canvassed the opinion of nearly a hundred physicians, surgeons etc. on the Palmer trial and they all, without exception, rejected the defence evidence. It finished by saying that even without the medical evidence, Smethurst would have been found guilty. Evidently, the newspaper endorsed the use of circumstantial evidence in a capital charge.

The *Morning Post* had a letter from an irate undertaker reacting to a piece in *The Times* saying that undertakers could assist the identification of potential murder victims if they suspected foul play.

The *Daily Telegraph* declared that the jury in the case had 'not improved their position' by saying that eleven of them had agreed on a conviction 24 hours before the conclusion of the trial. 'Tens of thousands of persons', it said, agreed that not only was 'the hypothesis of [Smethurst's] innocence' reasonable, but 'far more tenable than that of the prosecution'. His guilt was quite definitely 'not proven'. Smethurst was, however, a felon, and should be treated as such by the prison system. 'Never', the newspaper said,

> ...was a burst of opinion and feeling against the taking away of a life more entirely free from all that might be construed as morbid sympathy.

After a further barb aimed at Sir Frederick Pollock and his confidant, 'magician' Dr Taylor and his 'copper wand', the editorial referred to Dr Rodgers' letter in *The Times* of the previous day, debunking the 'new fact in chymistry' of potassium chlorate dissolving copper. It pointed out that Serjeant Ballantine, the principal prosecution barrister, had 'confessed himself unable' to prove that Isabella Bankes had been poisoned by arsenic or antimony, and a correspondent to one of the newspapers had claimed that she could even have been poisoned by Epsom salts. The *Daily Telegraph* had, it said, received hundreds of communications expressing dissatisfaction with the verdict, and not a single one declaring Smethurst's guilt. It then had another go at the prosecution case. '"Dr" Julius', it said, could not recognize a case of pregnancy when he saw it, but could recognize a case of poison; '"Dr" Bird, a military surgeon', had never seen a woman die under such circumstances,[10] and Dr Taylor was simply a bungler. The rest of the evidence was merely 'old woman's gossip'. The protest of the country would not cease, it said until Smethurst was reprieved.

Friday 26th August saw two substantial editorials in the *Morning Star*. The first one repudiated the charge made by an unnamed rival, that the newspaper was championing the Smethurst case because of its well-known opposition to capital punishment. The medical evidence presented in the case was analysed in the greatest detail; the medical practitioners for the prosecution were criticised, and praise was heaped on those for the defence. A second editorial was entitled: 'Dr Taylor on Poisons'. Dr Taylor had just brought out a second edition of his book, *On Poisons in Relation to Medical Jurisprudence and Medicine*. A review of the book lighted on Taylor's response to criticism he had received for his analysis of the organs of

---

10 Samuel Bird was awarded the degree of MD by St Andrews University in 1859, exact date unknown (Australian Dictionary of National Biography), although he was generally referred to as "Mr" during the Smethurst trial.

John Cook, the man allegedly murdered by William Palmer. Taylor had failed to find strychnine in Cook's body, but Palmer was hanged for poisoning Cook with strychnine. In the book, Taylor criticized two of the medical witnesses for the defence who claimed that they could have discovered the poison at microscopic levels, thus questioning Dr Taylor's competence in performing the analysis. They were Drs Herapath and Letheby. Herapath had a letter in *The Times* on Dr Taylor and the Reinsch test the same day the review was published; Dr Letheby had already written to *The Lancet* on the subject of the Reinsch test. In the book, Dr Taylor accounted for his failure to find strychnine in Cook's body by the poor state of the stomach when it was supplied to him, but his two colleagues were

> bent on making a trial for murder a scene of personal contention and rivalry.

The review went on to criticize the method Dr Taylor used in his analysis, the so-called Merck process, which for 'medico-legal' purposes was 'inconceivably clumsy and defective'. Naturally, this led on to a discussion of the Reinsch process he used to detect arsenic in the Smethurst case, 'not the most fitting for medico-legal purposes'. The editorial concluded by considering Taylor's book to display

> ...a want of candour, a defect of accuracy, an imperfect exposition of scientific truths, a suppression of important toxicological details, a rancorous partisanship and a dogmatic egoism, which render it peculiarly unsafe as a medico-legal handbook. We think that this edition is alike damnatory of Dr Taylor's reputation and injurious to the interests of judicial chemistry.

Elsewhere, there were 27 published letters about the case, 21 disagreed with the verdict, three were neutral and three supported it. Once more, the evidence was raked over, and again medical men reported cases similar to Isabella Bankes, where death was from natural causes. However *The Times* published two more letters central to the case. The first of these was from Dr Tyler Smith, another of the defence witnesses, and Physician-Accoucheur (obstetrician) to St Mary's Hospital. He commented that Isabella Bankes' pregnancy coincided very closely with the length of her illness. Every obstetric authority recognized, he said, that women are sometimes killed by vomiting in pregnancy, that diarrhoea is also a disorder associated with pregnancy, and that it was the early part of pregnancy where vomiting could be most severe and dangerous. He said that it was most likely to happen to a person like Isabella Bankes, pregnant for the first time in 'mature age', of 'bilious temperament and the subject of previous internal disorder'. He commented on the burning sensations she felt, and pointed out that pregnancy is constantly accompanied by heartburn. He said that in two out of four fatal cases of this kind of vomiting in pregnancy, the patient had been able to take food during the last two days of life – just as had Isabella Bankes, a fact that had weighed heavily against Smethurst who was then not caring for her. Dr Smith said the same had been true for Charlotte Brontë. On the question of Drs Julius, Bird and Todd:

> It cannot but be considered as remarkable that three medical men should have been in attendance upon a woman, 42 years of age, living for the first time as a married person, who had been suddenly seized with an illness of which vomiting was a prominent symptom, without detecting pregnancy.

He referred to his *Manual of Obstetrics* published in 1858, where he had stated that:

185

...an almost poisonous influence seems to be exerted
by the gravid [pregnant] uterus in some constitutions...

On the question of Isabella Bankes' expression, as emphasized
by Dr Todd, he quoted from Paul Dubois, Physician-Accoucheur
to the French Empress, who said that he had seen 20 cases of
death from vomiting in pregnancy in 13 years, referring to a
'marked change in the features', as a key symptom. It was an
exposition of the facts of the case, as known to Dr Tyler Smith,
and limited strictly to his specialization in which he could be
considered as being an expert; but it was a clear indictment of
Dr Julius, Mr Bird and Mr Todd.

Also in *The Times* was the letter from William Herapath, a
senior professor of chemistry at Bristol. He had been a witness
for the defence in the Palmer trial, his testimony having
implied neglect on the part of Dr Taylor who had appeared for
the prosecution (and he had just been criticized in Dr Taylor's
book). He launched straight into an attack on Taylor's evidence
in the Smethurst case. By his admission that the copper used
in the analysis contained arsenic, he destroyed all proof of
poison being present in the body, the evacuation, or the by now
famous bottle No 21. But Dr Taylor had also affirmed that he
had used the same copper for 20 years:

What shall be said of the justice of the convictions and
executions which have taken place during those years
upon Dr Taylor's evidence!

He commented on the amount of arsenic said by Dr Taylor to
have come from the copper:

Could the copper...deposit one grain of arsenic? In the
face of all England I say it could not; the hundredth
part of a grain of arsenic in that quantity of copper
would render it so brittle, it could not be drawn into

wire at all...the fact is, the whole set of operations were a bungle.[11]

He went on to say that the use of the Reinsch test simply proved the presence of one or more of the inferior metals, antimony, tin, lead, bismuth, mercury etc. Further analysis was needed to prove the presence of arsenic, and he warned juries that such analysis was needed to 'produce a body of evidence which it is impossible to gainsay'.

The communications from Dr Tyler Smith and Professor Herapath were very powerful testimony for the defence in the case of the Queen vs Smethurst.

There was also a letter in *The Times* from James Smethurst, Thomas Smethurst's older brother. He detailed Smethurst's financial position, and what he stood to inherit from Isabella, saying that they planned to get properly married after his current wife had died. He drew attention to the apparent contradiction between the evidence of Dr Julius and that of Mr Bird as presented during the trial. That was regarding whether Mr Bird had concluded that Isabella was being poisoned before or after Dr Julius spoke to him about it.

Saturday 27th August, ten days to the execution date, saw 26 letters against the trial outcome, and one in favour together with two editorials. The most interesting letter, surely pounced upon by anyone following the case, was that published in *The Times* from Smethurst's long-suffering wife Mary. Mary Smethurst was 74 years old, and had had much to endure in the previous year. There was her husband's 'inappropriate' relationship with Isabella Bankes, which must have caused tittle-tattle, among the other guests at the boarding house.

---

11 James Stephen in his book *A General View of the Criminal Law in England*, published in 1863, took a different view. Herapath's revelation that the arsenic could not have come from the copper could have meant that it was therefore really present in the sample, rather than proving Taylor's analysis was hopelessly wrong.

Then, after Isabella was asked to leave, followed shortly by Thomas Smethurst himself, there must have been more tittle-tattle, particularly when he was seen subsequently to be visiting from time to time to pay Mary's rent. And from early May onward, there were the newspaper reports of the various court hearings and the hurtful speculation about herself, her husband and Isabella, culminating in his death sentence. Finally, her brother-in-law, James, had announced the previous day in *The Times* that her husband and Isabella had planned to wait for her to die before getting properly married.

Mary Smethurst was still living at Rifle Terrace, and wrote from there on 25th August:

> It is with the most painful reluctance that I address you, but I feel bound, from a sense of duty and justice, to bring before you one or two facts...which, if known, may remove from my unhappy husband some of the unjust suspicions and prejudices which have fallen upon him.

They had been married for 30 years, she said, and had always lived together in perfect happiness and contentment. He had personally nursed her through several illnesses, and she had always received 'the most uniform kindness and attention'. He had received no property with her, and had supported both of them, as well as an invalid younger brother, from his income. She had long experience of her husband's humane character and amiable disposition, and until his departure with 'Miss Bankes', his moral conduct had been irreproachable. Mrs Smethurst went on:

> ...without wishing to cast any reflection on the memory of the deceased Miss Bankes...grounded on my observation...the first advance came from her... unhappily [meeting] with too ready a reciprocity on his part.

She had not visited her husband in prison, she said, only because he had forbidden her and many of their friends from doing so. Mrs Smethurst must have had great reserves of courage to write the letter, given the circumstances.

Mary Smethurst's letter was followed by another from a medical chemist, Charles J Shearman, MD. It was not enviable, he said, to criticize someone of Dr Taylor's 'rank and profession in chymical science...', but he saw it a duty, 'considering the life of a human being hangs on a very slender thread'. Dr Shearman's thesis ran somewhat contrary to that of Henry Letheby who had written to *The Lancet* about the use of the Reinsch test following Dr Taylor's evidence to the magistrates' court. Shearman advocated the use of potassium chlorate in the Reinsch test, saying that the process positively benefits, although Letheby had warned against its inaccuracy if it was used, some of the arsenic being freed as a gas. Shearman pointed out that the potassium chlorate and hydrochloric acid mixture used in the Reinsch test will dissolve copper, but Dr Taylor should have noticed this immediately from the green tint produced. However, other substances besides potassium chlorate produce the same tendency to dissolve copper, and

> ...some of these substances are the peculiar salts which occur in large quantities in the evacuations of dysentery...

Messrs Lehmann, Güterbock and Schmidt, 'men of the very highest position as physiological chymists' had pointed to the presence of large amounts of ammonium and magnesium phosphate, and sodium chloride in dysenteric evacuations. It was easy to prove, Shearman said, that these salts, when present, will cause the solution of copper gauze, thus freeing the arsenic... There was, therefore, no more ground for the suspicion of arsenic in the evacuation sample, than there was in the substance in bottle No 21. If copper gauze contaminated with arsenic were used in Reinsch's test on *any* evacuation in any case of severe diarrhoea or dysentery, the test would give evidence of arsenic, as in Miss Bankes' case, and poisoning would be suspected. Dr Shearman finished his letter by saying:

> I know of no other conclusion to be derived from the chymical investigation in this case than that there is not a trace of the existence of arsenic but in the copper gauze.

Dr Shearman had thus quite probably identified the mechanism by which Dr Taylor had identified arsenic in the sample of stool in bottle No 2. The letters from Professor Herapath and Dr Shearman (and the book review) surely demolished any lingering remains of Dr Alfred Swaine Taylor's reputation. He was revealed as a bungler, and Mr Brande was hardly better. Dr Taylor was shown to be criminally negligent in his apparent lack of knowledge of basic chemistry. These new revelations together with Dr Tyler Smith's comments on Isabella's pregnancy and the effect of that on her condition, rendered all vestiges of the medical evidence for the prosecution practically worthless.

An editorial in the *Daily Telegraph* demanded Smethurst's reprieve. It went on: 'A slur has been cast on trial by jury...' and 'the reputation of a judge for sagacity and impartiality has been brought down'. And referring to the hapless Dr Taylor, 'the fame of at least one professional man has been destroyed'. Drs Taylor, Julius, Todd and Bird were roundly condemned; their evidence was 'discreditable and worthless', Dr Taylor for reasons already examined, the other three for failing to recognize that Isabella Bankes was pregnant, a condition that could have entirely explained her illness.

The *Standard* quoted Dr Johnson:

> The supreme power has, in all ages, paid some attention to the voice of the people; and that voice does not least deserve to be heard when it calls out for mercy.[12]

The government should listen to the people, it said, and reprieve Dr Smethurst.

Again, many of the letters reanalysed the case in the light of the latest revelations. Dr Kidd had another ranting letter published in the *Morning Chronicle*, one of the newspapers less sympathetic to Smethurst. Again he was critical of Dr Taylor, in particular his evidence at the Palmer trial; he claimed that Taylor had subsequently recanted.

The following week, between Monday 29th August and Friday 2nd September there were more letters and more editorials. Monday's editorial in the *Daily Telegraph* is worthy of note. It started by saying that Dr Smethurst had been tried a second time by the Press, and 'by that great jury, he has been acquitted'. It claimed that within 48 hours of its original 'repudiation of the verdict' (on Saturday 20th August, the day following the end of the trial) *The Times* had become 'dubious and apologetic' and all other daily contemporaries, with one exception, had followed suit. (The *Standard* had also editorialized against the verdict on the first Saturday.) Many provincial journals had joined in 'detecting serious flaws' in the prosecution case, 'but the crowning fact', was that both the legal and medical press regarded the conviction as unsatisfactory.

---

12 This was a quotation from a letter Dr Johnson wrote to Charles Jenkinson, afterwards first Earl of Liverpool, pleading mercy for William Dodd, a clergyman convicted of forgery and sentenced to be hanged. Boswell reports that Johnson authored some lines for Dodd to use in his 'Convict's Address to his unhappy Brethren'. When doubt was expressed that the lines were Dodd's own, Johnson retorted with the famous line: 'Depend upon it sir, when a man knows he is to be hanged in a fortnight, it concentrates his mind wonderfully.' The plea was unsuccessful, and Dodd was executed at Tyburn.

Dr Todd, Dr Julius, Mr Bird and Dr Taylor were again severely criticized, 'bent upon sustaining a theory formed in a quarter of an hour in total ignorance of the patient's pregnancy'. On the question of part of the alleged motive for the 'putative crime', Isabella's money, the newspaper made the point, which had been made elsewhere, that Smethurst could probably have had it at any time had he asked for it. And as for the balance of the motive, fear of the consequences of his bigamy, Smethurst would have

> ...[run] the risk of being hanged to escape the chance of being transported...

The editorial went on to analyse the logic of those still calling for the capital sentence to be carried out:

> How do [those] scholastic quibblers, in their pompous summing up, pretend to arrive at the demonstration of Dr Smethurst's guilt?

(Seven days previously, the condemned man was being referred to as 'the convict Smethurst', then 'Smethurst' but now it was 'Dr Smethurst'...) The answer was,

> ...by ignoring two thirds of the proved facts, by forgetting that the...opinions of the three doctors are based on [an] error, by passing over the testimony... that the symptoms of Isabella Bankes...are frequently exhibited by patients suffering from natural disease...

Summarizing the argument:

> Jurymen are liable to err, and judges are not infallible... that...medical men and chemists may blunder has been painfully proved...and with public opinion decidedly averse from seeing the last sentence of the law carried into effect...

The *Daily Telegraph* wanted the Home Office to 'interfere between the gallows and the life of a man...'

The editorial had condemned those still calling for Smethurst's execution, calling them 'scholastic quibblers'. One of the scholastic quibblers, surprising for a man generally regarded as being sympathetic to the underdog, was Charles Dickens. He was incandescent with rage over the Smethurst affair. On 25th August 1859, he wrote from Gad's Hill to his friend John Forster:

> I cannot tell you how much interested I am in what you tell me of our brave and excellent friend the Chief Baron, in connection with that ruffian [Smethurst].

He commented on the 'miserable knaves and asses' who were calling for a reprieve, and declared that he would 'hang any Home Secretary...who should step in between that black scoundrel and the gallows'. In the letter, Dickens says that he had followed the case with much interest, so it is a little odd that he seemed to be unaware of the very telling arguments in favour of a miscarriage of justice.

There was an editorial in the *Morning Star* saying that the published editorials and letters in all the newspapers had now exhausted the 'topics of the trial', and it analysed the difficult options open to the Home Secretary, none of which was satisfactory. It concluded by calling for a Court of Criminal Appeal, commenting that it was monstrous that where a life was involved no such tribunal existed, whereas a civil case for a 'trumpery matter of £20 or £50' could be so referred.

The *Daily Telegraph* had said that the crowning fact of the press coverage of the Smethurst case was that the legal and medical press concurred with the prevailing view. On the previous Saturday, 27th August, *The Law Times* had had a long editorial entitled *The Law and the Lawyers*. It started:

> The conviction of Dr Smethurst is very unsatisfactory... among the lawyers experienced in the practice of the criminal courts, there is...scarcely a difference of opinion...that there was not evidence to support the verdict.

There was no proof of poisoning, and apart from the medical testimony, there was no case:

> ...[he] might have had a desire to kill his paramour because it was in his supposed interest to do so... but there was not the slightest proof...he had the opportunity...[but] there was no proof of the possession...or administration of any poison...

The fallibility of the medical evidence was shown by Dr Taylor; tests for poisons should be used only as an addition to other evidence. But there should also be unquestionable proof that the deceased did, in fact, die of poisoning:

> If there is the shadow of a doubt as to this, the accused is entitled, in justice and in law, to an acquittal.

On the verdict in Smethurst's trial:

> Looking at it with the eyes of a practical lawyer, experienced in criminal justice, we have come to the conclusion that it was a wrongful and unjustifiable verdict.

The article then commented on the letter sent to *The Times* by one of the jurors:

> This makes the case still more dreadful...eleven unscientific men "making up their minds" upon one of the most delicate and difficult questions...in a doubtful science, of which they were utterly ignorant!

It proved that the jury were guided either by the facts of the case irrespective of the medical evidence, 'and then there is no case whatsoever...', or by the medical evidence, 'upon which they were incompetent judges'. The article finished by saying:

> If Dr Smethurst is executed, it will be a disgrace to the administration of justice...there is no proof whatsoever of guilt, and if such evidence is to convict, there is no safety for the most innocent.

Both *The Lancet* and the *British Medical Journal* also had two-page editorials on the Smethurst trial. They both concluded that the execution should not be carried out. The BMJ commented on the enormous public doubt on the justness of the verdict, but the medical profession had made up its mind that there was insufficient evidence to prove the charge. Of the medical witnesses called, ten said that Isabella Bankes had been poisoned, seven that she had not. The BMJ pointed out the remarkable coincidence that Isabella's pregnancy coincided exactly with her illness. It questioned why, given the circumstances (she was newly married), Drs Julius and Bird had not examined her properly to see whether she might be pregnant. Dr Taylor's evidence came in for more criticism and 'the chemical evidence for the prosecution breaks down...' The judge too was criticised for his bias in summing up.

The Lancet commented on the chemical testimony, 'a grave subject for discussion', concluding, 'to execute a man upon such testimony would be perfectly monstrous'. Like the BMJ, it pointed out that Isabella's pregnancy had not been known of, and detailed the evidence of Dr Tyler Smith, an obstetrician, who had given evidence of a number of cases where 'vomiting had continued in pregnancy to such a degree as to cause death'. The editorial concluded:

> Doubt...of so serious a character attaches to the
> case, that the execution of Smethurst on the present
> conviction...is an impossibility.

And what was also an impossibility, was that the government in general, and the Home Secretary in particular, could possibly ignore such an overwhelmingly negative reaction to the trial outcome from the medical and legal establishments as well as the general public. By Friday 2nd September, 36 editorials and 261 letters about the Smethurst case had been published in the newspapers aforementioned. Of the letters, 21 were hostile to Smethurst, eleven were neutral but 229, 88% of the total, were critical of the verdict or process of the trial. Quite a number were from medical practitioners reporting cases very similar to that of Isabella Bankes, where death or serious illness, not attributable to poisoning, had occurred in pregnant women. Some were from barristers and lawyers highly critical of the legal process; many were anonymous, but of the two hundred and twenty-nine, all insisted that the death sentence must be commuted.

Sir George Considers...

The Home Secretary at the time of the Smethurst trial was Sir George Cornewall Lewis. Cornewall Lewis was the son of Sir Thomas Frankland Lewis and Harriet Cornewall. Like Gladstone and others, he had enjoyed a premium education at Eton and Christ Church College, Oxford, gaining honours in Classics and Mathematics, and becoming an expert in Ancient and Modern Languages. Between 1828 when he entered Middle Temple, and 1847 when he was returned unopposed for Herefordshire 'in the Liberal interest', he was variously a scholarly writer, a lawyer, an assistant commissioner enquiring into conditions in Ireland, and a Poor Law Commissioner. In 1844, he married Lady Theresa Lister.

Lewis became Parliamentary Under-Secretary at the Home Office in 1848, and Financial Secretary to the Treasury in 1850. After losing his seat in the 1852 general election he became editor of the *Edinburgh Review*. On his father's death in 1855, he inherited the baronetcy and a safe seat in the Commons. A few days later, Palmerston offered him the post of Chancellor of the Exchequer – vacant following Gladstone's resignation. He accepted reluctantly, worrying about following Gladstone, and having to produce a war budget in short order. Palmerston's administration fell in 1858, at which point Lewis was replaced by Disraeli. However, he was appointed Home Secretary in 1859, after Palmerston's resumption of power.

In addition to his activities in government, Lewis was a political scholar and classicist, whose books, '...prolix...' and '...written in the deliberately flat prose of...one who disliked "style" in writing...' are still read. And although he was described as '...grave and serious...' compared to his '... intelligent, vivacious and high-spirited' wife, he seems to have possessed a droll sense of humour. His comment '...Life would be tolerable were it not for its amusements...' suggests a cynical, detached, and languid attitude to life.[1]

As Home Secretary, Sir George had to decide whether to act on the considerable number of letters, memoranda and petitions for mercy he had received, and commute the death sentence on Thomas Smethurst. There was also the campaign in the press to consider. Editorial comment and letters to the newspapers were overwhelmingly in favour of a 'respite' (a delay in carrying out the sentence, which nearly always led to commutation), an opinion shared by medical and legal journals. In addition to this, Sir George was receiving visitors.

Mr Charles Humphreys, Smethurst's solicitor, had been having some trouble getting to see his client in Horsemonger Lane. Possibly the attendant publicity, care of the press, finally smoothed the way. He did then get to see him on Wednesday 24th August, and had a 'lengthy interview' following which a 'memorial' to the Home Secretary was published the following day. Its central thesis was that the prisoner

> has been convicted upon a tissue of probabilities, none of them inconsistent with innocence, and unsupported by that clear and indisputable medical testimony as to the cause of death...

The memorial requested Sir George to advise her Majesty to exercise the royal prerogative and commute the sentence.

On 25th August, Messrs Parry and Giffard, Smethurst's defence barristers, had an interview with Horatio Waddington, Under-Secretary of State at the Home Office. They told him that Sir Frederick Pollock had misdirected the jury, and that as a result, they had come to a conclusion 'against the weight of

---

1   Biographical details and quotations from ODNB.

evidence'. Waddington must have conveyed their concerns to Cornewall Lewis, who was at his family estate, Harpton Court, in Wales; he wrote back:

> Pollock may have shown too much of the spirit of an advocate, and too little of judicial calmness. Probably he had the image of Campbell, in Palmer's trial, before his eyes.[2]

He did say that considering Smethurst's conduct towards Isabella, it was difficult to believe that he didn't poison her. However, he was of the view that Smethurst was either guilty of 'aggravated murder' or quite innocent.

On the same day, Drs Richardson, Thudichum and Webb, three of the principal medical witnesses for the defence, all from the Grosvenor Place School of Medicine, addressed a letter to Sir George. They complained that through 'legal technicalities' or 'the manner in which the questions [were] put', they had been unable to convey all they knew and wished to impart to the court. Judging by the length and content of their communication, they must have done little else since the trial ended than research and collate a thorough analysis of Isabella's illness and the reasons for her death.

They produced 'new facts' on the case, confining themselves '...entirely to matters of science...' and deliberately ignoring the circumstantial evidence. Reading their letter it is difficult not to be impressed with the depth of their scholarship, and the skill of their advocacy. They systematically demolished the prosecution medical and scientific case for murder against Thomas Smethurst, leaving very little doubt that Isabella Bankes had indeed died of natural causes.

---

2   John Campbell, as Lord Chief Justice, was the judge in the trial of William Palmer; when Lewis wrote this, Campbell was Lord Chancellor, one of Lewis' cabinet colleagues.

They started by considering whether her symptoms were compatible with natural causes. Quoting from Abercrombie's, *Pathological and Practical Researches*, they listed the symptoms associated with chronic inflammatory disease of the intestinal canal. From the mouth ulcers, the appearance of the tongue, the burning sensation and the appearance of the faeces, to the part of the intestine affected, these were essentially identical with those seen on Isabella Bankes. They considered that 'nervous shock' occasioned by Smethurst's arrest may also have contributed to her death. Vomiting and diarrhoea were well-known to accompany early pregnancy, and of course there was Isabella's pre-existing condition of biliousness, delicacy of constitution and her womb complaint. 'Bilious diarrhoea' involving 'shreddy' and bloody mucus evacuations accompanied by 'tenesmus', they said, are well-established symptoms of natural disease, killing several thousand per month in England, with 13 deaths in London alone in the four weeks preceding Isabella's death.

They related details of a number of cases of excessive vomiting during pregnancy. Sometimes the patient had survived, sometimes they had died. In 1855, Pedro Maria Cartaya had published an essay in Paris on uncontrollable vomiting during pregnancy; of 58 cases, 24 had proved fatal. Professor Stoltz of Vienna had recorded eleven cases where the mother had died. Considering the fact that Isabella had suffered from both vomiting and dysentery, 'what surprise is to be expressed at a fatal termination?'

Then there was the reaction of Dr Julius, Mr Bird and Dr Todd, to the fact that none of their medicines seemed able to abate the symptoms. To this the authors commented:

> It is a universally admitted fact that the sympathetic disturbance of the alimentary canal in pregnancy defies, in severe case, all curative measures, and is aggravated by...medicines of a metallic character.

They posed the question: was death due to arsenic or antimony poisoning? Seven symptoms specific to arsenic poisoning were listed; none were present in Isabella Bankes:

> ...the entire absence of [all] is decisive against arsenic poisoning.

This was reinforced by the post-mortem results. In arsenic poisoning, the stomach received the 'primary and specific action', the large intestine far less, if any at all. In Isabella Bankes' case, the results were reversed; it was the large intestine that had suffered severe damage; the stomach was unaffected. The same arguments applied to antimony and to arsenic in combination with antimony. The latter hypothesis was tested on four dogs; all four animals exhibited symptoms specific to the two poisons. They added that there was no case on record since 1808, when a procedure was first developed for identifying arsenic in organic tissue, that in a case of slow arsenic poisoning, the poison had not been found in the body.

The proposal that potassium chlorate had been used to eliminate the arsenic from the body they had proved to be wrong by experiments with dogs. The arsenic found in the evacuation came either from the copper used in the Reinsch test, or existed as a known impurity in the medicines Isabella had received – copper sulphate, *Grey powder* and bismuth trisnitrate. It was pointed out that Dr Taylor had estimated the weight of arsenic detected in the evacuation by visual comparison with another sample, a very inexact method. The hypothesis of arsenic as an impurity in medicines they put to the test by dosing a patient with bismuth trisnitrate for six days. Arsenic was duly found in the patient's urine.

The doctors now turned to the question of antimony. There was no case on record, they said, where slow poisoning with antimony had not resulted in its being found in the liver. Finding antimony in the blood and not in the liver threw doubt over the validity of the test used, 'which...was unknown to all but the experimenters...' However, even assuming antimony to have been present in the body, it had been shown to have been an impurity in *Grey powder* as well as bismuth, both of which had been administered to the patient. Antimony was known to be slow in being expelled from the body, having been shown to have been present at least three months after last being administered.

Finally, they addressed the possibility of other poisons. On the question of corrosive sublimate being used:[3]

It was as fair to assume that death was produced by iodine or lunar caustic.[4] The specific effects of these two substances were not more absent than were the specific effects of mercury.

They added that the gentlemen who had suggested it were 'so little cognisant of [Isabella's] symptoms' compared with those of corrosive sublimate, that their opinions regarding poisoning should be taken with 'the most solemn reserve'.

Their letter had been very long, but its summary was succinct and to the point:

1. The symptoms and pathology of Isabella Bankes were consistent with dysentery occurring in a pregnant and previously unhealthy woman; and her death is fairly ascribable to producing such causes.

2. The symptoms and pathology of Isabella Bankes are not consistent with the hypothesis of poisoning by arsenic, by antimony, or by both these poisons; nor is death fairly ascribable to them.

---

3 Corrosive sublimate is mercury bichloride; Dr Todd and Mr Bird had suggested that it might have been used to poison Isabella Bankes.

4 Lunar caustic is silver nitrate.

3. There is no chemical proof whatever that either antimony, arsenic, or any other irritable poison, was ever feloniously administered to Isabella Bankes.

Drs Richardson, Thudichum and Webb had produced the definitive analysis of what probably had, and what almost certainly had not, happened to Isabella Bankes.

On Saturday 27th August, Lewis was summoned to London for a cabinet meeting. He took the overnight train on Sunday via Shrewsbury, arriving back at 5:15 am on Monday morning. After the meeting he had lengthy discussions with Sir George Grey, Lord John Russell and Lord Palmerston, the Prime Minister. They had all held the post of Home Secretary, and he consulted them for their views on the Smethurst case.

On the same day, Dr William Baly and Dr William Jenner wrote to the Home Secretary requesting an interview. They enclosed with their letter a letter of introduction from Sir James Clark, a physician and close friend of the Queen and Prince Albert. They were, themselves, eminent physicians; Dr Baly had just been appointed Physician Extraordinary to the Queen and Dr Jenner was to be appointed to the same position a few years later. Cornewall Lewis called them in to see him on Tuesday 30th August. They presented him with an account of their 'remarks' on the trial. Their conclusions were virtually identical to those of Richardson et al., and they made many of the same points, albeit without experimentation – although they referred to Dr Richardson's experiments on dogs to gauge the effect of potassium chlorate. They were most critical of Dr Julius and Mr Bird in suspecting poisoning yet continuing to treat for diarrhoea and dysentery until shortly before the patient died. They condemned of the use of copper sulphate and silver nitrate, which, they said, would increase rather than allay intestinal irritation. Had Dr Julius and Mr Bird realized that Isabella Bankes was pregnant, Baly and Jenner said, poison would never have been suspected. They censured Dr

Taylor, saying that the arsenic found by him in the evacuation almost certainly came from his copper gauze.

However there was an unaccountable error in Baly and Jenner's account of the case. They claimed that Dr Julius was treating Isabella Bankes for some days 'before he heard about vomiting'. This was clearly wrong, as can be ascertained from the court transcript. Nevertheless, the two communications, from Richardson et al. and from Baly and Jenner, were most powerful advocacy against the medical case that Isabella Bankes died of poison.

The Times reported that all the papers relating to the case had been submitted by the Home Secretary to the Lord Chief Baron for his consideration, and that he had an interview with him (on the same day as Baly and Jenner). Sir Frederick had arrived at the Home Office at a quarter to one carrying a 'huge red bag' containing the 'voluminous papers relating to the case'. He stayed all afternoon. He wrote to Sir George the following day briefly summarizing the key points of evidence in the trial. He was unrepentant of the outcome, his note ending by saying:

> The question was I believe fairly left to the jury – and
> by them was decided and I see no ground to believe
> that their decision was erroneous...

Also on the same day, 31st August, Sir George received a formal petition presented by Mr Augustus Newton, a barrister, on behalf of Thomas Smethurst, requesting a pardon. In 36 articles, Smethurst laid out his case. He asked for a full pardon rather than just a reprieve. Much of the petition is a repeat of material related to the case that has already been extensively covered in this narrative. In summary, he complained that it was not Sir Frederick Pollock's 'turn' to preside over his trial, and Sir Frederick was biased because he was a friend of Dr Taylor, an important prosecution witness. The evidence of Drs Julius and Bird was inconsistent, and Dr Taylor's blunder on the arsenic had created extreme prejudice against him. He complained about Sir Frederick's bias and his misdirection during the eight-hour summing-up. He explained how the last-minute will-making had come about. He detailed his background and financial affairs and those of Miss Bankes, pointing out that the financial motive for her murder was non-existent. He branded a 'malignant falsehood' that vomiting had always occurred when he had administered food to the deceased. He had been contacted by one of the jurymen, Mr Follett, of Mayfair, who insisted that no discussion or expression of opinion had taken place by the jurymen until they had heard the whole charge (summing-up) from the judge. He also freely admitted to the bigamy.

There was, however, one item of interest. Article 26, which commented on Isabella's illness, stated that the sickness, which came on in the middle of March, was a

> bilious attack, caused by a chill, received, I think, in
> cold-bathing night and morning, at that cold season...

It seems, therefore, that Smethurst may have been using the Water Cure on Isabella in an attempt to treat her various ailments. If she really did catch a chill, a chill which led ultimately to her death, then in a way Thomas Smethurst really was responsible for the death of Isabella Bankes...

A second petition was sent in the following day. This consisted of details and afterthoughts pertaining mainly to the evidence given by the landlady and Drs Julius, Bird and Todd. Smethurst also petitioned Prince Albert.

On 1st September, Mary Smethurst produced a petition for mercy, also asking for a free pardon. The petition was presented to Sir George by Henry Brinsley Sheridan, MP for Dudley, who also presented Mary Smethurst herself together with Mrs Smith, the landlady at Rifle Terrace where the Smethursts had first met Isabella Bankes. The ladies had a

90-minute interview with Sir George, who listened to them 'with the greatest attention and patience'. The substance of Mary's petition was that Smethurst was a kind and caring man who received no property with her. He had always supported her and a crippled brother, and had personally nursed her several times during illnesses. For thirty years Smethurst had been of irreproachable moral conduct until 'tempted' by Miss Bankes.

The following day Samuel Wilks wrote to Sir George; the letter was probably received the same day. Wilks was one of the senior medical witnesses for the prosecution. Along with Dr Taylor, he had examined the viscera of the victim removed post-mortem, and had stated in court that the appearance was most probably due to an (administered) irritant. Now he was concerned that his considered medical judgement had been misrepresented. His actual opinion was no more than that

> ...the post-mortem examination threw no light on the cause of the disease found...and owing to the rarity of acute dysentery, the probabilities were in favour of an irritant.

He amplified the opinion in an article sent the following day to the *Medical Times and Gazette*. The journal printed it on 10th September. He further stated that the appearances could have been due to a vegetable irritant administered to procure abortion, but he was of the opinion that there was substantial and sufficient doubt as to the cause of the post-mortem appearance, and the prisoner should have had the benefit of that doubt. Samuel Wilks' letter was the first crack in the wall of the prosecution medical opinion. It was also the first time anyone had suggested that Isabella's death could have been the result of a botched abortion attempt.

Sir George Cornewall Lewis spent between Tuesday 30th August and Friday 2nd September considering the Smethurst case, reading correspondence, conducting interviews and listening to 'long' arguments. There were over 200 separate communications to be read and considered. One of Sir George's main problems, though, was the question of the medical evidence. Neither he, nor his cabinet colleagues had any medical experience, and he needed an unbiased objective view. On Friday 2nd September, Sir George made a call on Dr Robert Ferguson. Ferguson had been the first professor of Midwifery and the Diseases of Children at the new King's College Hospital in 1839. The following year he was appointed physician-accoucheur to Queen Victoria. By 1859 he had resigned his position with the Queen, and had become a general physician, numbering among his patients Lords Palmerston and Derby, Wordsworth and Sir Walter Scott.[5] Cornewall Lewis may also have been one of his patients since his wife was later to be treated by Dr Ferguson. Ferguson had taught obstetrics for many years and contributed extensively to the literature on the subject. He and Sir George 'had a conversation...on Smethurst's case'. Sir George may have shown him the letters he had received from Richardson et al. and Baly and Jenner. What Ferguson's view was on the cause of death of Isabella Bankes was not recorded but evidently it made up Sir George's mind, and after returning to the office he signed the respite document for Thomas Smethurst 'During the Queen's pleasure'. The respite was sent to the High Sheriff of Surrey, and communicated to the governor of Horsemonger Lane Gaol who immediately passed the message on to the prisoner.

The respite granted to Smethurst was, as the editorial in the *Daily Telegraph* of the following day made clear, only a stay of execution, not a full reprieve. Nevertheless, many persons (not including those who had hoped to make money by leasing premium grandstand views of the execution) would be

---

5 ODNB

relieved: the public, the 'partial judge...[who] forgot the duties of his high office...', the jury, the witnesses, Dr Taylor,

> ...whose murderous mistakes...imperfect analyses, [and] pertinaciously fallacious statements, so nearly tied the halter round the neck of Dr Smethurst...

And of course, Dr Smethurst himself. The newspaper congratulated itself, with some justification, on the part that it had played in the process. The editorial finished:

> Our bitterest opponents will not now deny that we commenced and have carried out the popular movement, and that we have directed the pressure from without which has at last resulted in the respite of a man unjustly sentenced to the gallows.

However, even though Thomas Smethurst had received the respite, he had still been found guilty of murder and the authorities had to decide what to do with him. At the Home Office, over the weekend, a long memorandum summarizing the Smethurst case and the reasons for the respite was prepared and this, together with a covering letter from Sir George, was sent to the Queen. On Sunday 4th September, Sir George, still in the office, wrote a note to Waddington regarding the next steps in the Smethurst affair. He asked him to consult 'any legal authority' regarding the possible granting of a free pardon; there was the question of the bigamy and the proper legal procedure. He also asked him to engage a

> ...good detective [to investigate] Mrs Gibson and her language as to the veneficous[6] tendencies of the Smethursts...

---

6 Veneficous = venefical, 'Practising, associated with, malignant sorcery or witchcraft', OED

Mrs Gibson was James Smethurst's landlady, and certain allegations had been made...

On 6th September, Sir George, now back at Harpton Court, wrote again to Waddington. The long train journey had allowed him time to reflect and he had concluded that the verdict in the Smethurst case was 'altogether erroneous' and a free pardon was the only option. He did not want to take that step, however, until he had heard from the Queen and the Lord Chancellor. On the bigamy charge, he wanted to avoid the appearance of persecution:

> ...seeking to punish for one crime when you indicted for another...

He asked Waddington to look into the 'false affidavit' (when Smethurst swore on oath at Doctors' Commons in order to get the marriage licence), to ascertain whether he should be charged with perjury as well as bigamy. And although the Lord Chief Baron had caused the Home Secretary considerable trouble, he wanted to avoid the free pardon casting a slur on him. He proposed to write to Sir Frederick, pointing out that the pardon was granted on the basis of new medical evidence coming to light since the trial. He also wanted to avoid setting a precedent. He finished:

> I am glad that Pollock takes the decision in good part. He ought in fact to see that it has had the effect of extricating him from an immense scrape...

Sir George wrote to Waddington again the next day. The Lord Chancellor had approved the course of action, and it awaited only the Queen's response. He wanted to know whether Waddington had made any progress regarding precedent on the question of an indictment after a free pardon, and was unsatisfied with the cases Waddington had suggested. He pointed out that the 'entire verdict of the jury had been discredited', and there was considerable doubt as to whether Isabella Bankes had been poisoned at all. He further commented:

> It appears that the perjury fails – but it strikes me that after all that has happened, the government had better prosecute for bigamy. At any rate, the matter must not be left to chance.

Evidently it had been concluded that prosecution for perjury as well as bigamy was not appropriate. A few days later he wrote again. He wanted the free pardon to be issued simultaneously with Smethurst being taken before a magistrate to answer the bigamy charge. Smethurst's lawyers were to have sufficient time to prepare for the bigamy trial before the next session at the Old Bailey but,

> ...so short a time as to prevent any good reason for liberating him on bail.

He reflected on the 'general feeling of society' being much divided over the Smethurst case, but 'the medical profession in general think the verdict wrong'. He commented on an article in the *Saturday Review*, highly critical of the respite. It had claimed that the Home Secretary had overturned the proper verdict of the jury, yielding to an 'ignorant popular clamour'. Lewis thought that the piece, 'mischievous enough', represented the opinions of 'a good many people in the upper classes...' However, he now had the consent of the Queen, as well as the Lord Chancellor, to proceed with the free pardon, and it remained only to decide how to handle the bigamy charge. He wanted to avoid the possibility of Smethurst being released on bail.

The Times had a story to the effect that the Home Office was in great difficulty in deciding what to do with Smethurst. Normally, it said, persons reprieved from hanging had the sentence commuted to penal servitude or transportation for life, and it cited several precedents. However 'a good many persons' were of the view that the reprieve implied a serious question of doubt, in which case a free pardon ought to be granted. Perhaps the story had been leaked to them.

The press appeared to be unaware that the Home Secretary had not only received many communications in support of a reprieve, he had also been sent a number of letters, some anonymous, accusing Smethurst of a variety of wrongdoings, some of which involved his brother James. Sir George had ordered the police to investigate the more credible of these before any further decision could be made regarding the prisoner's fate.

'A friend to Justice', undated but probably sent in late August, had written stating that James Smethurst was living with a 'Nymph of the Pave', and being supported by her prostitution; the 'Nymph' in question was Mrs Gibson, James Smethurst's landlady.[7] Thomas Smethurst was then accused of having taken apartments in Trinity Square for a young lady alleged to be his wife. Mr Mayther and another medical student had been living in the same house. Shortly afterwards the lady was confined and gave birth to a healthy child which died suddenly. She left and was never heard of again. At the time, which had been some years previously, Smethurst was said have been living in Clapham.

On 1st September, the day before the reprieve was announced, Laura Willis, a widow, of No 7 'Richmond Villas', Brompton, whose husband had died in 1858, made a long statement, some of which she said had been made to Inspector McIntyre following Smethurst's first trial for murder. Mrs Willis was James Smethurst's next-door neighbour; their gardens were separated by a low wall. He lived at No 6 York

---

7 A 'Nymph of the Pavé' was a term for a prostitute, literally, 'lady of the street'.

Cottages with a woman calling herself 'Mrs Gibson'.[8] About three years previously Mrs Gibson had spoken 'in a highly excited state' to Mr Willis in the garden. She had been suffering from diarrhoea for three days, so severe that it 'actually ran through the sacking of the bed...' Mrs Gibson had said:

> ...those two villains, the Smethursts, were all night with me with a sheet of paper...wishing me to make my will saying why not leave what I had to them in preference to others...

Mrs Willis said that Dr Smethurst visited his brother at the house two or three times a week. She remembered in the previous December seeing Dr Smethurst in the garden with a lady,

> ...of rather tall stature somewhat sallow and ladylike looking...

Dr Smethurst introduced her as the future Mrs Smethurst... Apparently Mrs Willis had said to her when Smethurst's back was turned, 'Do not know anything of those people in there...' The lady looked surprised but said nothing. Mrs Gibson had told Mrs Willis previously that Smethurst had left his wife and gone to live with another person, adding with a coarse laugh, 'I believe he calls it attending on her as a medical case'.

On one occasion since the first trial, Mrs Gibson had been taken ill and Mrs Willis had called a doctor on her behalf. When he had left and Mrs Gibson was drinking tea in bed she said: 'I have not taken tea for a year and a half ever since those men played tricks with it'. Finally, Mrs Willis said that on a number

---

8   The Post Office directory indicates that the ten houses, probably terraced, in this group were called 'York Cottages'. Mrs Willis lived in No 7; James Smethurst and Mrs Gibson lived next door in No 6. Mrs Willis' house may have been called 'Richmond Villa', which is why she gave her address somewhat confusingly as 'No 7 Richmond Villas'.

of occasions they had had cause to complain about 'a smell of drugs' emanating from No 6.

Since James Smethurst was now being implicated in wrongdoing, it is appropriate to say something about him. From around 1832 until 1850 he was a chemist and druggist, but he was also listed in the census as a 'Stock-Jobber',

> An outsider or intermediate agent between the buyer and seller of public securities, who makes a marginal price at which shares &c are to be bought or sold in the Stock-exchange.[9]

Possibly he carried on both occupations simultaneously, at least until 1850.

James too had had an unpleasant encounter with the Law. In January 1839, he was accused of sexually abusing a fifteen-year-old boy by a shop window close to the *Tower Tavern* in the Borough, an inn he was in the habit of frequenting. He was tried at the Quarter Sessions in April and acquitted, his brother Thomas giving evidence on his behalf. There was a suspicion that the boy had conspired with another boy together with the constable who had made the arrest. James brought a charge against the three of them for conspiracy but although they were found guilty they received a fine of one shilling each and were discharged. He then brought an action for perjury against the police constable who had arrested him but the charge was dismissed. This brush with the law and its perceived injustices, might explain James' uncompromising support for his brother twenty years later. Nevertheless, the fact that he too was now implicated along with his brother meant that the police were possibly dealing with a conspiracy.

On 24th September 1859, Detective Sergeants Smith and Tanner made a report having followed up another communication: Between the years 1845 and 1846, Dr

---

9   From Dictionary of Trade Products by Simmonds, 1858

Smethurst, his wife and 'idiot brother' (William), occupied the first floor of No 11 Beak Street, Regent Street. At the same time, James Smethurst 'was in business as a chemist' at 25 Warwick Street, an address which was directly opposite 11 Beak Street. James and Thomas visited each other frequently. A Mr & Mrs Gibson lodged with James Smethurst, and Henry Gibson died there on 5th November 1845 making a will in favour of his wife. His mother and two sisters came from Croydon to the funeral but were refused leave to attend by Mrs Gibson and James Smethurst. The cause of death was *Phrenitis Chronica*, no doctor's name appeared on the death certificate, and the medical man who attended Henry Gibson had not been identified. However, according to some of the neighbours it was thought to be the 'convict Smethurst'. Mary Whitty, 'present at the death', had also not been found. The police had attempted to trace the family of Mr Gibson to corroborate the account, but all were dead except a nephew who was at sea at the time, but remembered his mother telling him the story. Immediately after Henry Gibson's death, Mrs Gibson had 'cohabited' with James Smethurst, and they lived together now (1859) at 6 York Cottages, Brompton.

These were very serious allegations and the police sergeants' superior, Inspector S Thomson, went to interview Mrs Gibson. He reported three days later. Mrs Gibson confirmed the death of her husband, who worked as a 'carver', in 1845 after an illness of approximately three years duration. He did make a will in her favour, but by the time of his death, he had nothing to leave. Dr Brett had attended him 'for some considerable time' before his death. But then:

> Mrs Gibson further stated that during her husband's lifetime, in consequence of their poverty, she was obliged to receive the visits of gentlemen, to enable her to procure the necessaries for her husband during his illness...

However she denied 'most positively' that now or at any time had she ever 'cohabited' with James Smethurst. She also denied Laura Willis' story that she had been ill, with Dr Smethurst pressing her all night to make a will. Inspector Thomson tracked down Dr Brett, who confirmed that he had attended Henry Gibson at James Smethurst's house. He also confirmed the cause of death, *Phrenitis Chronica*, or softening of the brain, brought on by excessive drinking. Brett expressed the opinion that Gibson was in straitened circumstances, but his wife always appeared to be very attached to him.

On the same day, Inspector Thomson also reported the results of the investigation of two more of his men, Sergeants Lockyer and Williamson, into the anonymous letter from 'A friend to Justice'. The medical student, Mr 'Mayther', was now Dr Mather, and was a police surgeon to G Division, living at Essex Street, Islington. He referred them to a 'Miss Smith', who had been staying at a house at 15 Trinity Square some twenty years previously. (Dr Mather had also stayed at the house a few years before that, and had become acquainted with Miss Smith.) She told the sergeants that while she was there, a lady and gentleman calling themselves 'Mr and Mrs Smethurst' came to reside at the same house. She stayed there permanently, he visited her, staying all night 'at intervals of two or three days'. Mr Smethurst was in practice at Clapham as a surgeon. The lady gave birth to a still-born child and left the lodgings shortly afterwards. Miss Smith had no idea where she went. However, the lady did inform Miss Smith that she had eloped from a school in Clapham...

Two weeks later, Inspector Thomson reported the contents of a letter he had received from Superintendant Linck of the Ramsgate police. This letter contained two statements; the first one was from John Watson, a grocer in Ramsgate. Smethurst had treated his wife for some post-natal problem, using his fee to defray a grocery bill. He claimed that the medicine Smethurst had prescribed was analysed by a Dr Barry, who advised that had she taken any of it, she would have gone mad. Watson accused Smethurst of trying to keep his wife ill in order to settle the outstanding debt. He sued Smethurst for the debt, and won, and then sought out his patients telling them not to take any of his medicine. He claimed that he 'hunted' Smethurst out of Ramsgate, ignoring lawyer's letters and a writ. Following up the story, the police found that the nurse who attended Watson's wife during her confinement was dead, and Dr Barry, who had analysed Smethurst's medicine, could not recall the 'circumstances of the analysis'.

The second statement was from a tailor, Mr Evans, who sent his son to Smethurst for treatment by hydropathy under which he appeared cured. Smethurst then suggested medicine, which seemed to make the boy worse, and told him that he was consumptive. The boy was sent to the hydropathic centre at Malvern under Dr Gully where he made a complete recovery and was told that he was not consumptive at all. The arrangement with Evans was, as with the grocer, that Smethurst's fee was to be settled in the form of goods, in this case clothes. Evans was of the opinion that Smethurst put something in the medicine to extend the boy's sickness in order that he could get a good stock of clothes. Smethurst visited the boy twice a week for nineteen weeks at half a guinea a visit.

The police had invested considerable effort in following up these various allegations, but what, in fact, did the findings amount to? The apparent allegation that Thomas Smethurst had a hand in Henry Gibson's death was plainly untrue; the doctor attending Gibson was found and confirmed the circumstances of his illness and death. Mrs Gibson denied that she had told Laura Willis or her husband that Smethurst tried to get her to make a will in his favour when she was ill. Naturally that charge was highly suspicious given the circumstances of Isabella Bankes' death, and it is certainly odd that Laura Willis should have made such a detailed statement without some of it being true. Mrs Gibson even denied being ill. Mrs Gibson, Julia Emma Gibson, was certainly a singular individual. She was evidently at pains that the police should understand that she did not 'cohabit' with James Smethurst, yet she freely admitted 'entertaining gentlemen' in order to make ends meet.[10] It might also be suspected that she used her talents to good effect. In the 1851, 1861 and 1871 census returns, she and James Smethurst occupied the same dwelling, but she was designated the head of the household, implying that he was lodging with her. And when she died, intestate, in 1879, having been left nothing by her husband, the value of her estate was in the region of £2,000.

As for the charges from the grocer and tailor, that Smethurst was a bad doctor with questionable ethics, such a circumstance was not a crime. Alternatively, both gentlemen could have simply mistaken his actions for poor judgement or a poor outcome of his treatments. After all, Isabella Bankes had *died* under Dr Julius' care. In different circumstances, Smethurst could have had him charged with murder. The fact that Smethurst may have fathered a child with the lady who eloped from a school in Clapham, was no more than the Prime Minister, Viscount Palmerston, had already done several times over. He had been nicknamed *Lord Cupid* for his womanizing...

Evidently, Cornewall Lewis concluded that none of the allegations really amounted to anything, but before the case could be concluded by issuing the free pardon and prosecuting Smethurst for bigamy, there was a need for a grand summary of all the facts relating to the Smethurst affair. This would be sent to the Queen and others as a record of the events leading up to the pardon and the justification for it. Sir George decided to ask Sir Frederick Pollock, the trial judge to produce this summary. Pollock must have been seriously fed up with the Smethurst case and all the press criticism he had had to

---

10 It is by no means clear why Julia Gibson found it necessary to make this admission to the police, unless her neighbours had already told them that she earned money in this way.

endure since the trial. In truth though, if the whole mess was anyone's fault, it was Pollock's. Whatever the witnesses had said, and Dr Taylor's mistakes notwithstanding, it was he who unequivocally directed the jury to a guilty verdict.[11] Sir George asked him for a full report into all aspects of the case.

Sir Frederick Pollock started requesting information and writing to Lewis' Under-Secretary of State, Horatio Waddington. He also visited him. On 7th October, Waddington wrote to Lewis:

> Pollock has just been here again and is most laboriously employed upon his report which he promises in 5 or 6 days...

But Pollock had read William Herapath's letter damning Dr Taylor's analysis, and wanted the Home Secretary to ask Dr Taylor for a formal response. Waddington was concerned that this would lead to a 'violent controversy between the two adepts' which would delay Pollock's report. Lewis agreed:

> ...it is sufficient for my purpose that the case is envisioned with doubt...

The decision not to invite Taylor to respond to Herapath's letter was given to Pollock when he called to see Waddington on 11th October. He was not satisfied, and wrote to Waddington on 13th October reiterating the request, pointing out the importance of Herapath's comments and the fact that they had been referred to by Baly and Jenner, and others. Pollock's note was long and rambling, and written in bright blue ink. The handwriting was quirky with much underlining and annotation, and it

---

11 One of the jury had written to *The Times* saying that he and ten of his colleagues had 'made up their minds' before the judge's summing up, although this was refuted by another juryman who contacted Smethurst after the case. Whichever was true, it was up to the judge to summarize accurately and fairly the evidence both for and against the prisoner immediately before the jury retired to consider their verdict.

looked more like the work of a schoolboy than a senior judge. Waddington's patience with the Chief Baron was starting to wear thin; 'What answer is to be given to this rigmarole?' he wrote to Lewis. Lewis agreed with the sentiment, replying that if Taylor 'voluntarily' communicated any remarks, he would be happy to read them but he would not compel him to respond.

Pollock wrote again on 17th October regretting the Home Secretary's decision. The letter was timed at 4:45 in the morning (all his letters were written very early in the morning), and as before executed with variable handwriting, blue ink and lots of underlining. He was now convinced that Herapath's arguments would have 'blown to atoms [and] sent to the winds' all of Dr Taylor's analysis and calculations had they been used in court. He went further, saying that the verdict could well have been altered. The Chief Baron was changing his tune and seemed to have latched on to Herapath's letter as a mechanism for getting him off the hook for his conduct of the trial. Cornewall Lewis annotated the judge's letter with the observation:

> The Chief Baron is a strange correspondent – but the period of his participation seems now happily to be terminated.

He further commented to Waddington that his decision on the Smethurst case (regarding the free pardon) could not be delayed any longer.

On 18th October, Pollock's summary of the circumstances of the trial and aftermath were finally sent to the Home Secretary. The document consisted of 67 pages of foolscap, and was written by a clerk using clear copperplate and black ink, but there was no doubt of the authorship. It summarized the views of the trial judge in the light of the subsequent medical evidence and all the criticism the case had attracted. It is most illuminating as to Pollock's view of the Smethurst case. He used the report to reiterate his opinion of Smethurst's guilt, emphasizing again the incriminating circumstantial evidence relating to the bigamous marriage and the will. He made passing reference to Smethurst's diary which had never been mentioned in the trial. He also engaged with tedious detail any fact or opinion that appeared to upset his own interpretation of events. No mention was made of the various police reports acting on information received about Smethurst and his brother James. Cornewall Lewis may have concluded that to send such potentially incriminating material to Pollock would only have fuelled his apparent obsession with the circumstantial evidence against Smethurst.

The document started with a summary of the 200 plus separate communications on the Smethurst case that had been addressed to the Home Office:

> From petitions and memorials signed by many individuals (some of great respectability) to anonymous communications entitled to no attention whatsoever...from remarks made by medical men of the highest reputation, to the idle dreamings of an insane old woman...[12]

There were 39 petitions of varying sizes, and already by page 3 of the document, Pollock had detected a conspiracy. The largest petition, containing around 5,000 signatures, was from the offices of the *Morning Star*, owned by Mr Bright (the 'Manchester Radical' who had started it along with Mr Cobden), and edited by 'Mr Dymond'. The paper, 'of considerable circulation', had taken up the Smethurst case 'with much ability' and published some

> ...very strong and powerful but not very scrupulous or accurate articles against the judge, the jury, and the witnesses for the prosecution...

---

12 This was a lady whom Pollock made reference to several times in spite of his description of her as '...the insane Mrs Whiteside...'

Cornewall Lewis had written in the margin that the *Morning Star* and members of the Grosvenor Place School of Medicine were probably responsible for many of the petitions.[13] The circulation of the *Morning Star* was only around 13,000 in 1856, to Cobden's disappointment, and far less than that of the *Daily Telegraph* at the time of the trial. The *Daily Telegraph* had been very aggressive in its condemnation of the trial outcome, yet it was the *Morning Star* that attracted the attention of the judge. Pollock questioned the objectivity of the petition, claiming that it had been orchestrated by the *Morning Star*.

The summary went on to detail various other general petitions received, containing in total 1,100 signatures. Then there were 10 petitions from medical men with around 120 signatures. There were 30 letters from medical men and chemists, 11 of whom had experience of cases similar to that of Isabella Bankes. There was an article in *The Lancet* of 17th September, 'written in great moderation', which Pollock thought 'quite incorrect'. There was a petition from 21 members of the Bar, '[none of whom was] present at the trial'. There was also the long letter from Drs Richardson, Thudichum and Webb.

There were nine letters, including one in pencil from Putney, from persons who thought Smethurst to be guilty. Pollock detailed these too. Then there were 15 anonymous letters which were also summarized, after which Pollock commented, somewhat inconsistently, that 'any anonymous communications...are unworthy of any attention' and 'I myself never read anonymous communications at all'.

There was a petition from James Smethurst, another from Mary Smethurst and four communications from Smethurst

---

13 There were a number of annotations in the margin. One of them was signed 'GCL', although the handwriting was clear and legible and quite unlike the scrawl the Home Secretary used for his diaries. Since this was an official document for the scrutiny of the Queen and Prime Minister, Lewis may either have smartened up his handwriting, or they were made by a clerk at Lewis' direction.

himself, one addressed to the Prince Consort. On Thomas Smethurst's offerings, the Lord Chief Baron focussed on his claim that a friend of Isabella Bankes had witnessed a conversation where Isabella wished for the marriage so that she would not appear to be Smethurst's mistress. Smethurst claimed that the friend was available to give evidence, but Serjeant Parry had deemed it unnecessary. Pollock doubted very much whether this was the case. 'Why,' he asked, 'is not her statement...now offered?' Then there was the question of the will. Smethurst had claimed that the barrister who drew it up (James Mellor Smethurst) was in court as a witness, but according to Smethurst, Serjeant Parry 'would not go into it'. Both facts were, he said, highly suspicious.

There were four communications that Pollock thought 'worthy of special notice'. There was a letter from Mr Bright, MP for Birmingham, one of the co-founders of the *Morning Star*. There was the communication from Drs Baly and Jenner. There were some observations from a former judge at the Sudder Court, and there was the letter from Messrs Parry and Giffard, Smethurst's counsel.[14]

Mr Bright, '[who] is sure to be attended to' was of the opinion (in the context of the supposed injury to Isabella Bankes' reputation by the bigamous marriage) that Isabella shared the guilt equally with Smethurst. Bright justified this by claiming that

> ...hundreds of married men keep mistresses and thousands are unfaithful to their wives...

Pollock observed that this was a 'view of society and the female character' with which he could not agree. He disputed Bright's view that the 'pecuniary motive' had been disposed of, and dismissed the point that no poison had been found in

---

14 The 'Sudder Court', Sudder = Supreme (OED), was a high court or court of appeal in Calcutta.

Smethurst's possession, since he was a medical man with a brother who was a chemist. Bright had also commented that no poison was found in the body except traces of antimony. Pollock disagreed with him on his view of the public and the press, claiming that the majority of the public journals, 'the unthinking as well as the thinking part' were against Smethurst. Pollock went on with much underlining:

> The opinion of any journalist or of any private individual is of no importance unless it be the result of a calm, dispassionate and accurate consideration of the whole of the evidence, and I have found nothing of the kind in the entire mass of papers before me.

Now he came to the 'remarks' of Drs Baly and Jenner. It is notable that the long, carefully argued, and very convincing letter from Drs Richardson Thudichum and Webb, principal medical witnesses for the defence, was not considered 'worthy of special notice' by Sir Frederick. They, of course, were relative unknowns, and as the newspapers had observed, 'bullied' by him during the trial and 'tainted' by their allegiance to the Grosvenor Place School of Medicine.

Baly and Jenner though were two members of the 'highest branch of the medical profession' and 'deservedly entitled to great respect'. Their conclusions were virtually the same as those of Dr Richardson and his colleagues, and Pollock went on to detail them. They concluded that Isabella Bankes 'laboured under spontaneous disease' and no satisfactory proof had been 'adduced' as to her having been poisoned. Pollock commented on the mistake in their analysis; they had claimed that Isabella could not have been poisoned since she had not started vomiting at the time when Dr Julius was first called to her. This was plainly wrong, as has already been noted. It was a serious error, more serious even than that of Dr Taylor over bottle No 21, as Cornewall Lewis commented in the margin.

However, Pollock was disposed to deal kindly with Baly and Jenner's shortcomings (there were other errors), attributing them to the haste with which the letter was prepared (dated 29th August, just eight days before the execution).

The letter from the Sudder Court judge, Pollock appeared to include simply in order to ridicule its contents, which included the suggestion that Isabella Bankes might have poisoned herself out of shame and remorse.

It was in responding to the letter from the prisoner's counsel, Messrs Parry and Giffard, that Pollock again revealed something of his thought processes. They had accused him of committing an error on a point of law, saying:

> The fact of death by poison was not established beyond all doubt...as a matter of law, [Pollock] ought to have told the jury...that death by poison could not be inferred either from motive or from the conduct of the prisoner, but must be proved by medical or scientific testimony...

Pollock thought they were wrong, and was willing for the question to be submitted to the Court of Criminal Appeal for a ruling.[15] He justified this by claiming that the doubt could be resolved by reference to 'collateral circumstances'. He went on to claim, apparently quite seriously, that the prisoner's suspicious conduct was of equal weight in law, as if he had written in a diary his intention to commit murder, and then written on a later date that he had actually committed the murder.

Half of Pollock's report had been devoted to a review of the communications received by the Home Office on the Smethurst

---

15 This was not a full Court of Criminal Appeal such as some of the newspapers had called for; that was not instituted until 1907. Pollock was referring to a court set up purely to rule on points of law.

case; now however, the Chief Baron came to the actual evidence. And addressing the Home Secretary, he declared:

> ...the effect of the medical evidence now before you, is very different from that which was before the jury...

Pollock thought that the medical witnesses for the prosecution were of

> ...much greater weight as to station, experience and standing in the profession, than the medical witnesses for the prisoner...

Moreover, he thought it was 'very indiscreet', and had prejudiced the prisoner's position, for the defence to use witnesses who had been on the 'losing' side in the Palmer case, and to produce them as the first and third witnesses. He was referring to Drs Richardson and Rogers; Dr Richardson had repeated in the Smethurst trial that he had thought Palmer's so-called victim might have died of angina rather than poison.[16] Pollock thought that this was 'exceedingly unfavourable' both to Smethurst and to the witness, since the public were 'universally and deeply impressed' with Palmer's guilt. In vain, he said, he had instructed the jury that they could not consider Palmer guilty for the purposes of the Smethurst case. Because of this, the medical evidence for the defence did not go to the jury 'in so favourable a way as it might'. The medical evidence since received made it clear, firstly, that far more weight should have been given to the effects of Isabella Bankes' pregnancy, and secondly, the post-mortem appearances were ambiguous; indeed some had claimed that the 'symptoms and appearances were inconsistent and incompatible with poison'. He then conceded that 'according to the practice of the Home Office' the life of the prisoner should be spared, however:

---

16 Actually Richardson and Rogers were the first and second witnesses for the defence in Smethurst's trial.

...beyond this it seems to one that the mass of ignorance, presumption, inaccuracy and inattention, of confusion and contradiction, to say nothing of downright blunder, misconception and misrepresentation (mixed up no doubt with some learning, science and good sense) which I have before me, has no tendency to establish the innocence of the prisoner, so as to entitle him to a free pardon.

This was written with no sense of irony regarding Pollock's own apparent contribution to the 'presumption...inaccuracy... misconception and misrepresentation' attaching to the Smethurst case. He added that the disclosures since the trial:

...tend to confirm the prisoner's guilt, but to give a different direction to the object of it.

He conceded that arsenic was not administered to the victim, but thought that antimony might have been...

Having dealt, for the moment, with the medical evidence, Pollock now sought to influence the Home Secretary on what he always thought had most incriminated Smethurst, the circumstantial evidence. In civil actions, he said, it was normal for the jury to rule on individual and subordinate aspects of the case. This was not done in criminal cases; the defendant was either guilty or not guilty of the charge. Nevertheless, Pollock thought it appropriate, and for the Home Secretary's consideration only, to consider individually how guilty Smethurst appeared from the lesser aspects of the case. He reproduced Smethurst's unsent letter to Mary, where he told her 'I shall see you as soon as possible...' and '...should any unforeseen event prevent my leaving...' He went on to analyse the phraseology of the letter seeking to show that Smethurst knew that Isabella would be dead in a day or two after which he would return to Mary. Of equal importance, Pollock claimed, was the relation in which Miss Bankes stood towards the prisoner...did she altogether share in the sin, crime and profligacy of the transaction...

Pollock considered it most improbable that a

well educated woman of 42 years of age, of respectable connections, of independent fortune...and hitherto unblemished reputation...would commit the crime of bigamy and the sin of adultery...

He thought it 'next to an impossibility' that Isabella should have been party to a felony. However, he conceded that Isabella's 'levity' at Rifle Terrace, when she was asked to leave for flirting with Smethurst, was 'unfavourable' to her. He went on to claim that her statement to her sister, 'If you will be quiet it will be alright', could only mean that it would turn out that she was properly married to Smethurst. Her signing of the will using her maiden name, he suggested was because of her weakened state, since she had died 'of weakness' only 48 hours later.

Then there was the question of poison. Many of the communications to the Home Secretary claimed that no poison was found in the body. In fact Dr Taylor, assisted by Dr Odling, claimed to have found between one quarter and one half of a grain of antimony in the entire body, and none was found in the liver. Arguments against this evidence were a) that Dr Taylor was unreliable following his blunder with bottle No 21, b) that the quantity found was too small to be significant and c) that some ought to have been found in the liver. And it was shown that bismuth, copper and mercury, all given to Miss Bankes as medicine, contained arsenic and antimony as impurities.

On point a) Dr Taylor was careless and bungling, although 'Dr' Brande said he would have made the same mistake. However, if impartial scientific persons thought that his finding of the antimony was valid, Pollock thought it 'decisive of the case'. On point b) Pollock thought it a spurious argument. He reminded the Home Secretary that Dr Richardson 'could not state' there was even half a grain of arsenic in the dog that had died. How much, Pollock asked, would be needed to disturb the system of a pregnant woman? Taylor and Odling thought it was sufficient to account for Isabella Bankes' death. On point c) Pollock was, unusually, unable to offer an opinion. On the question of the poisonous impurities found in the medicines, he thought that that ought to be 'the subject of distinct and specific enquiry...' He thought Dr Thudichum's evidence on the poisonous impurities he claimed he had found in medicines not candid or honest. He had no memorandum of his experiments, and Pollock thought his evidence was presented merely to raise doubts in the minds of those who would take a 'loose and ignorant view of the subject'.

Now the issue of Isabella's pregnancy was addressed. Pollock thought that Smethurst *did* know that she was pregnant, and sought to conceal it; moreover, he thought this to be crucial evidence against Smethurst. When Dr Julius had asked Smethurst if Isabella might be pregnant, he was told that 'her monthly courses were on her'. But a diary had been found in which Smethurst noted the dates of Isabella's periods, Pollock called them her 'monthly sexual visitations'. The diary *proved* that Smethurst was lying (Pollock didn't go into detail), and was trying to conceal the pregnancy from the other doctors.[17] He suggested that Smethurst had wanted to procure an abortion, but wanted to hide the fact from Dr Julius

---

17 Presumably either no note was made in the diary of Isabella's period when it should have been due, or Smethurst noted that it hadn't appeared. However, if Isabella was between five and seven weeks pregnant at her death on 3rd May, her 'missed' period should have been approximately sometime between Tuesday 29th March and Tuesday 12th April. Dr Julius' first visit was Sunday 3rd April and subsequent days. Assuming that he questioned Smethurst on Isabella's possible pregnancy on the first or second visit, Smethurst's response, 'her usual periods were on her...' may well have been perfectly true – at the time she may not have missed a period.

and the others. If Isabella had become pregnant, it would be a 'great impediment' to Smethurst's plans. She would want her relations around her, and the illegal marriage was sure to come out. Pollock was of the opinion that pregnancy and an attempted abortion explained all the 'mystery and secrecy of the bedchamber' and the absence of a nurse. He claimed that the pregnancy was the motivation for the last-minute will.

Pollock conceded that the medical evidence obtained since the trial did 'materially' alter the case, 'apparently' in Smethurst's favour, although he claimed that the majority of the medical profession, 'competent from practice and experience', agreed with Drs Julius, Bird and Todd. There was, he said, a strong and almost universal perception in the 'thinking sensible' public that Smethurst was guilty; an acquittal would have created 'alarm...and distrust' in the public mind. He thought a free pardon was not warranted in view of the diary Smethurst kept of Isabella's 'monthly visitations', in spite of the new medical evidence.

Of all of the communications received, he said, the one from Drs Baly and Jenner was the most trustworthy, although the 'unaccountable mistake' in it needed to be rectified before it could be used for making a decision. Pollock concluded that the judgement of 'medical and scientific persons' selected by the Home Secretary should consider the symptoms and appearance of Isabella Bankes, as well as Dr Taylor's analyses. He finished his report by declaring that the points raised by Dr Herapath should be pursued; had Taylor been cross-examined on these, 'the result of the trial might have been quite different'. He signed himself 'Fred Pollock'. Sir Fred Pollock's report had been long and detailed, but it was clear that in his view, and despite the medical doubts and Taylor's bungling, Smethurst was guilty by virtue of the circumstantial evidence. But the judge was mindful of difficulties with the medical evidence, and he did, at least, recommend a medical and scientific review.

The Home Secretary decided to call in Sir Benjamin Brodie and ask him for an independent assessment. Sir Benjamin was, by this time, perhaps the most eminent surgeon in the land. In 1844 he had been elected President of the Royal College of Surgeons, and in 1859 he became the first President of the new General Medical Council. He was also the first surgeon to be elected President of the Royal Society. In addition to that, he had provided prosecution evidence during the Palmer trial. If the Home Secretary was aware of Brodie's previous spat with the Grosvenor Place School of Medicine, he evidently decided that Sir Benjamin's current eminence overrode any consideration of bias.

Sir Benjamin wrote to Sir George on 28th October. Considering the wealth of medical testimony both during and after the trial, his findings were hardly profound. And he irritated Sir Frederick Pollock by not limiting his comments to the medical evidence in which he was supposed to be the expert. His report consisted of six articles supporting Smethurst's conviction and eight against. Smethurst had, he said, an indifferent moral character and a financial motive (for murder). Smethurst had objected to others but himself attending Isabella; but Sir Benjamin observed that many symptoms of arsenic poisoning were absent in Miss Bankes' case. Antimony had been found in the body, and the poison was likely to have caused the symptoms and post-mortem appearances observed. Smethurst's suggestion of testing prussic acid on sparrows pointed to knowledge of poisoning and experimentation.

Set against this was the fact that antimony is an 'uncertain poison' and where only a trace was discovered, allowance should be made for error; in any case, antimony is likely to be present in the body for a long period, so the traces detected could have been there for months. Also, no antimony had been found in the liver. Isabella's symptoms in life and appearance after death were compatible with natural causes and Brodie considered the effect of pregnancy had been much exaggerated. No poisons were found in Smethurst's possession, nor was there any evidence that he had ever purchased any. Smethurst was not in need of money, and the will had been made at the last minute when the actual time of death was uncertain. Sir Benjamin concluded that '...there [was] no absolute and complete evidence of Smethurst's guilt'.

On 15th November 1859, Sir George informed the Lord Chief Baron of Sir Benjamin Brodie's opinion, stating that in view of the doubt of his guilt, it was his duty to grant him a free pardon. He would, however, institute proceedings against him for bigamy. He said that his decision was not

> due to any defect in the constitution or proceedings
> of our criminal tribunals [rather] the imperfection of
> medical science, and from the fallibility of judgment,
> in an obscure malady, even of skilful and experienced
> medical practitioners.

Pollock replied on the same day. Considering that the Home Secretary had let him off the hook for responsibility in what was looking more and more like a legal shambles of a case, Sir Frederick was remarkably grudging in his response. 'Fred' Pollock's letter conceded nothing. An initial tribute to Brodie's 'general talents...good sense...and intellectual superiority', was followed by a "but", indicating Pollock's rejection of Brodie's qualification to give an opinion, the opinion itself and Sir George's decision to grant the free pardon.

Firstly, Sir Fred grumpily commented that he couldn't provide a 'lawyer's opinion' on Brodie's letter, since he didn't know what Brodie had been asked or what his terms of reference were. Then he complained that Brodie's conclusion was not based purely on medical evidence; he (Brodie) had assumed that *all* of the evidence, including motive, had been referred to him for a ruling. That, Pollock insisted, '...overrules the conclusion of the jury'. On the question of Smethurst's obtaining the poison, he observed:

> ...as if the brother of a chemist required to go to anyone but his brother to get it...

Pollock then criticized Brodie for failing to comment on the suggestion that Smethurst administered poison in order to procure abortion, saying that this had been legally 'demonstrable' (underlined very hard). Pollock went on to complain about the 'improper practice of suppressing evidence':

> ...[had] the parchment-covered book...been in evidence, I think Smethurst would have been hanged long ago.

That was a reference to the diary in which Smethurst had noted the occurrence of Isabella's periods. Apparently a decision had been made not to present it as evidence during the trial. Perhaps the entries were ambiguous... Pollock pointed out that death following an attempt to procure abortion was still murder, and asked whether Brodie had considered whether there was not 'reasonable' (underlined) evidence that that was what had happened. He ended his letter by saying that the lack of 'absolute and complete evidence' was not grounds for a pardon, as there was lack of 'absolute and complete evidence' in nine cases out of ten. This, he said, had been true of the Palmer case, where two of Smethurst's defence witnesses had appeared for Palmer's defence, and had stated that the victim did not die of strychnine. The letter was a *tour de force* of prejudice and reaction. After all that had been said about the case, much of it detailed by 'Sir Fred' himself in his report, Sir Frederick Pollock, the Lord Chief Baron, was entirely unmoved. It was a shabby and grudging response, entirely lacking in good grace.

Sir George wrote back to Pollock. He said that the medical evidence was inconclusive one way or the other, and the question of abortion was not raised at the trial. In any case, the jury were influenced by the financial motive and the making of the will:

> ...[if] some deleterious medicine was given for the purpose of destroying the child, it is impossible that the desire of obtaining the woman's money could have had anything to do with the act.

In any event, the Home Secretary had made his decision; Thomas Smethurst was to be granted a free pardon by the Crown.

Bigamy

Sir George Cornewall Lewis had written to the Lord Chief Baron informing him of his decision to grant the free pardon on Tuesday 15th November, but he had already started the chain of events. The Pardon was dated 14th November, but even before that, on Saturday 12th November, Thomas Smethurst was brought before the Southwark Magistrates' Court on a writ of *Habeas Corpus* served on the governor of Horsemonger Lane gaol to answer a charge of bigamy.

The use of a writ of *Habeas Corpus ad Subjiciendum*, literally, 'thou (shalt) have the body (sc. in court)' seems a sledgehammer mechanism to use to bring Smethurst to the magistrates' hearing.[1] *Habeas Corpus* was an ancient legal instrument, in use in England since the twelfth century, designed to ensure that no-one could be arbitrarily imprisoned without having had a hearing in a court of law. In fact, it might have been the only way to proceed. There may have been no other way to release a convicted murderer from prison at the time. Sir George wanted to make sure that Smethurst was duly charged, arraigned and committed for trial *before* the free pardon was issued. In that way he avoided any chance of him being set free, if only for a short while, and all the potential press melee and publicity that would have resulted.

One report called it a 'semi-official announcement' that Smethurst would be brought before the police court. In any event, people crowded the entrance for two hours before the

---

1 From the OED. Sc. is short for scilicet = that is to say, namely. OED.

doors opened. When they did, the space assigned to the public was 'immediately filled to inconvenience'. Smethurst was brought into court in the custody of Mr Keene, the governor of Horsemonger Lane. He wore a dark green or black Chesterfield overcoat buttoned to the neck, a black satin stock (cravat) and kid gloves. He still retained his 'conspicuous' moustache. He shook hands with his brother James who was near him in court.

Mr Combe was the presiding magistrate; Mr Clerk conducted the prosecution. Mr H G Robinson, a solicitor of 6, Half Moon Street, was present to 'watch the proceedings in the interest of the prisoner', who was then charged that he, Thomas Smethurst,

> on the 9th December last, within this district, did unlawfully and feloniously intermarry with one Isabella Bankes, his wife Mary being then alive.

Mr Clerk said that it was not necessary to 'allude to the circumstances under which the charge arose...' other than that the prisoner was tried and convicted of murder, but that the sentence was not carried out. He then summarized the circumstances of Smethurst's marriage to Mary Durham, meeting Isabella Bankes, and marrying her while Mary was still alive.

Mr Clerk called William Easter, the parish clerk of St Mark's Kennington who proved Smethurst's marriage with Mary Durham. He called Charles Laporte and his son, who were relatives of Mary. Laporte proved the signature in the register was that of Mary Durham. His son had seen Mr and Mrs Smethurst together within the last 18 months. Mr Smith, the landlord at Rifle Terrace proved that the Smethursts and Miss Bankes had resided at his house until Miss Bankes left, followed shortly by the prisoner. James Sprice, parish clerk at Battersea proved the marriage between Smethurst and

Isabella Bankes, and Louisa Bankes was called to prove that the signature in the register was that of her sister.

Inspector McIntyre, who had arrested Smethurst, identified the letter found on him, addressed to Mary Smethurst, and unsent. Mr Laporte, the elder, was recalled, and identified the handwriting as that of Smethurst. And that was the case for the prosecution.

Mr Robinson, who had not questioned any of the prosecution witnesses, reserved his defence for the 'other tribunal', but asked for bail for the prisoner, which would be provided by 'persons of undeniable respectability and responsibility'. Mr Combe, the magistrate, said that the prisoner was brought to court under a writ of *Habeas Corpus*, but was in the custody of the governor of Horsemonger Lane Gaol. 'No bail...would justify his being taken out of that custody'. Mr Robinson said that a pardon would very likely be given to the prisoner, 'In that case, would your worship take bail?' Mr Combe responded that the application could be made after the pardon had been given. Smethurst was then committed for trial at the Central Criminal Court, and taken back to Horsemonger Lane. One report stated that there was immense excitement in court at that point, but that the prisoner 'retained the same calm demeanour' he had shown throughout.

The free pardon was duly signed on Monday 14th November, and on Thursday 17th, Mr Robinson was back in front of Mr Combe requesting bail.

Mr Combe:

I cannot accept bail.

Mr Robinson:

You were pleased to say on Saturday that if a free pardon was granted to my client you might accept bail.

Mr Combe:

> I said that under the circumstances before me. Where is your free pardon?

Mr Robinson:

> I have it here sir...

> *The Seal of Our Lady the Queen, 'Victoria R'*

> *Whereas Thomas Smethurst was at a session of the Central Criminal Court, holden in August last, convicted upon a certain indictment there and then preferred against him for the wilful murder of Isabella Bankes, and had sentence of death passed upon him for the same.*

> *We, in consideration of some circumstances humbly represented unto us, are graciously pleased to extend our grace and mercy unto him, the said Thomas Smethurst, and to grant him a free pardon for the crime of which he stands so convicted upon such indictment as aforesaid.*

> *Our will and pleasure therefore is, that you do take due notice thereof, and for doing so this shall be your warrant.*

> *Given at our Court of St James's the 14th day of November, 1859, in the twenty-third year of our reign.*

> *To our trusty friends and well-beloved Justices of the Central Criminal Court, the High Sheriff of the County of Surrey, and all others whom it may concern.*

> *By her Majesty's command, G C Lewis.*

> *I certify this to be a true copy of her Majesty's pardon to Thomas Smethurst for the crime of wilful murder of which he was convicted in August last. John Keen,*

Governor of the County Gaol, at Newington, in the county of Surrey, Nov 17, 1859.[2]

Mr Combe read the document through, then said:

I tell you I cannot accept bail. Whatever the government has done, I have to do my duty as a magistrate. This man is charged with bigamy.

Mr Robinson:

But you have power to accept bail in such cases.

Mr Combe:

In this case, I will not. Go to a judge in chambers if you like.

Mr Robinson:

Then you refuse to accept bail here, sir?

Mr Combe:

Yes certainly. I cannot interfere.

Mr Combe may have been empowered to accept bail under the circumstances, but it was clear from the Home Secretary's correspondence with his Under-Secretary of State that he did not want Smethurst released before the bigamy case was heard. Perhaps someone had had a quiet word in Mr Combe's ear...

The trial of Dr Thomas Smethurst for bigamy took place on Wednesday 30th November 1859 at the Central Criminal Court.

---

2 Horsemonger Lane Gaol had officially changed its name to the County Gaol at Newington, on account of the name of Horsemonger Lane being changed to Union Road. Most people still referred to the prison as 'Horsemonger Lane'.

The judge presiding was Baron William Bramwell; prosecuting were Mr Clerk and Mr Beasley, and defending Smethurst were Mr Sleigh and Mr Talfourd Salter. Smethurst, who presented a 'depressed and careworn appearance', pleaded not guilty in a low voice.

Mr Clerk opened for the prosecution, and with commendable understatement observed that it would be 'idle to suppose that the jury were not well acquainted with all the circumstances [of the case]...' His case was very much like that conducted during the magistrates' hearing two weeks previously. After the marriage of Smethurst and Mary Durham was proved, he produced a clerk from the London and Westminster Bank, Mr McCrosty, who identified Smethurst's handwriting. So far, so good, but then the hearing which had promised to be a repetitive affair, virtually all of the evidence having already been heard during the murder trial, suddenly came alive with the next witness. Charles Laporte was called; he was a fifty-two year old artist.

Charles Laporte:

> I am acquainted with Mary Durham...she is a relative of mine...this is her handwriting...I have seen her repeatedly since 1828 as Mrs Smethurst...she called upon me...my son [Charles] has repeatedly seen her, in my presence...

Mr Sleigh (or Mr Salter):

> ...I understand you to say when you are speaking of Mary Durham, you mean Mrs Smethurst?

Charles Laporte:

> Yes...I am a son of hers...[but] the defendant is not my father...my father was living on 10th March 1828 [the date of Smethurst's marriage to Mary Durham]

239

So, Mary Smethurst, née Durham, had a past... Mr Clerk continued with his questions:

Your father's name I believe was Laporte?

Charles Laporte:

It was...Mary Durham passed by the name of Johnson when I first knew the prisoner, before he married her [it was Charles Laporte who had introduced his friend Thomas Smethurst to his mother Mary]...I had also gone by the name of Johnson until after the prisoner married my mother...Mr. Laporte, my father, also went by the name of Johnson to me...it was after the marriage of the prisoner that I discovered that my father's name was Laporte, and not Johnson...after that Mr. Laporte introduced me to his family...he had an elder son of the name of [George Henry] Laporte...he is here.

Mr Clerk then asked whether the wife of Mr Laporte, senior, was alive at the time, but Mr Sleigh objected. Charles Laporte continued:

There was a lady living with Mr Laporte who was to all appearance his wife...after the prisoner's marriage with my mother I passed by the name of Laporte, and dropped the name of Johnson at my father's request...I then for some time became a member of my father's family...my half-brother, Mr. Laporte...is a good deal older than I...in the year 1828, Mrs. Smethurst, who had been Mary Durham, shewed me the certificate of that marriage...

The reports in the press do not mention gasps from the public gallery at these revelations, but the prosecution case did seem to have backfired somewhat in revealing that Mary Smethurst had a past almost as shady as that of Thomas Smethurst...

Mr Sleigh continued:

> Mary Durham your mother...was living with a person calling himself Mr. Johnson, she being called Mrs. Johnson?

Charles Laporte:

> Exactly so...Mr. and Mrs. Johnson, my father and mother, appeared to me to live as man and wife previous to 1828...

Before clarifying this curious ménage, one more witness needs to be heard; he was George Henry Laporte...

George Henry Laporte:

> I am a son of Mr. Laporte, and, in some sense, the half-brother of the last witness...I did not know Mary Durham; she was a servant in our family when I was an infant; my sister knew her...I had never seen her at our house.

The Judge:

> You know nothing of her yourself, then, of your own knowledge?

George Henry Laporte:

> No; my sister does, I do not.

Mr Clerk:

> When did you first see the last witness Charles Laporte?

George Henry Laporte:

> In the summer of 1828, at Cambridge...my mother
> was living at that time...I was twenty-six years old...
> my mother died in the year 1840 ...I had seen Mary
> Durham, under the name of Johnson, at Johnson's or
> Laporte's house; I only saw the back of her, and a slight
> view of her face...I think that was in 1837 or 1838, I
> cannot say the date exactly...she would of course pass
> by the name of Smethurst then...I had never seen her
> before she married the prisoner.

Mr Clerk:

> Did your father live in London?

George Henry Laporte:

> Yes, with my mother...relations of my father and our
> friends visited us, and also my mother's friends...she
> was introduced into society as Mrs. Laporte...my father
> regularly resided with the family...he was occasionally
> absent from home certain days of the week, which we
> could not account for...

This was an extraordinary revelation, and handed messrs
Sleigh and Salter an opportunity for a defence of sorts.
However, in the interests of clarity the relationship between
Mary Durham and the Laportes should be explained.

John Peter Laporte, (1761 – 1839), was a well-known
watercolour artist, specializing in landscapes, who had
exhibited at the Royal Academy and British Institution. He may
have been acquainted with Turner.[3] In December 1783, he
married Martha Henderson and they had at least four children,
of whom only two seem to have survived into adulthood;

---

3 ODNB

these were Mary Ann, born around 1788, and George Henry, born 1802. George Henry Laporte also became an artist, specializing in animals, and he too exhibited at the Royal Academy. According to George, Mary Durham was a servant in the house and it is likely that his sister, Mary Ann, knew her, because there was just three years between them in age.

John Peter Laporte took a fancy to his servant Mary, and when she fell pregnant, he set her up somewhere as 'Mrs Johnson', he being 'Mr Johnson'. Their son Charles was born in 1807 or thereabouts, and was christened Charles Johnson. John Peter used to absent himself from the family home and visit Mrs Johnson and Charles several times a week. Charles Johnson grew up, and became acquainted with Thomas Smethurst whom he brought home to meet his mother, while 'Mr Johnson' was still around. At some point, it was said, Mary nursed Smethurst through an illness, and despite the fact that she was nearly twice his age and Mr Johnson may still have been on the scene, they decided to get married. Perhaps by 1828 (the year Mary married Thomas Smethurst) John Peter Laporte had decided that at the age of 67, he was getting a little old for leading a double life. Naturally, Mary had to explain to her son how it was she could marry Thomas Smethurst when she was already 'married' to Mr Johnson. But when Charles learned that his father's real name was John Peter Laporte, a well-known artist, he was delighted. He was introduced into his father's family, changed his own name to Laporte, and became an artist himself.

Thus Thomas Smethurst had married a much older woman, who had not only been carrying on with a married man for years and had had an illegitimate son by him, but was living under a false name. Mary must have been very grateful to have found a breadwinner at the precarious age of 44, and this goes a long way to explain her selfless loyalty to her husband. Her loyalty was undiminished even after Isabella Bankes had 'lured him away' from her in the same way that she may have lured John Peter Laporte away from his wife.

Back to the trial, and Charles Laporte junior, aged 32, deposed that the last time he had seen Mrs Mary Smethurst was at Rifle Terrace, about a fortnight after Smethurst had been taken into custody. Joseph Smith, who kept the boarding house at Rifle Terrace, was called. After some confusion in the questions and answers it was established that Isabella Bankes associated with the Smethursts, and addressed Mary as 'Mrs Smethurst'. Everyone in the house also knew her as Mrs Smethurst. Louisa Bankes used to visit when Mrs Smethurst was in the drawing room. She conversed with Smethurst but not Mrs Smethurst. Joseph Smith did say of Smethurst:

> ...his conduct was quite that of a gentleman; it was...
> of an amiable, well-behaved, kind person...he was very
> attentive towards his wife.

After the parish clerk at Battersea proved the marriage between Isabella Bankes and Smethurst, Louisa Bankes was called, and when asked to identify the signature, understandably upset, she said 'with great emotion':

> I see the name of Isabella Bankes to the entry in
> the book before me...that is the handwriting of my
> murdered sister...

Charles Laporte was recalled. He confirmed that he had introduced Smethurst to his mother; subsequently he visited his mother at the house while his father was still there. 'Mr and Mrs Johnson' had a proper establishment, but none of Mr Johnson's relations ever visited. Occasionally, he said, his father and mother would go into society, 'into parties of pleasure'; they used to go to Richmond or Greenwich, 'with strangers that they would pick up...'

In his closing speech for the defence, Mr Sleigh adopted a high-risk strategy. There was no case to answer, he said. He claimed that there was 'reason to believe' that Mary Durham was already a married woman when she met the prisoner, in which case her marriage to the prisoner was not legal. Mr Salter added that if it was suggested by the prosecution that 'Mr Laporte or Johnson' was a married man, evidence should have been presented to prove it. In the absence of such evidence they could only conclude that when Mary Durham married the prisoner, she was already married. The judge left court to consult with a colleague on this point. On his return, he said that 'there was hardly any evidence to go to the jury in support of that defence...'

Mr Sleigh then addressed the jury. He said the circumstances under which the trial had come about were matters of history. On the question of bigamy, it was usually one of the wives who instigated the prosecution, more often the second wife, as she was a victim of delusion, seduction and fraud. In this case it was clear that the first wife took no part in the prosecution, and neither did the friends of the 'unhappy lady who is no more'. The prosecution was under the direction of the Secretary of State. Under these circumstances, he said, the defendant was entitled to sympathy and commiseration, and he thought that the jury, 'would not press the evidence too harshly against him...' and give him the benefit of the doubt. He reminded the jury of the agony and suffering the prisoner had endured, but he should now be treated on the basis that he was perfectly innocent of murder as the Home Secretary had confirmed by the free pardon.

The judge, clearly unhappy with the line that the defence counsel was taking, remarked that 'a pardon is no more a certificate of innocence than a verdict of not guilty'. This comment received applause in court which angered the judge, who directed that anyone seen to 'misconduct himself' should be taken into custody.

Mr Sleigh soldiered on. He said that the charge was not proven, and that Dr Smethurst was entitled to an acquittal. No person could be convicted of bigamy unless it was established 'in the clearest possible manner' that the first marriage was legal. It had been proved that Mary Durham had been living with a 'Mr Johnson', and passed as Mrs Johnson before she married the prisoner. Their son had no idea that they were anything else until years later. The prosecution, he said, had attempted to show that Johnson was already a married man, but there was as much evidence that Mr and Mrs Johnson, or Mary Durham, were man and wife as that Mr and Mrs Laporte 'stood in that relation to each other'. If there was any doubt on the point, the prisoner was entitled to the benefit of it.

The judge summed up. He said that this was a clear *prima facie* case of bigamy, and outlined Mr Sleigh's defence to the charge. If the jury believed the defence case, then the woman now called Mrs Smethurst was guilty of bigamy and the prisoner was innocent of the offence when he married Isabella Bankes. The judge called the jury's attention to the circumstances of the two establishments, Mr Laporte and his wife and family, and Mr Laporte/Johnson and Mary Durham/Johnson. Mr Laporte

> had a family by a lady who passed by the same name, and who was recognized as his wife, and visited as such by friends and relatives of both.

Mrs Johnson, on the other hand,

> was visited by no relatives, and Laporte appeared to have eventually given her up to the prisoner...

And:

> The prisoner appeared to have been married to the woman in the name of Mary Durham.

Would these facts, he asked the jury, justify concluding that Mrs Johnson was a married woman when she married the prisoner?

One of the jury asked whether there was any evidence that the maiden name of Mrs Smethurst was Mary Durham. The judge replied that there was no legal evidence, although it might be 'fairly taken that it was so'. The jury 'deliberated on their verdict and almost immediately found the prisoner guilty'. Upon being asked for comments, Mr Sleigh reminded the judge that 'no fraud or deception' had been practised on Isabella Bankes.

Once more the judge left court to consult with one of his colleagues. On his return he addressed the prisoner (called 'Dr' Smethurst in the press reports). He had been found guilty of the crime of bigamy. Reference had been made to the circumstances of the death of his second wife, but the fact that he had been absolved from that crime could not diminish the punishment received for another:

> If the original charge had been unfounded, [you cannot] be compensated by having the just punishment for another offence remitted...

It was his duty, he said, neither to augment nor to diminish the sentence. The crime of bigamy varied much in its circumstances. It was comparatively minor when committed by

> two abandoned persons who were perfectly aware of what they were doing.

On the other hand it was far more serious, where a man deserted a

> virtuous and respectable wife and married another woman in order to gain possession of her property or her person.

In the present case, the prisoner had deserted his first wife, although in her view, she probably wished him to receive no further punishment. But the object of punishment was, he said, to 'prevent a repetition of the crime'. The second wife undoubtedly knew that the prisoner was married, and went through the ceremony voluntarily. As far as she was concerned, he said, the case did not call for severe punishment. However, the prisoner had made a false oath in effecting the second marriage (that had been by licence, so Smethurst would have sworn that there was no impediment etc.) Taking into account, the judge said, that the prisoner deserted his first wife, had sworn a false oath, and then

> endeavoured to impute to [your] first wife the crime of
> bigamy without any probable justification...

The judge concluded that the case required a

> more severe punishment than was usually passed in
> similar circumstances.

He had consulted Judge Byles and other officers of the court on the sentence he was about to pass, and they agreed that it was proper. He sentenced Smethurst to one year in prison with hard labour.

Smethurst, who had not said a word apart from his plea during the proceeding, was led away and taken to the New Surrey House of Correction on Wandsworth Common, to serve his sentence.

Probate

Thomas Smethurst had been sentenced to one year in prison with hard labour, a severe sentence for consensual bigamy. It had been suggested that Isabella Bankes agreed to marry him because he told her that he and Mary were not really married. Mary's unconventional life before she married Thomas could have provided sufficient material for a credible story. He might even have introduced Isabella to Charles Laporte... In fact the evidence told against that. The solicitor who drew up Isabella's will stated that she was of sound mind and un-coerced when she signed herself 'Isabella *Bankes*, *Spinster*', and left her property to her 'dear *friend*, Thomas Smethurst'. If she had been convinced that the marriage was genuine, she would surely have signed herself 'Isabella Smethurst', and left her money to her 'dear husband...'

It seemed then, that Judge Bramwell might have been settling scores between Smethurst and the legal establishment. His brother judge, Sir Frederick Pollock, had come in for much criticism of his conduct during Smethurst's trial for murder. And even after all of the revelations in the press regarding the medical and scientific testimony, he remained largely unrepentant. It was the Home Secretary, a member of the Executive, who had overruled the Judiciary, and awarded Smethurst a free pardon. There may have been some quiet score-settling in Judge Bramwell's sentence. It certainly ran counter to the wishes of the Home Secretary who had stated that he did not want the perjury action to appear to be persecuting Smethurst.

A few days later, the *Law Times* had a short news report on the trial and criticized the harshness of the sentence. It summarized the case, commenting that the defence team might have been wiser, without proof, not to have adopted the position they took. Nevertheless, 'Dr Smethurst has had a very fair trial'. Not so the sentence. The sentence for the offence, since it was clear that Isabella Bankes was a willing participant, should have been a week or a month:

> Nor can we admit the justice of the motive assigned for inflicting a severer punishment than the offence of which he was convicted deserved.

He had not been tried for the other offence – that of swearing a false declaration when he applied for the marriage licence. It was like

> the old Quarter Sessions practice of convicting a man for a petty theft, and punishing him for being a poacher.

The report went on to say that it wanted to

> see the law administered strictly with reference to the particular case before it, suffering itself to be swayed by no extraneous considerations.

The *Morning Post*, which had adopted a neutral position on the question of the murder trial, also thought the sentence far too harsh considering the circumstances. It went further, and suggested that the government, after having granted the free pardon, might have left the indictment for bigamy 'to be performed by any hands but its own'. It concluded by calling for a Court of Criminal Appeal to be set up. After 'such a case as that of Dr Smethurst', a change in the law was a matter of necessity.

An editorial in *The Times* pointed out that the charges for murder and bigamy were quite different and separate.

Smethurst was an 'innocent victim of circumstance' in the capital charge, but the charge for bigamy stood on its own merits. The editorial summarized the extraordinary arrangements of Mary Durham's establishment before she married Thomas Smethurst, but concluded that the verdict and sentence fairly satisfied 'the requirements of justice'. A few days later, the newspaper had a piece to the effect that since Smethurst had been convicted of a felony, all his 'goods, chattels and land' reverted to the Crown. This meant that he would not get a 'single farthing' of Isabella Bankes' money.[1] The newspaper was obviously unaware that Smethurst had already made over his property to his brother James before his conviction for murder, precisely to forestall such an eventuality; just before the trial for bigamy, he had similarly made over any benefits from Isabella's will to his brother. Whether he would be able, successfully, to claim probate to Isabella's will remained to be seen.

The New Surrey House of Correction on Wandsworth Common, where Smethurst was to spend the next year, could have been far worse. It had opened in 1851, and operated the Separate System of prison discipline. This consisted of housing each prisoner in a separate cell to prevent any contact between them. The intention was to stop the old lags and time-servers from corrupting the first-time offenders. The prison chaplain was supposed to effect the prisoners' reform and rehabilitation; apart from the guards, he was the only person they had any contact with. The cells were fitted with flushing lavatories and gas lighting, a luxury most homes of the period were without. Some cells had their own labour machines; a box with a crank that had to be turned 12,000 times a day. The box contained nothing that did any useful work, just a system of wheels, belts and weights, to enable the effort needed to turn the crank to be adjusted. This was done to the instruction

---

1   A farthing was one quarter of an old penny.

of the prison surgeon according to whether the prisoner was able-bodied or not. Apart from the labour machines, there was oakum-picking, pumping water and grinding grain to be done.

Smethurst may or may not have been aware of it, but the New Surrey House of Correction was going through a crisis just at the time he was admitted. The former chaplain, the reverend Henry John Hatch, was awaiting trial at the Old Bailey for the indecent assault of two young girls under his care. In fact he was tried the day after Smethurst's trial for bigamy. Reverend Hatch was convicted and sent to prison for four years, a sentence that was to be served at Newgate.[2] In any event, Smethurst spent the next year at Wandsworth under conditions that some thought were bordering on the luxurious.

So much for Thomas Smethurst for the moment, but what about his long-suffering and elderly wife Mary? She had been without any visible means of support for eight months now. Even after Smethurst had run off with Isabella Bankes, he continued to pay for Mary's board and lodging at Rifle Terrace. But since early May 1859 he had been in custody, and Mary had no income. She may have had some modest savings, but they would have been unlikely to have lasted her more than a few months. However, since Smethurst had made his money and property over to his brother to prevent it being sequestered by the Crown, he probably instructed James to look after his wife and pay her board and lodging. In addition to that, there was little doubt – at least until the bigamy trial when her past was raked over in indecent detail – that Mary Smethurst was regarded by the public as having been the innocent pawn in the Smethurst affair. She was the 'virtuous deserted wife'. Since her address at Rifle Terrace had been widely reported in the newspapers, it would not be surprising if she had received financial gifts large and small from a sympathetic public.

---

2   Rev Hatch was released under the Royal Pardon after six months when his main accuser, a twelve-year-old girl, was convicted of perjury. An account of his story is contained in my book *Henry's Trials*.

Thomas Smethurst was imprisoned in Wandsworth with hard labour, but if he was cowed, he was certainly not beaten. In April 1860 he again petitioned the Queen from prison, this time it was for an early release from his sentence. He claimed that the sentence of the judge had been far too harsh; in any case he had already served a year in prison, having been in gaol continuously since early May of 1859 when he was arrested for murder. He pointed out that had not the first 'foul and unjust charge' been preferred against him, the second one, for bigamy, would never have been heard of (a highly dubious argument, surely not sanctioned by any legal advice). The defence offered in the bigamy trial, suggesting that his wife Mary had actually committed bigamy on him, was cooked up by his brother and solicitor without his knowledge. He said that his health was now ruined; he had a dislocated right knee (his childhood injury), chronic disease of the left kidney, chronic asthma, rheumatism 'involving the heart' and an 'apoplectic seizure' two years previously which nearly cost him the use of his right hand, was now starting to trouble him again. The prison surgeon had taken him off hard labour, and he was permanently on the sick list. It was a long and rambling document poorly presented. Unsurprisingly, no action resulted from it.

But the following month, May 1860, Sir George Cornewall Lewis received a letter from Messrs Symes, Teesdale and Sandilands, the solicitors originally engaged by the Crown to prosecute Thomas Smethurst, and now representing the Bankes family. Their communication was to the effect that Smethurst's solicitors had subpoenaed them to bring Isabella Bankes' will to the Probate Court. On behalf of the Bankes family they had previously lodged a caveat against the will on the grounds of undue influence (by Smethurst), but now he appeared to be calling on them to make good their objections in the Court of Probate. The solicitors thought that Smethurst ought not to be able to acquire a 'beneficial interest' under the will, due to the law on felons' property being forfeit to the Crown. His solicitors had told them that he had, indeed, assigned his property to his brother James Smethurst, but they thought that that should not interfere with the rights of the Crown. The Bankes family would not contest the will, provided that the property would pass to the Crown and not the 'Criminal'.

Three weeks later a letter from Henry Reynolds, a solicitor to the Secretary of the Treasury, set out the position in law. If Smethurst had assigned his property to his brother James, then that would probably include any benefit under Isabella Bankes' will. And even if the Bankes family assigned the proceeds of the will to the Crown, Mr Reynolds

> ...[could not] advise, whether the property of Miss Bankes would pass to the Crown under the will.

In other words, although the law stated that the 'goods and chattels' of any felon became Crown property on the felon's conviction, a proper assignment of those goods, including apparently wills not yet subject to probate, meant that any benefit accruing would pass to the assignee, in this case James Smethurst, Thomas Smethurst's brother.

Thomas Smethurst was released from Wandsworth Prison in November 1860 having served the full twelve months of his sentence. The *Morning Post* reported:

> ...[he] is considerably reduced in bulk, but his bodily health does not appear to be impaired...

And on his release, Smethurst went back to live with his wife Mary. Mary was now 75 years old and her reputation must have been damaged by the revelations of her past in the bigamy trial. As previously noted, she was almost certainly being supported by James Smethurst using the money that

Thomas Smethurst had previously assigned to him. Thomas Smethurst, of course, also had no financial resources so it may be that he initially went to live with Mary as his only option. Perhaps though, since they had, after all, been married to each other for 32 years, they were able to provide mutual support and comfort. But Mary can hardly have been pleased with what happened next. Days after Smethurst's release from prison, *The Times* reported:

> Court of Probate and Divorce...Smethurst v Tomlin and Others... Dr Thomas Smethurst, propounded the will of the late Isabella Bankes...

Isabella Bankes' will had left everything except a brooch to her 'friend' Thomas Smethurst. After her death, and with Smethurst in prison, Isabella's family had claimed undue influence in the execution of the will. Now that he had paid his debt to society, Smethurst was determined to obtain what had been left to him, and he launched an action to prove his right to probate.

The case was heard in the new court of Probate and Divorce, before the unimaginatively named Sir Cresswell Cresswell. Thomas Smethurst was the plaintiff; the defendants were Isabella's sister Elizabeth Tomlin, Elizabeth's husband, Friend Tomlin, and Louisa Bankes. The proceedings dragged on for two years. There were at least three preliminary hearings before the case was heard in court before a jury.

The initial hearing in December 1860 related to the fact that Isabella's friend, Miss Jenkins, to whom she had left the brooch had waived her claim, presumably not wanting to be sucked into a costly litigation. In May 1861, the question whether a felon could act as executor and claim probate was argued. This was 'demurred' to by Smethurst's counsel.[3] The judge said the question required 'great consideration', and judgement was deferred until July. In that month judgement was given to the effect that a convicted felon *could* act as executor and claim probate. Finally, on Friday 25th April 1862, the case was heard in full before Sir Cresswell Cresswell and a special jury. Smethurst fielded a formidable legal team consisting of Dr Phillimore, QC, Dr Swabey, Mr Downing Bruce and Mr B Webster. Serjeant Ballantine and Mr Merewether appeared for the defendants.

Smethurst, as plaintiff, propounded the will of Isabella Bankes, he being named as executor. Probate was contested by members of Isabella's family on the basis of undue (inappropriate) execution, want of capacity (legal competence) and undue influence. The hearing did not get off to a good start. A key witness for the plaintiff, Mr Senior – the solicitor who had drawn up the will – was found not to be in court. A hastily drawn up affidavit requesting a postponement, was said by the judge to be the 'least satisfactory he had ever seen'. However, a 'sharp discussion' between Dr Phillimore and Serjeant Ballantine was quickly terminated when Mr Senior was seen to have arrived.

Dr Phillimore opened his case, and addressing the jury he said:

> It would be an affectation of idle pedantry, to assume that you are wholly ignorant of the previous history of the plaintiff [Smethurst]...

But he said that he had no doubt that they would give an impartial verdict 'in conformity with [their] oaths'. He went on to detail the history of the case. On the question of the

---

3 A 'demurrer' was a 'pleading which, admitting for the moment the facts as stated in the opponent's pleading, denies that he is legally entitled to relief [costs]...' OED.

bigamous marriage, Dr Phillimore said that it was not for him to defend the morality of the transaction, but he submitted that

> ...the great affection, however unlawful, which existed between the parties, [affords] a strong prima-facie presumption that the will before the court was likely to contain the expression of [Isabella's] real wishes...

He went on:

> If it is her will, it is entitled to probate...it is competent to all persons in this country to dispose of their property as they please, however immoral, however whimsical, however foolish that disposition might appear to be.

The will was then read out in court. The key elements being that Smethurst was the sole executor, everything except a small brooch was left to him, Isabella called him her 'sincere and beloved friend', she signed herself 'Isabella Bankes', and she described herself as a 'spinster'. If Isabella had died intestate, her estate, amounting to around £1,800, would have been shared between her three sisters, Louisa Bankes, Elizabeth Tomlin and Jane Haffenden and their brother, George Vernon Bankes.

The first witness, Mr Frederick Senior, was called and examined by Dr Swabey and then cross-examined by Serjeant Ballantine. He had been a prosecution witness in the murder trial. Smethurst had called on him on Sunday, 1st May 1859, and asked him to come to Alma Villas at ten o'clock to make Isabella's will. He wanted him there at that time to avoid the doctors who usually came at half-past ten. Smethurst had told him that the doctors did not need to be there when the will was drawn up, because Isabella was 'perfectly right in her mind'. Mr Senior said that he deliberately delayed his arrival so that the doctors should be present, but in fact they did not arrive while he was there. He described what had happened. He was shown into Isabella's bedroom:

Smethurst:

My dear, this is the gentleman who has come to make your will.

Isabella bowed and handed Mr Senior a piece of paper.

Mr Senior:

Is this what you wish? Perhaps you will allow me to read it to you?

Isabella nodded assent, and Mr Senior read the will through to her.

Mr Senior:

Is that correct?

Isabella:

Yes, except I wish to leave a brooch to a friend, but I don't know how to describe it...

Smethurst:

Well but, my dear, it contains the hair of your late father, does it not?

Isabella:

Yes, and it is set in brilliants and pearls.

Mr Senior:

Oh, that'll do. I'll describe it for you.

Mr Senior then wrote out the will, and went back to Isabella's bedroom with Smethurst. He read the will through to her and she said it was all right. Then they called up Susannah Wheatley, the landlady's daughter, to witness the signature. Mr Senior now changed the evidence he gave. In the murder trial he had said that Smethurst had wanted to tell Susannah Wheatley that it was a 'Chancery paper' that she was to witness. Mr Senior had then told Smethurst that she must be told that it was a will. Now, he said that he told Susannah, 'That lady wishes you and me to see her sign a paper'. At which point Smethurst had said: 'You have not told her that it is a will'. Mr Senior said that he then said to Isabella:

> This is your will, is it not, and you wish Miss Wheatley
> and myself to witness your signature to it?

Isabella said 'yes', whereupon she signed the will in their presence, and they both signed as witnesses.

He said that Isabella was deadly pale, prostrate, and very feeble, but she understood perfectly what he said to her. Her manner was 'perfectly placid and calm', but he thought that she was dying. He asked Smethurst who were her doctors. Smethurst told him Dr Julius and Mr Bird adding, 'She's in first-rate hands don't you think?' On the question of Isabella's signature, 'Isabella Bankes', he said that Smethurst offered no explanation of that, other than that they were living as man and wife but were not married. He said that Smethurst told him that a barrister friend of his in London had made the original draft of the will.

Frederick Senior's evidence was the most important testimony of the trial. It established that the will was properly drawn up and executed, and as far as Mr Senior could tell, Isabella was lucid and able to make decisions. That was clear from the fact that she wanted the draft changed to include the bequest of the brooch. It was odd though, and a point not apparently picked up by Serjeant Ballantine, that Mr Senior's evidence in this hearing, where he was a witness for Smethurst, was significantly different from that given during the murder trial where he was a witness for the prosecution. Then, he had made a point of saying that Smethurst had wanted to misrepresent the will as a 'Chancery paper' to the landlady's daughter who was to witness it. The fact was mentioned by the judge during the summing-up, contributing to the mass of circumstantial evidence against Smethurst. Now, Mr Senior claimed that it was Smethurst himself who called his attention to the fact that Miss Wheatley should be told that it was a will. Susannah Wheatley was now called, and confirmed that she had properly witnessed the signing of the will.

Thomas Smethurst himself was next in the witness box. This was the first time in all of his court appearances that he had been able to give formal evidence, and if he was determined to tell the truth, he did not start well:

> I am the plaintiff in this cause. My age is about 50 years...

At Smethurst's first trial in the summer of 1859, his age was given as 48. There was a suspicion that he was older, and the newspapers uncovered the fact that in 1828, he had been in custody at Horsemonger Lane Gaol for around a week. The charge was obtaining goods by false pretences, and his age at the time was given as 24. He was subsequently discharged following a magistrates' hearing. If he was 24 years old in 1828, his year of birth would have been around 1804, and his application to the Society of Apothecaries confirms his date of birth to have been 2nd January 1805. It seems rather odd then that at 57 years old, he should give his age as 'about 50'. The only conclusion to be drawn is that he was insufferably vain. He went on to say that he married (Mary Durham) in 1828 (when he would have been 16), and since he said later in his evidence that his wife Mary was now (in 1862) 77, she would have been 43 years old when they married. Was he really asking the court to believe that a 16 year-old boy would marry a 43 year-old woman, someone almost old enough to be his grandmother? Smethurst went on to detail his time with Isabella Bankes:

I have been very intimate with her, but not improperly so till after the marriage...

A somewhat unfortunate way of putting it. Smethurst related the conversation he had had with Isabella on the subject of the will. 'Doctor,' she said, 'I wish you to do me a favour.' Apparently, she was concerned that she had the same disease that killed her 'dear papa' and wanted Smethurst to arrange to make her will. 'You're the only true friend I have on earth,' she said, 'and I wish to leave you all I have.' He claimed that he told her it was not necessary; he had sufficient money for his needs, and in any case her sisters would contest the will... He said that he declined to have anything to do with it, apparently relenting on the Saturday before her death when Isabella said:

Call on the solicitor, and have the will executed today, before she [Louisa Bankes] arrives.

He was cross-examined about his relationship to James Mellor Smethurst. They were not related; Smethurst had treated James Mellor Smethurst with the water cure at Moor Park. They had been on 'very intimate terms', and called each other cousin and 'coz'. A few days after the probate trial, James Mellor Smethurst wrote to *The Times* to correct a minor inaccuracy in its reporting of his evidence (see below) relating to the will. He said that when Smethurst had treated him at Moor Park he was 'seriously unwell', and remained there for some weeks:

From his kind and skilful treatment I derived much benefit, and to it I believed I owed my recovery...Though in no way related to Dr Smethurst, I entertained a

> strong feeling of gratitude towards him for the more
> than ordinary care with which he attended me...

Thomas Smethurst continued with his evidence. Isabella had given him around £71, being the first dividend due to her under her uncle James Rhodes Bankes' will. The 'Smethursts' had used a false address:

> ...because we did not wish either of our families to
> know where we were.

One of Smethurst's friends, Mr Treherne, who was bailiff to 'Lord Delawarr', near Tunbridge Wells, agreed to receive and forward letters and a cheque for the dividend had been forwarded on 12th or 15th April.[4]

Smethurst went on to deny that he had ever represented to Isabella or anyone else that his marriage to Mary Durham was illegal. He claimed that the defence (at his trial for bigamy) had been concocted by his counsel and attorneys and managed by his brother James who knew Mary Durham's circumstances. He said that during the trial he had written a note to Mr Sleigh, his defence counsel, asking him, 'not to expose [his] wife's antecedents'. The judge pressed him on the point:

> Did you know her former position?

Smethurst:

> I did. I never believed that she had been married.

The Judge:

> But why did you not tell Mr Sleigh that the story
> was false, and ask him to state publicly that it was a
> mistake?

---

4   'Lord Delawarr' was George John Sackville-West, fifth Earl De La Warr, who
lived at Knole Park, ten miles or so from Tunbridge Wells; he cannot have
been very pleased to see his name in the newspapers associated with the
Smethurst case.

Smethurst:

I was in his hands...I did not wish to expose her.

The Judge:

There was nothing to expose if it were untrue.

Smethurst:

My wife had been living with another gentleman when I married her. The defence [was] that she was herself guilty of bigamy. There was no other defence made for me. [They]...tried that on, of course (a laugh)...I was very sorry for it.

He went on to say that his wife Mary was a perfect wreck when he was released from prison, and 'out of kindness and good feeling for her' he went back to live with her 'and protect her'.

The relationship with Isabella had 'commenced mutually', although when prompted by the judge, Smethurst maintained that it was Isabella who had asked him to marry her:

She paid me attentions and followed me up...I can't say that I objected.

The Judge:

Do you mean to say she asked you to marry her?

Smethurst:

Yes, I am certain of that, my Lord.

Isabella had told him that she had two friends who were secretly married, one was a cousin named Tomlin, presumably a relation of Friend Tomlin. She had asked Smethurst in Kensington Gardens if he would not like such a marriage with her. He had also heard her say to a lady boarder, Mrs Firth, at

Rifle Terrace, that she should like to have a private marriage with 'the doctor'.[5] At Isabella's bidding, Smethurst had visited Doctors' Commons to read the will of her uncle, James Rhodes Bankes, in order to confirm her financial expectations. Then after Isabella had been given notice by the landlady to leave, she and Smethurst had a meeting. Isabella said that she was very wretched, and asked him again if he would object to a secret marriage, adding:

> It can't injure you, doctor, because only your wife or I could appear against you. I am sure your wife would not, and I could not, because I know already that you are a married man.

Smethurst said that he made no answer to this, but they met again a few days later when she said:

> I am very wretched, doctor; let us go away into the country, from all our friends.

(It is further evidence of his vanity, that Smethurst continually reported Isabella as referring to him as 'Doctor'.) He then said that if they did that, then first they should go through the ceremony of marriage as she had suggested. He commented:

> I did not think I should ever be punished for such a bigamy as that, as it was perfectly mutual. My wife [Mary] knew nothing about it...

His next comment drew laughter from the court:

> I intended to leave her [Mary], but I meant to protect her so far as allowing her money and watching over her comforts went.

---

5   Subsequently, Smethurst also claimed that Isabella had said to Mrs Firth that she knew he was already married. Mrs Firth was in court ready to give evidence, but was not called.

He told his wife when he left the boarding house that he was going on a 'tour' and seeing friends. He said that he had written to her every week until Isabella fell ill. The letter he had written to his wife, found on him, not posted, when he was first arrested (the day before Isabella died), was read and entered as evidence. There was also a letter written the same day to his brother James:

> D[ea]r James, dear B lies now in a most dangerous state. I fear there is not a single hope. Her sister is staying with us. Two or three days I much fear will place the dear soul beyond all human aid...God grant that she may recover! Seal your letters and call Miss Bankes B only...

He described Isabella's illness, claiming that she was suffering from bilious diarrhoea from 16th April until her death. He kept a diary, showing the notes to Mr Bird, '...her regular attendant...' He did not show the notes to Dr Julius. He claimed that Louisa was alone with her sister for half an hour on at least three separate occasions, and Mrs Wheatley, the landlady did sometimes bring medicines into Isabella's room. He never took them from her at the door, as she had claimed in other evidence. The letters between Smethurst and Louisa regarding her visits, including the ones forbidding her visits for the time being, were read out in court. He described a conversation when Louisa first visited Isabella and Smethurst on 19th April. Isabella had said to Louisa:

> If you will be quiet, it will be all right by-and-by, won't it dear? [the last addressed to Smethurst]

He replied that it would, understanding her to refer to what would happen in the event of Mary's death, although he claimed that he had not discussed that circumstance with her. He then proceeded to explain matters between himself and

Isabella Bankes. From her perspective, the bigamous marriage was one of conscience that removed the stain of being Smethurst's mistress; it was something that she could 'pass off to her friends as a lawful union'. They had already agreed that if Mary Smethurst died, they should be privately married again. Initially, Smethurst said, they had agreed to be lovers until Mary died, but after Isabella had received her notice to quit Rifle Terrace, 'she preferred to be married to me'. He went on to describe various conversations he had with Isabella on the subject; things he might, with advantage, have left unsaid. Isabella had 'often' conversed with him about the probabilities of Mary dying. She said that Mrs Smethurst was very aged, and she asked Smethurst whether he thought she would live for a long time. He had watched his wife's health 'as carefully as Miss Bankes...'; he knew the state of her health but claimed that he expressed no opinion about it. She was over 70, he did not wish her to die – and did not wish so now, but he did 'wish to perform [his] engagement to Miss Bankes'. Here, the judge helpfully interjected:

> The gentleman wished to leave the case to the course
> of nature...

Smethurst went on, describing his dismay when he went to Doctors' Commons to get a marriage licence and was required to swear an affidavit:

> I am very sorry for it...I was quite taken aback...I
> nevertheless swore the affidavit.

He conceded that he had received the dividends from Isabella's legacy, but he then paid for everything. He did not know whether Louisa Bankes was aware of his marriage to her sister.

Smethurst now described his visit to Doctors' Commons to view the will of Isabella's uncle, James Rhodes Bankes, the main source of her income:

> I cannot tell why she wished me to go...and satisfy myself that she had money. She had previously concealed the fact in order, as she said, to test my affection...

And that completed Smethurst's testimony. The court action over probate was going to be expensive. There were solicitors' costs, four barristers and at least four separate hearings. It was also by no means certain that the case was winnable. If he lost, Smethurst would be liable for his costs as well as those of the defence, so what he said in court on his behalf would be critical in persuading the jury in his favour. But his testimony can hardly have done him any favours. He came across as vain, calculating and cynical – to a quite astonishing degree in respect of the discussion of his wife Mary's age, and the prospect of her death enabling him and Isabella to be together. He also freely admitted his perjury in swearing the affidavit for the marriage licence, as well as his bigamy with Isabella, while saying that he never thought that he would be punished for it. If he was given advice by his counsel regarding what to say and what to leave unsaid, he must have disregarded it. Anyone in court, or reading the press reports, would have been confirmed in the view that most of the newspapers took at the time of the murder trial: Thomas Smethurst may have been innocent of the crime of murder, but he was an amoral scoundrel.

Next to be examined was James Mellor Smethurst, the lawyer who had advised Thomas Smethurst on Isabella Bankes' will. He had collected rents for Isabella Bankes for a short while – whether he was introduced to her by Thomas Smethurst was not stated. He had not kept the correspondence he had had with Smethurst over the will. He had not redrafted the will, but merely added an attestation clause and a note to the effect that the will should go through the hands of a solicitor. It was the fact that he had destroyed the correspondence with Thomas Smethurst that engendered some comment in the newspapers, smelling a conspiracy. The evidence from James Mellor Smethurst closed the case for the plaintiff.

Serjeant Ballantine opened the case for the defence. He acknowledged the absence of evidence of undue influence, saying that the question of coercion revolved around the characters of Isabella and Smethurst, and 'the position in which they stood one towards the other...' According to *The Times*, he then 'thundered against his [Smethurst's] character...' Smethurst was, he said, a perjurer and bigamist,

> ...who had not been ashamed to make...an attempt to get possession of Miss Bankes' property, although in order to do so he was obliged to...expose himself to the scorn and detestation of his fellow men.

Then,

> He had even imputed to that unhappy, weak-minded woman that she had made love to him, and had proposed the marriage; but he had been actuated throughout by the love of lucre...before he gave his consent to the marriage he went to Doctors' Commons in order to satisfy himself that she had money...not a single word of Dr Smethurst's evidence was to be believed.

Here, the judge interjected, detectably with some amusement, 'Not even when he speaks against himself?'

Ballantine:

> I confess, my lord, I should feel some difficulty in doing even that...there are some men so steeped in falsehood that they will tell lies against themselves (laughter)...

He went on to condemn the 'calumnies' Smethurst had heaped on the memory of Miss Bankes. The defence that had been tried at the bigamy trial – that Smethurst's original marriage to Mary Durham was void because she was already married – was very likely the story Smethurst had told Miss Bankes. He added that it was a 'wicked falsehood' that Louisa Bankes had any real opportunity of seeing her sister, 'while there was any probability of his victim escaping from his influence...'

At this point the judge drew Serjeant Ballantine's attention to the fact that there was no plea of fraud in the defence case, whereupon Ballantine requested that the plea be added. Dr Phillimore did not oppose the request, reserving the right to call further witnesses, if necessary, to refute the claim. Serjeant Ballantine continued with his address. He said he would show that

> the whole nervous system of the deceased had been
> so shaken, that she was unfit to transact any matter of
> business at the time the will was made.

He finished by saying that he had never known a case 'of so singular a character', hoping that a court of justice would never again be disgraced by 'such an exposure as Dr Smethurst had made'.

The first witness for the defence, and the last one of the day, was Susannah Angelina Wheatley, landlady of 10 Alma Villas where Isabella had died. Her testimony was largely as before; she made Isabella's bed every day, but Smethurst received food and medicines at the door, and removed the slops himself. She never spoke to Isabella except in Smethurst's presence, although she did say under cross-examination that Isabella and Smethurst lived 'on the happiest terms' while they were there. Smethurst was affectionate and attentive, and Isabella reciprocated the affection.

The court reconvened the next day, Saturday 26th April. Louisa Bankes was called. She had been with Isabella when she died. Louisa Bankes must have been thoroughly sick of the whole business not to mention deeply upset. This was to be the sixth occasion on which she was called to give evidence against Smethurst.

Louisa was four years younger than Isabella; they had lived together for a number of years in Notting Hill after their father had died. It was clear from her distress during the bigamy trial, when she talked about her 'murdered sister', that she was convinced that Smethurst *was* a murderer. She spoke about her background. There were five sisters and a brother; her sister Ann was dead, sister Jane had married Alfred Haffenden and sister Elizabeth was married to Friend Tomlin. Elizabeth had also lived with Isabella and Louisa until she got married. Isabella had decided to leave also, although Louisa insisted that they did not quarrel. Isabella went to stay with an aunt, and then moved in for several months with her married sister, Elizabeth, before she went to Rifle Terrace. Louisa described their financial arrangements; under their uncle's will, £5,000 had been left to each of the three sisters, Isabella, Louisa and Elizabeth. They had no power of disposal over the money, being able to benefit from the interest only for the period of their lives. In the event of the death of any of them, their interest would be shared among the surviving sisters. On Isabella's state of health, she said:

> My sister had always been a very nervous, excitable person; she always had very good health.

Once more, she described visiting her sister at Rifle Terrace. She spoke to her about her 'apparent intimacy' with Smethurst, a married man. She said that Isabella told her that Smethurst was not married. She also visited Isabella at Kildare Terrace (where Isabella moved after the landlady at Rifle Terrace had given her notice to leave). The next time she saw her was at Richmond when she was very ill, 'much changed' since she had seen her last. She then described, as before, the events leading up to her sister's death.

Next on the stand was Friend Jennings Tomlin, Louisa's brother-in-law and co-defendant and married to her sister Elizabeth. Isabella had lived with him for three or four months, leaving in September 1858 because he was 'giving up housekeeping'. He had looked after her business affairs for some time having little regard for her financial judgement:

> I looked on her as a lady of very weak mind...I had the greatest difficulty in making her understand anything relating to her property out on mortgage, or her property under her uncle's will, of which I was an executor...

And on the question of the will,

> ...I should not say that while she was living with me she was capable of making a will without the advice of others. If she was told how much money she had she could say whom she wished to have it; but she could not have dictated a will...

To which the judge caused some laughter in court by commenting, 'that is a very different matter...' Tomlin continued by saying that, in his opinion, Isabella would be liable to be 'very influenced by others' in deciding to whom to leave her property. He finished by saying that he had no personal interest in the suit; any money involved would go to his wife.

Dr Julius was now called. His evidence was largely as before, except that he was now the only medical man in court who had seen Isabella alive. Mr Bird had emigrated to Australia for his health, and Dr Todd was dead.[6] He had succumbed to cirrhosis of the liver, a probable consequence of his drink

---

6   Samuel Dougan Bird, suffering from tuberculosis, settled in Melbourne in Australia for his health, arriving there in 1860.

habit. Dr Julius' evidence was not greatly different from before, except that now he claimed:

> ...[there was] a kind of wildness about her eyes. There was an expression of terror about her...most peculiarly on that occasion [when Dr Todd examined her]...the expression on the deceased's face was much more than one of anxiety...

During the murder trial, it was Dr Todd who particularly remarked on the 'expression of terror' in Isabella's eyes; Dr Julius hadn't mentioned it.

'Professor' Taylor was called, and repeated the evidence that he had found antimony in the body; he had also found arsenic (in the sample of stool) but insisted that there was no mistake about it. And amazingly, when describing the 'mistake in one analysis', the arsenic 'set free from some copper gauze', he persisted in claiming that it was 'a new [fact] in chemistry'. Taylor's evidence closed the case for the defendants.

What happened next was rather curious. Mr Robinson, Smethurst's solicitor, was called by Dr Phillimore 'in reply' to the defence case. He had managed Smethurst's defence during the bigamy trial, and he presented the brief he had prepared for Smethurst's barristers for that trial as evidence. The judge, having read through the brief commented that although it contained 'hints' for cross-examination, there was 'nothing about bigamy in the statement'. The next witness was Mr W Campbell Sleigh. He had been the senior barrister defending Smethurst during the bigamy trial and was now called 'at his own request'. He started by saying that the brief that had been presented as evidence was that of his junior barrister on the case, Mr Talfourd Salter, and he (Mr Sleigh) had certainly received other instructions, including the calling into question of the validity of Smethurst's marriage to Mary Durham. There had been a long consultation meeting at his residence the night before the trial attended by himself, Mr Robinson, Mr Salter, James Smethurst and Henry Brinsley Sheridan, MP for Dudley. He added:

> It was, of course, not attended by Dr Smethurst. I would not have had him there under any circumstances. (A laugh.)

It had been a long meeting, and 'all the antecedents of the two ladies' had been disclosed, at which point Mr Sleigh decided that there was a defence case to be made. But:

> If I had not had those instructions, I should have been ashamed myself to raise such a defence...

And:

> I see it stated in the papers that Dr Smethurst sent a note down to me not to go into his wife's antecedents. I have not the slightest recollection of receiving any such note. If such a note had been sent to me, I should at once have felt it my duty to abandon the defence.

Serjeant Ballantine had no questions, saying: 'I anticipated your statements yesterday'. An attempt was made to applaud Mr Sleigh as he left the witness stand but this was 'instantly suppressed by the officers of the court...'

Mr Sleigh's evidence was quite prejudicial to Smethurst's case, and the fact that some of those present in court tried to applaud him suggests that what he had to say garnered popular support. Procedurally though, the order of the last two witnesses was strange. Two separate and different (i.e. not syndicated) press reports make it clear that Mr Robinson was called by Dr Phillimore to support Smethurst's case, followed by Mr Sleigh 'called at his own request' rather than by Serjeant Ballantine. Why was Mr Robinson not called initially as part of Smethurst's case? And since Mr Sleigh's evidence clearly supported the defence case, why did Serjeant Ballantine not call him immediately after Dr Taylor?

What might have happened is that Mr Sleigh was reacting to Smethurst's evidence given on the first day of the trial; he may have been in court, he may have read the trial report early the following day, or someone might have informed him of what was said. There had been some criticism in the newspapers of his conduct of the defence case during the bigamy trial (in suggesting that Mary Durham committed bigamy on Smethurst). Smethurst's evidence in this new hearing that he had sent down a note asking Mr Sleigh not to reveal his wife Mary's antecedents during that trial, which he must have then ignored, was felt by him to be a charge that could not go unanswered. Mr Robinson's evidence was presented (*before* that of Mr Sleigh) in an attempt to mitigate what he was anticipated to say.

Serjeant Ballantine proceeded to sum up. He ridiculed the 'air of disinterestedness' with which Dr Smethurst had described the making of the will, 'dwelling upon the repeated falsehoods...and the suspicious circumstances' attending the execution of the will:

> Who could doubt that over a woman of a naturally weak mind, and with a nervous system enfeebled by doses of antimony...Dr Smethurst's very glance would exert a power like the fascination which the human eye was said to produce over the brute creation?

He went on:

> If the plaintiff was acting honestly in regard to the will, why did he not, as a prudent man, require her to explain her wishes to her medical man and to her sister?...by terror and fraud he had obtained an undue influence over her, and had kept her carefully secluded

from anyone whom she might have informed of her real intentions...

On the 'unspeakably filthy' details of the sick chamber he declined to comment but:

> ...remembering the probable effect of Smethurst's continued presence upon a weak-minded woman at the point of death, and the abject manner in which she turned towards him and watched his eye whenever any other person was present...[I] contend...that the plea of undue influence [has] been satisfactorily established.

He accused Smethurst of having tricked Isabella into marriage in order to acquire her property. It was true, he said, that Smethurst would have benefited from the interest on the £5,000 during her life and only acquired £1,800 on her death but:

> ...how much longer could Smethurst have hoodwinked his real wife and continued the cohabitation with the testatrix?...it was clear from Miss Louisa Bankes' testimony that the plaintiff had really made the testatrix believe that he was not legally married to his first wife.

He reminded the jury of Mr Sleigh's testimony which contradicted that of Smethurst in respect of his explanation of the defence offered at the bigamy trial. If he would try 'such a trick' to avoid gaol, would he also not 'try it on' to acquire Miss Bankes' property? He had made Miss Bankes believe that he was her husband, and the will had been obtained by fraud – admitting that she had executed it willingly. He finished:

> ...if such a scheme as this succeeded, a court of justice would be made an instrument of injustice...crime would flourish, and virtue would look down.

The press report stated that: 'The learned serjeant resumed his seat amidst some cheering'.

Dr Phillimore stood to make his reply. It was a matter of 'public notoriety', he said, that Dr Smethurst had been tried for murder and sentenced to death. It was no less well known that the sentence had been reversed by the crown after

> such an exhibition of the fallacy of medical evidence as had never before been seen in the course of a judicial investigation.

Then,

> There was nothing...incredible that the testatrix had preferred to make Dr Smethurst the object of her testamentary bounty rather than any one of her relations...

He (Dr Phillimore) protested against the idea that Miss Bankes, 'a lady of forty-two', was a victim of Dr Smethurst's 'seductive arts':

> If ever there had been a case of a lady throwing herself into a man's hands it was surely the present. There was...no reason to believe that the testatrix had done anything in executing the will that she would not gladly have done a fortnight sooner, when her acts would have been unquestioned.

If the crown was correct and Dr Smethurst was innocent of murder, the evidence pointed to the will having been perfectly voluntary. And on Dr Smethurst himself:

One of our poets had truly said – "Entire affection
scorneth nicer hands..."[7]

Dr Phillimore pointed out that 'no greater proof of love' could
be found than for a person to perform 'such menial offices' as
were required in a sick room. He reminded the jury that that
was initially the opinion of Louisa Bankes after she visited
her sister. So, if so 'warm an attachment' existed between
Isabella and Smethurst, 'what so natural' for Isabella to give
her 'paramour' what 'little wealth' she had?

On the question of fraud, the fact that Isabella had
described herself in the will as 'Isabella Bankes, Spinster', and
had signed herself 'Isabella Bankes', disposed 'at once' of the
allegation. The case did present difficulties, he said, but he had
confidence in the jury. 'It would be easy', he said, for the jury
to give a 'popular verdict', punishing Dr Smethurst, but such a
verdict

> would not...increase either the public respect for the
> administration of justice, or the public regard for that
> peculiarly English institution – trial by jury.

He went on:

> It would be easy [for you] to give a verdict that would
> meet with applause without, and perhaps within the
> court...

He said that he felt they would be able to resist that temptation:

> If [you] are satisfied that Isabella Bankes was in a
> condition legally to transfer her property on the

---

7 The quotation was from Book I of Edmund Spenser's The Faerie Queene. In
fact Dr Phillimore had remembered it slightly incorrectly; the actual words
were: 'Entire affection *hateth* nicer hands', an interpretation of which might
be, 'true love transcends (unpleasant) circumstances'.

partner of her guilt, [I] am satisfied that [you will] establish that fact by [your] verdict.

The judge now summed up. Compared with Sir Frederick Pollock's summing-up during the murder trial, his speech was the epitome of balance and rectitude. It was done with 'unusual minuteness', because:

> It would be idle of me to pretend that I am not aware that you [the jury] must have formed a most unfavourable impression of the plaintiff [Smethurst]. He has admitted himself to have been guilty not only of gross immorality, but of the crimes both of perjury and bigamy.[8]

Smethurst was, the judge said:

> ...a man against whom human nature must revolt. All the best feelings of the heart will be roused by the idea of a claim...being made by that man, and there is a danger...lest you should be led away by the emotions which his appearance...will so naturally excite.

Nevertheless, he said, Smethurst had a right, as executor, to claim the property:

> If he could obtain the money, he might say "populus me sibilant, at mihi plaudo!"[9]

From the evidence of Mr Senior, the solicitor, the judge said, there could be no doubt that the will was properly executed. But on the question of undue influence, 'absolute control', the jury must decide for themselves from the evidence. He contrasted the plaintiff's stated reluctance to allow the will to be made, with his

---

8   The judge's words have been changed into the first person.
9   'People may hiss me,' said he, 'but myself I clap...' Horace, *Satires*, I, 1, 66.

pains...to have it executed without the knowledge of either the lady's family or of her physicians.

He pointed to the evidence that Smethurst had acted as a 'kind and tender nurse' to the deceased, but had kept her in 'a most remarkable state of seclusion', a circumstance, he said, that ought to 'excite the vigilance of the court'.

On the question of fraud, he said that if the plaintiff had misled the testatrix into thinking that they were legally married, the will would be invalid. But 'had he done so?' The signature on the will was 'Isabella Bankes', but Louisa Bankes had told the court that her sister had told her that Smethurst was unmarried. He added:

> For the life of me I cannot understand why a woman should enter into a private marriage to satisfy her friends; or how it could satisfy her conscience to add to the immorality of an illicit connection with a married man, the mockery of a solemn religious service for which Dr Smethurst could have been prosecuted, and she...punished likewise as an accomplice.

Finally, he told the jury that 'whether...justice' had been done at the previous trial was of no concern to them. They had to decide simply whether the will had been properly executed, whether Isabella was of 'testamentary capacity', whether it had been obtained by undue influence, and whether it had been obtained by fraud.

The jury were out for fifty minutes. When they returned, they found for Smethurst on all counts. Isabella Bankes' will was valid, and Dr Thomas Smethurst was the sole beneficiary.

Aftermath...

The outcome of the action for probate was extraordinary. It certainly ran contrary to public opinion – the applause in court for Serjeant Ballantine and Mr Sleigh demonstrated the level of feeling against Smethurst. And even though the evidence was strong that the will had been properly executed and Isabella had acted of her own free will, Smethurst's testimony must have sickened the public at large. His casual admissions of perjury and bigamy, and particularly his revelations of the discussions he and Isabella had about the likelihood of Mary Smethurst dying and enabling them to get married, reinforced the contempt in which he was held by most people. During the press campaign following his murder conviction, the majority who thought him innocent of murder, concurred that morally he was beyond the pale.

Still, in modern parlance the result meant that Smethurst could laugh all the way to the bank, or rather Isabella Bankes' bank. In fact the outcome was not quite an overall victory. Isabella's assets were initially said to have been worth between £1,700 and £1,800, and when probate was first granted in November 1862, the value was duly given as being 'under £2,000'. However, Isabella's money was lent on mortgage to Mr Tarte, and the matter was 'in Chancery', and had been there since 1st February 1858. In 1848, the four Bankes sisters, Isabella, Jane, Louisa and Elizabeth, had each lent between £1,740 and £1,760 to William Tarte, initially without security. The total amount lent was £7,000 and the agreed interest was 5%. Mr Tarte had subsequently been compelled to invest the money in three houses, Nos 6, 7 & 8 Hyde Park Gate South, which were made over as security for the loan. Jane Bankes had subsequently married Alfred Haffenden, and he had used her mortgage as collateral against another loan. He now wanted the mortgage repaid, although Jane's three sisters apparently did not. The Chancery suit was between Alfred and Jane Haffenden as plaintiffs, and William Tarte, the other three Bankes sisters and Elizabeth's husband Friend Tomlin as defendants. The case dragged on but was apparently decided by the summer of 1864 in the Haffendens' favour, when the houses were advertised for auction. Mr Tarte's business acumen was seen to be poor; the dwellings were said to have a rental income of £310 a year, but he appeared to be paying the Bankes sisters £350 a year in interest on the loan... It was another two years before the matter was finally closed, and the probate to Isabella Bankes' will was re-sworn in May 1866. After the costs of the case and disposal of the houses had been settled, the value of her assets had fallen to less than £800. This was confirmed by James Smethurst some time later, since Thomas Smethurst had made over any benefits arising from Isabella's will to his brother.

As a footnote to Smethurst's overall legal expenses, he made a further petition to the Queen in June 1867, this time on the question of financial compensation. He summarized his conviction for murder and the subsequent free pardon, mentioning the six months spent in prison on remand between his arrest in May and pardon in November 1859. He said that the consequences of the prosecution were 'fatal to [his] reputation and prospects'; the cost of defending himself 'exceeded the sum of one thousand pounds' and he now found it 'impossible to resume his [medical] practice'. He pointed out that the prosecution was conducted at the 'expense and with all the power of the Crown'. He stated that the verdict in the Court of Probate concerning Isabella's will established his innocence of the murder.[1] The property thus acquired was, he said, 'almost wholly absorbed in litigation' – just a little exaggeration there – and he therefore asked Her Majesty to order

> proper compensation...for the great costs and expenses...and sufferings...during the said six months of his imprisonment upon the said [murder] charge... and...the loss of his professional...reputation...

Naturally, the petition made no reference to the conviction for bigamy. The petition was also poorly drawn up. It stated that judgement in the 'Probate Court' in April 1862 had been given by 'Sir James Wilde'. The presiding judge had actually been Sir Cresswell Cresswell. Sir Cresswell had died in July of 1863, and was succeeded by Sir James Wilde at the end of August of that year. Whoever had drawn up the petition had not checked his facts. Unsurprisingly, the petition was endorsed with the following note:

> It is not very probable that the House of Commons will compensate this gentlemen – most people think that he had a very lucky escape...

There remain two further incidents relating to the Smethurst affair that deserve examination. The first of these occurred two years after the probate hearing when the issues were again fought over, this time in the pages of *The Times*. Since the duellists were Smethurst and *The Times* itself, and editorial control was in the hands of the latter, the outcome was not favourable to Dr Smethurst.

In 1864, Franz Müller, a 23-year-old German tailor, was convicted and subsequently hanged at Newgate for the murder

---

1   The result of the jury verdict in the probate case, in granting probate to Smethurst, effectively proved in a court of law Smethurst's innocence of the charge of murder.

of Thomas Briggs, a banker. The crime was unique, having been the first murder to have taken place on a railway train, in addition to which the murderer fled to America on a sailing ship. The British police set off in pursuit in a steam ship which arrived in New York first. Müller was arrested and deported back to Britain. Following his conviction and sentence a petition requesting mercy, prepared by 'some of his countrymen', was presented to Sir George Grey, the Home Secretary (who had replaced Sir George Cornewall Lewis in 1861). *The Times* was critical of the petition, and three days before Müller was due to be executed, published a long editorial on the subject. The newspaper, having summarized the evidence presented in court against Franz Müller, reproduced the conclusion of the petition for clemency:

> ...Müller was condemned by public opinion before he was brought to England [from the USA] at all, in the same way as, but in a stronger degree than Dr Smethurst was. This gentlemen was convicted of poisoning before the Lord Chief Baron, who expressed himself satisfied with the verdict, and gave him no hope; yet when, on a memorial like this, he was respited, the accusation was found to be false, and no one ever since doubted that he was wrongfully convicted of the crime for which he was adjudged to death...

The Times was having none of it, commenting on 'so unfortunate an illustration...' The editorial continued:

> Dr Smethurst's case is the very last which ought to be quoted as a precedent for the interference of the Home Secretary...while the circumstances under which a pardon was granted were peculiar in the extreme, the reference of the matter to one eminent surgeon, after

a solemn investigation in court, has been reprobated ever since by the whole legal profession.

And:

> ...[it is] the reversal, and not the non-reversal, of sentences [that] involves responsibility...the verdict of a jury who have [seen] the witnesses [and] every disputed particle of evidence sifted before their eyes, and have listened to the counsel and the judge, will be more trustworthy than the report of an informal inquisition...

Furthermore,

> ...allegations which might have been made at the trial, and there submitted to the ordeal of cross-examination, should be received with the greatest suspicion...

Smethurst wrote in protest to *The Times* on Tuesday 15th November – the day after Franz Müller had been hanged. His letter was published two days later. He would have been wise to have restricted his comments to a few lines. In the event, *The Times* allowed him considerable rope...

Smethurst referred to the conclusion of the Müller petition and *The Times*' response in which the process of Smethurst's free pardon was criticized. He detailed an exchange in parliament, reported in *The Times* on January 28th 1860, between Edwin James, QC, and Sir George Cornewall Lewis, the Home Secretary. Edwin James had called Sir George's attention to Smethurst's pardon, the case having 'engaged a large share of public attention', and called for an enquiry. Sir George's reply, which was contained in Smethurst's letter and duly reproduced in *The Times*, occupying itself nearly 40 lines, outlined the sequence of events. He had called for the transcript of the trial, plus evidence from Smethurst's friends and legal advisors. These were then referred to the trial judge,

Sir Frederick Pollock. Pollock suggested that Sir George call in an 'eminent medical practitioner' for a report, and the relevant papers were sent to Sir Benjamin Brodie. The Home Secretary went on:

> After full consideration given, I can assure the House, with the utmost attention of which I was master, and after hearing a variety of opinions from different persons, I came to the conclusion that the proper course for me to adopt was to advise the Crown to grant a free pardon...nothing which has occurred since...has made me entertain any doubt as to its rectitude.

Sir George did add that Pollock had thought that Smethurst should not be hanged, but that he (Pollock) considered that drugs might have been administered to Isabella Bankes in order to procure an abortion. Such a 'hypothesis' had not been presented in court, and he had no idea what the verdict would have been had it been so presented.

In his letter, Smethurst pointed out that the commencement of Isabella's sickness coincided exactly with the onset of her pregnancy. If the former was the result of poison given to her in order to terminate the latter, he must have known she was pregnant the instant it had commenced. He went on:

> I challenge the whole medical profession to say that I, or any one, could know of the pregnancy at this early period...

And having made a very powerful argument in his favour, Smethurst proceeded to destroy any remaining sympathy for his position by what he said next:

> ...is it likely that such deadly mineral poisons would be used for such a purpose by a medical man of many years' experience, when it is generally known in the

profession that a stiletto would have done the business
in the course of an hour or so?

He quoted from *Ryan and Beck's Medical Jurisprudence*, which
stated: 'There are no signs by which pregnancy can be detected
before the third month'. Having, as he thought, dealt with
that issue, and the validity of his Royal Pardon having been
called into question, he now quoted what he claimed that Sir
Frederick Pollock himself had said on the subject:

> The Royal Pardon is a most authoritative declaration
> that the party has been wrongly convicted, and that he
> was an innocent man – May 14, 1861.

And:

> I say this, that I think it must be taken, according to
> the administration of our criminal laws, that when a
> person has been convicted, and the Secretary of State
> has advised Her Majesty to grant a free pardon, that
> individual has established his innocence in the only
> way he can according to the administration of the
> criminal laws of this country, and that he is entitled to
> the full benefit of that fact – Nov 6, 1861.

Smethurst finished his letter:

> These facts at once put an end to the will motive, and
> the case altogether, by the Chief Baron's own showing.
> A case of greater hardship and cruelty, or one more
> strikingly illustrating danger to the life of the people,
> can scarcely be imagined. I therefore ask you, for the
> sake of truth, justice, and the satisfaction of the people,
> to insert this communication in your next impression.
> T Smethurst MD, London Nov 15.

The response from *The Times* was printed the same day. It was an unequal contest. The newspaper was determined to get its own back for the various barbs, obviously still painful, that the *Daily Telegraph* and other newspapers had aimed at it for its 'disingenuousness' and equivocation when Smethurst was first convicted. It was a long, analytical and sustained attack on Smethurst's version of events. The leader-writer engaged all his powers of rhetoric and invective to put Smethurst very firmly in his place. It is sufficient to report part of what was said. It started:

> We cannot...be...surprised that Dr Smethurst should have thought fit to try himself over again at the bar of his own opinion, and should have seized an opportunity to publish the verdict in our own columns. What... fills us with amazement, is that he should venture to represent our passing allusion to him in connexion with Müller's case as "alike injurious to myself, the Government and the people". If our remarks were "injurious" to himself, it must have been the fault of the facts, for we...confined ourselves to censuring the particular method in which the sentence was reviewed by Sir G C Lewis.

It went on:

> Dr Smethurst...demands something more than neutrality and suspension of judgment; he claims the expression of a judgment in his own favour. We take the liberty of informing him that such a claim will never be recognized by us.

The newspaper took issue with Smethurst's view that the Royal Pardon reversed the verdict of the jury, making him innocent of the crime. It was not as simple as that:

> We find nothing in the Common Law which gives a pardon the effect he attributes to it. It makes the offender "a new man", it relieves him from "all corporal penalties and forfeitures", it gives him a right of action against any one who shall call him felon or traitor, but that is all...It leaves his character where it found it...

And just in case the point had not been sufficiently understood:

> Not only may the recipient of it have been guilty of crimes as odious as the one to which it applies; he may have been proved guilty of that very crime in the opinion of the Home Secretary himself, but under circumstances different from those inferred by the jury from the evidence.

The quoted comments from the Lord Chief Baron, the newspaper was unable to find, 'unless...used in reference to Mr Hatch'.[2] In any event, the newspaper said, they meant no more than that

> a pardoned man...[has been] either convicted of a crime he did not commit, or on inadequate evidence of a crime he did commit, and that in either case he is thenceforth "innocent" of that crime in the eye of the law.

The newspaper accused 'Dr Smethurst' of trying to 'mislead the public by his own version of the facts', and clear himself of having tried to procure an abortion, when that was not the evidence on which he was tried. The evidence presented in court was again raked over. *The Times* commented that the Lord Chief Baron's stated opinion that Smethurst 'ought not to be hanged', was quite different from a 'testimonial to his

---

2   Henry John Hatch, who also came under judgement from the Lord Chief Baron during an action against his solicitor for negligence.

innocence'. Finally, the editorial reiterated its main objection to the Royal Pardon having been granted to Smethurst, that the Home Secretary relied on the opinion of Sir Benjamin Brodie considering topics 'far beyond the province of a physician', and constituting a 'single arbiter' into a Court of Criminal Appeal.

It would have been as well to have let the matter rest there, since Smethurst was never going to win a contest with *The Times* in its own columns. Perhaps he felt, with some justification, that the response to his letter had been so damaging to his reputation and so dismissive of his own arguments that he had to respond. After an initial statement in which the word 'treacherously' figured several times, he commented:

> As you intimate in your leader of 17th inst., the taint of a most loathsome suspicion still hangs over me...

He reported the words of Mr McMahon, MP, in February 1860, when arguing in favour of a Court of Criminal Appeal:

> ...this mercy [the Royal Pardon] is but a miserable relief, if obtained, for the injury he [the one pardoned] has suffered. It may save his property from forfeiture and himself from...the gallows, but the foul blot remains on his reputation.

Smethurst commented on Dr Taylor's 'murderous blunder', and then took *The Times* to task for suggesting that his (Smethurst's) 'expression of a judgement in his favour' would never be recognized by it, by quoting from its own leader of 2nd December 1859:

> It is perfectly competent for any man to conclude that all the suffering through which Smethurst has passed was undeserved. He may be regarded as an innocent victim of circumstances in the case of the capital charge.

Smethurst went on to state that he was convinced that the jury should never have convicted him. He quoted from a letter Professor Herapath had written to the *Pharmaceutical Journal* on the subject of arsenic in copper wire. Herapath again insisted, as he had done in his letter to *The Times* when Smethurst was under sentence of death, that the quantity of arsenic that Dr Taylor claimed to have found in bottle No 21 could not possibly have come from the copper wire (gauze). He also quoted from a letter Dr Odling had sent to the same journal. Odling was also a prosecution witness at Smethurst's trial, and had worked with Dr Taylor and checked his analyses. Now, however, he claimed that his participation had been minimal, and that it was he, not Dr Taylor, who had discovered the 'error' of arsenic in the copper wire; he talked about Dr Taylor's 'want of candour' and disavowed any 'complicity in Dr Taylor's production'.

The Times had claimed that:

> One scientific witness after another swore that the abnormal appearances...could hardly have resulted... from any known disease. This conclusion was identical with that [of the] three medical men...by an observation of symptoms during life.

But, Smethurst pointed out, Drs Julius, Bird and Todd, had never seen a case of poisoning by arsenic or antimony, and never seen such a case post-mortem. After commenting that he had no readier means of acquiring arsenic or antimony than *The Times* itself, Smethurst reproduced a letter sent on 29th August 1859, by a barrister, Mr Leonard Gent, to Henry Sheridan, the MP who had taken an interest in the Smethurst case:

> ...I was present during a greater part of Dr Smethurst's trial...My declaration throughout was that the trial was

a 'sham', a 'mockery'. In my whole experience I never witnessed, nor I dare say ever shall witness, anything so extraordinary. Spectators, witnesses, prisoner's counsel, judge, jury, prosecuting counsel, one and all, seemed weighed down, absolutely unable to escape from some mysterious weight...which impelled them to a belief in the prisoner's guilt. Even the prisoner's counsel put his questions as though this evil influence led him every time to expect an unfavourable answer, and he got it[3]... On considering all the evidence, I now not only think he ought to have been acquitted, but I am convinced of his innocence...

The Times responded:

To vilify the judge, jury, and witnesses for the prosecution, imputing treachery to all and infamy to the first, is the worst possible way of bespeaking charitable consideration for himself...

The newspaper pointed out that Smethurst's perceived 'universal prejudice' against him,

...might have its origin in other motives than the malevolence of society...

These 'other motives' were then detailed:

The truth is that, rightly or wrongly, there is a rooted conviction in the minds of most people that a man who not only cohabits with a mistress in the lifetime of his wife, but goes through a sham ceremony of

---

3 Whether it was true that even Serjeant Parry was 'weighed down' with belief in the prisoner's guilt is impossible to gauge. He certainly clashed with the judge on several occasions, and it is not obvious that he pulled his punches in his cross-examinations, particularly with Dr Taylor and his blunders. He also charged the judge afterwards with misdirecting the jury.

marriage with her, after swearing that there is no legal impediment to it, must be a very heartless person, and is more likely to be guilty of another crime than a man of unblemished character.

And,

The circumstance that the lady thus connected with him executed a will in his favour just before her death, and that Dr Smethurst got that will prepared, was not calculated to weaken this impression.

The editorial then proceeded to rebut at length the other charges made in Smethurst's second letter, which, since old ground was again covered, need not be reported. If Smethurst wrote to *The Times* again, his letter was not printed. Most likely he recognized the truth of the origin of the 'universal prejudice' with which he was regarded by the public at large and decided, no doubt seething with indignation, that it was a contest he could not hope to win.

The second 'incident', occurred many years later after the affair was all but forgotten. Thomas Smethurst was dead, and his brother James would be dead within months. Serjeant Ballantine published his memoirs in which he related a story about the brothers which, if true, would have been a sensation in 1859. He claimed that Thomas and James Smethurst were a gang who preyed on vulnerable women; Thomas married them for their money, after which James, in his capacity as a druggist, provided the wherewithal to poison them. Ballantine prefixed the tale with the comment:

I am about to tell a story the circumstances of which would be thought improbable in a romance, and yet every word of it is true; and there are incidents which I believe to be connected with it that would add to its strangeness, but which I suppress because I do not possess the proofs requisite for their authentication.

Ballantine started by relating the circumstances of Isabella Bankes and Thomas Smethurst, their brief time together, her death and his trial. The account was generally accurate except that he claimed that arsenic was found in Isabella's body when none was. He went on to say that Smethurst had used potassium chlorate deliberately to defeat the Reinsch test for arsenic. According to Ballantine, when Smethurst was allowed to return to his lodgings unsupervised after the first arrest he contrived to lay a trap for Dr Taylor. This consisted of a bottle of 'innocent' liquid containing a solution of potassium chlorate and arsenic. At the time of the murder trial, Ballantine said, one of the medical witnesses for the prosecution had forwarded a copy of *The Lancet*, dated June 1844, to the solicitor acting for the Bankes family.[4] It contained a letter from Thomas Smethurst concerning a case he had dealt with involving a tooth infection and subsequent extraction. According to Ballantine, on the page opposite to that containing Smethurst's letter was one part of an on-going series of articles by Dr Karl Remigius Fresenius. Fresenius was a Lecturer in Chemistry at the University of Giessen, and the article reviewed the methods available for the detection of arsenic post-mortem. In this article, Ballantine said, it was stated that 'wherever chlorates were used, Reinsch's test would invariably be defeated'. The implication was that the article gave Smethurst the idea of how to conceal the presence of arsenic. When he was released by the magistrate, he laced the arsenic solution being used to poison Isabella Bankes with potassium chlorate, knowing that it would cause the Reinsch test to fail.

During Ballantine's address to the jury at the beginning of Smethurst's second trial for murder, he had stated:

---

4   From the description, it is clear that the witness in question was Dr Buzzard.

> The prisoner [is] a man of considerable chemical and medical skill, well acquainted with the nature of different poisons...[and he has] made use of this knowledge to baffle, to a considerable extent, the tests [used] to discover the presence of poison.

Having initially made this statement, the matter was not followed up during the prosecution case. No doubt it was pointed out to the serjeant by one of his colleagues that since Dr Taylor now admitted that there had been no arsenic initially present in the bottle (No 21), the argument that Smethurst had laid a deliberate trap for the person conducting the test was entirely specious. In any case, all of Smethurst's bottles and packets were confiscated when he returned to the lodging, and there was a police constable stationed at the house. Ballantine's memoirs were published nearly 25 years after trial, and he had evidently forgotten these critical details.

A simple scrutiny of the article by Dr Fresenius in *The Lancet* further undermines Serjeant Ballantine's story. The fact that it is not on the page opposite Smethurst's letter, but some nine pages earlier, is perhaps less important than the absence of any claim in the entire paper that chlorates will defeat the Reinsch Test.

Ballantine presented this story in his memoirs, when a simple check of the details shows it to be complete fiction. But he was sexing up his account in preparation for the climax. This was the report of a statement, apparently made to the Bankes family's solicitor, by a lady present at Thomas Smethurst's first trial; this trial, it will be remembered, was terminated after a day and a half when one of the jurymen fell seriously ill. The lady in question, identified only as 'witness', had lived with her husband in a house in Brompton next door to James Smethurst; another lady, 'Mrs G', lived in the same house (as James Smethurst), and Thomas Smethurst was constantly visiting his brother in the house. Approximately three years earlier (around 1856) Mrs G had come into the witness's house accusing Thomas Smethurst of trying to force her to make a will in his favour. On another occasion a servant fetched her when Mrs G was having a 'fit', and in the presence of a doctor, she 'made statements' indicating she was in 'great apprehension as to the food she was taking'. Mrs G appeared to be about forty years of age.

It was further stated that some years earlier, a lady 'assumed to be Mrs G', together with her husband – the lady 'possessing some attractions' – had lodged with James Smethurst in the West End. Mrs G's husband had fallen ill and had been attended by Thomas Smethurst, who was living with his wife and practising in an adjacent street. He used drugs supplied by James Smethurst from his business. The husband died 'in mysterious circumstances', after which 'both brothers disappeared from the neighbourhood'. The husband's death certificate indicated death from kidney disease, no medical man's name was attached, and according to Ballantine,

> ...the application of arsenic would produce symptoms
> that might be mistaken for this disease.

A statement of all of this was made to 'Sergeant' McIntyre at the time.

The climax of Serjeant Ballantine's story was taken, of course, from the various police reports following investigations made in September 1859. 'Mrs G' was Julia Gibson, James Smethurst's landlady and 'Witness' was Laura Willis, Julia Gibson's next-door neighbour. No action had been taken following these reports, since as previously stated, all they really proved was doubtful ethics on the part of Thomas Smethurst, and the highly questionable behaviour of Julia Gibson.

The story about Julia Gibson telling Laura Willis that the brothers tried to get her to make her will in their favour was definitely suspicious, but since Mrs Gibson denied that it had happened that was an end to the matter. But the 'mysterious death' of her husband, Henry Gibson, was entirely manufactured by Serjeant Ballantine. Henry Gibson's cause of death was given as *Phrenitis Chronica*, chronic phrenitis. The OED defines phrenitis as:

> Delerium esp. when associated with or attributed to inflammation of the brain...

Dr Brett, who attended Henry Gibson, clarified the condition as 'softening of the brain' brought on by excessive drinking. So quite definitely not 'kidney disease with symptoms similar to those of arsenic poisoning'; perhaps Ballantine confused *phren*itis with *nephr*itis, inflammation of the kidney, the first syllables being anagrams of each other. There was no 'medical man's name' attached to the death certificate, but that was entirely normal practice at the time as a survey of contemporary death certificates shows. Since Dr Brett, the medical man who treated Henry Gibson was found and interviewed by the police, there was no mystery. It was quite definitely not a suspicious death.

The charge that 'both brothers disappeared from the neighbourhood' after Henry Gibson's death was plainly untrue. James was still living at the same address three years later, and Thomas had only moved a mile or so to Mornington Place.

What prompted Ballantine to wheel out this collection of wild stories and plain falsehoods? Serjeant Ballantine was 71 years old when this edition of his memoirs was published (1883), and within four years he would be dead. Did he carry such a grudge against Thomas Smethurst and his perceived 'escape from justice', that he was determined to throw every last vestige of half-truth, innuendo and downright fabrication at his memory in order to demonstrate that he really was guilty of murder? Ballantine knew that the allegations had been fully investigated by the police, since his account in some respects follows closely what was written in the police reports. Furthermore, he knew that there was no arsenic mixed with potassium chlorate in bottle No 21, since the whole story had come out in court when Dr Taylor gave his evidence.

Serjeant Ballantine's account was always going to be improbable. After all, both James and Thomas in their respective professions traded on their good names and reputations. Was it really likely that they would have risked all of that *and* the gallows in order to make some money in the way described? Julia Gibson died intestate in 1879, and her £2,000 estate went to the Crown. But even for that amount, would respectable, professional, relatively wealthy men (Thomas possessed £3,500 in cash and property in 1859, James left over £1,000 when he died) be likely to risk the gallows? And in the unlikely event that the brothers *had* decided to act in that way, would they have carried out their schemes in the very centre of London where they were both well known? If Julia Gibson's husband had died in mysterious circumstances, attended by Thomas Smethurst who was using drugs supplied by James, would she not only have stayed at the same address with James Smethurst for several years, but then have moved to Brompton with him where they continued to live together for at least the next 20 years? It seems hardly likely that Mrs Gibson would have retained James in her house for any time at all if he had either been implicated in her husband's death, or he or his brother had tried to induce her to make a will to his benefit (or had tried to poison her).[5]

---

5 It might be suggested that Julia Gibson would have stayed with James Smethurst if she was, after all, having a relationship with him. While this cannot be discounted, it does not detract from the fact that her husband had died of natural causes, and there was no evidence of James or Thomas' involvement in his death. On the other hand, Julia Gibson denied, most emphatically, that she was involved with James, while freely admitting to the police that she had 'entertained gentlemen' for financial gain.

In fact Serjeant Ballantine condemned his own credibility in a postscript added to the story; in his words:

> ...I am perfectly clear that there existed a secret understanding between husband and wife [Thomas and Mary Smethurst]...a very intimate friend of mine, Captain Ward, who had been a distinguished officer in the Indian Service...read certain correspondence that had passed between the two. He was much struck by the similarity it bore to the communication between the Thug[gee]s, which body of assassins he had been largely instrumental in suppressing.

Serjeant William Ballantine was an eminent, intelligent and accomplished lawyer who numbered many well-known persons among his friends and acquaintances. He had earned praise for the tact he displayed in declining to cross-examine the Prince of Wales, the future King Edward VII, when he appeared in the witness box as a suspected co-respondent in the Mordaunt divorce case in 1870.[6] Yet here he was advancing, quite seriously, the most absurd argument in order to justify his position on the Smethurst affair. Such a proposition would have been quite literally laughed out of court had he presented it during his professional life.

---

6 ODNB

Epilogue

The Smethurst affair was a true cause célèbre. Thomas Smethurst's name had hardly been out of the newspapers between May and September of 1859. At least one critic had observed that it was because Parliament was in summer recess and the press were looking for stories to print that the case had generated so much apparent interest, the period shortly to be christened the 'Silly Season'. But the response to the Smethurst trial was very much more than frivolity and summer madness. The trial and aftermath generated an enormous amount of comment, particularly during the period between Smethurst's conviction and 'respite'. Questions were subsequently asked in Parliament, and there were calls for the establishment of a full Court of Criminal Appeal – calls that went unanswered for another 48 years. Popular interest was fuelled by cheap flyers with details of the trial gleaned from the newspapers, some with doggerel verse – one accusing 'Smithurst' of poisoning 'Elizabeth Banks'. There was a chapbook, *Scenes from the life of Dr Smethurst, the Richmond Poisoner,* with an elaborate, but entirely fictional, drawing of Smethurst sitting by a bed-ridden Isabella Bankes. The *Liverpool Mercury* reported that a full-length 'perfect and faithful likeness' of Dr Smethurst was on show in 'Mr Allsop's magnificent exhibition of waxwork[s]' in the Teutonic Hall. Over three days more than 5,000 people had paid sixpence to visit the 'very gorgeous and interesting' exhibition.

The consensus of opinion in the 150 years that have elapsed since is that Smethurst was definitely not *proven* guilty, and the Home Secretary was right in first reprieving and then pardoning him. And yet in much of the published comment it is possible to detect a barely concealed view that Smethurst might, after all, have done it. Some commentators declare that he definitely was guilty and got away with it. In the words of the anonymous annotator of his application to Parliament for compensation, 'most people think that he had a lucky escape...'

The two persons who most contributed to the verdict of guilty during the trial for murder were Dr Alfred Swaine Taylor, who conducted the chemical tests for poison, and Sir Frederick Pollock the trial judge. Dr Taylor had reported at the magistrates' hearing the detection of arsenic in Isabella's stool, as well as in a mixture in Smethurst's possession (bottle No 21), which had caused the Reinsch test to fail, a so-called 'new finding in science'. Clearly, this created enormous prejudice against the prisoner who was already regarded with great suspicion on account of the last-minute will in his favour, the bigamous marriage and Isabella's pregnancy. Subsequently, almost every aspect of Taylor's analysis was found to be faulty. His 'new finding in science' was shown to be nothing of the sort, his use of the Reinsch test for arsenic was inappropriate, and his copper gauze was contaminated with arsenic. Even the amount of arsenic he claimed to have found (from the copper) was disputed, Dr Herapath pointing out that had the copper contained that much arsenic, it would have been far too brittle ever to have been pulled into a wire. Taylor admitted the mistake over his arsenic-contaminated copper in court (although Dr Odling subsequently claimed that it was he, not Dr Taylor, who had discovered the mistake), but by that time the damage had been done. Taylor always insisted that the arsenic found in Isabella's stool was not a mistake, although Dr Shearman had pointed out a credible mechanism by which other chemicals known to be present in dysenteric evacuations could have precipitated the arsenic present in the copper gauze.

At least one newspaper commentator, in the flurry of editorials and correspondence following the conviction, had said that Dr Taylor's fame was destroyed. If his reputation was dead it refused to lie down, because just a few years later, in 1865, Taylor published the seminal work on his subject, *The Principles and Practice of Medical Jurisprudence*. On the title page, was a quotation in Latin:

In Certis Unitas. In Dubiis Libertas. In Omnium Veritas.

A translation of which would be: 'In certainties unity; in doubts, liberty (to argue, debate etc.), and in all, truth'. But for two letters in the final word, this motto is identical to a well-known quotation attributed to St Augustine, which ends with the word 'Caritas' (charity) instead of 'Veritas' (truth). Dr Taylor had been privately educated, and was apprenticed to a medical practitioner at the age of sixteen. It is said, though, that he had a 'knowledge' of Latin and Greek.[1] Was he trying to be clever in substituting 'truth' for 'charity'? What he said about the Smethurst affair in his book lacked both truth and charity and hardly allowed for any doubts. He briefly related the facts of the case, commenting that Drs Julius, Bird and Todd (who had seen Isabella while she was still alive), and he himself, had concluded that she was poisoned by arsenic and antimony. Drs Tyler Smith, Richardson and others (who did not see her alive), concluded natural causes. He commented on the arsenic discovered in an 'evacuation' and the antimony found in the intestines post-mortem (not mentioning his mistake with the Reinsch test and the copper gauze). He then described another case, where a number of members of the same family were found to have been slowly poisoned with antimony. Sixteen similar cases had been referred to him since 1847, suggesting

---

1 ODNB

...grave reflections on the insecurity of life, when poison is used with skill and cunning [demonstrating] the inefficiency of the present system of recording death.

He quoted from the *Law* Magazine which, commenting on the Smethurst case, had said:

All that is requisite for future murderers by poison to do, is to use small doses, combine the use of various destructive drugs, and subpoena the proper medical witnesses for the defence.

So, no doubts from Dr Taylor, plenty of certainties but little real truth.

The bias of Sir Frederick Pollock during the trial was palpable; he bore the lion's share of responsibility for bringing Smethurst to within four days of the hangman's rope. There was also the fact that it was not his 'turn' on the bench rota. Did he pull strings to ensure that it was he who tried Smethurst for the second time, determined to see justice done as he saw it? It was said of Pollock that among his few shortcomings were '...a tendency to make up his mind early in a case...'[2] In Smethurst's case, he had made up his mind before he had heard the evidence; his antagonism towards the defence witnesses and his one-sided summing-up has been extensively detailed in earlier chapters. He spent far more time going over the circumstantial evidence than the carefully considered opinions of twenty medical practitioners and chemists. He declared that the defence medical testimony was less credible than that of the prosecution, when a simple perusal of the court transcript shows that the former was properly 'evidence' based, rather than consisting of just opinions. At one point during the summing up Sir Frederick Pollock said:

2   ODNB

> It may be that no arsenic, no poison is traced to the possession of the accused, it may be that no poison is found in the body, and yet it may be the easiest thing in the world to put a case where no sensible man could doubt that the accused had possessed the poison, that he had used it, and that the deceased had died of it.

If the judge could make such an extraordinary statement during his instruction to the jury, it is difficult to see what evidence the defence could possibly have presented that he would have believed.

Again and again the judge stressed Smethurst's immorality, as if that alone confirmed his guilt. Smethurst had objected to being tried by Sir Frederick Pollock on account of the fact that he and Dr Taylor were friends, and Pollock did not deny it. Just how good their friendship was is not known, but both were Fellows of the Royal Society and both were very keen amateur photographers. Even though the Royal Society had several hundred Fellows at the time, a common obsession with a new and absorbing hobby was very likely to have cemented their acquaintance with each other. And as Pollock admitted during the trial, he had welcomed Dr Taylor into his house just a few days previously. Pollock left no memoir of his time as a judge, but his view of the outcome of Smethurst's trial was almost entirely unchanged after the event. That is quite clear both from the long analysis of the case submitted to the Home Secretary and the bad-tempered and unrepentant letter following the decision to pardon Smethurst. Pollock was very well aware of the welter of criticism in the press of his conduct of the trial, some of it from his own lawyer colleagues, not to mention the almost universal condemnation of the chemical evidence. Although he did, in the end, concede that Smethurst should not hang, he made virtually no other concessions, either in his conduct of the trial, or the guilty verdict. There is little doubt that a different trial judge would have produced an entirely different verdict.

In 1931, Dr Leonard A Parry, a Fellow of the Royal College of Surgeons, published *The Trial of Dr Smethurst*. The account contains comprehensive transcripts of the various court hearings together with a 'modern' medical assessment of Isabella Bankes' condition. He considered the clinical (symptoms in life), pathological (causes and effects of diseases) and toxicological (presence of poisons) evidence. Dr Parry concluded that Isabella's symptoms in life were very much like those of arsenic poisoning, and only superficially resembled vomiting in pregnancy:

> ...from the clinical evidence...the case was remarkably like one of irritant poisoning, and...not merely a severe case of vomiting in pregnancy, complicated by dysentery, though...it would [not] be possible to definitely deny the latter.

The pathology, he said, was inconclusive; the appearances could have been due either to irritant poisoning or dysentery. Poisoning by arsenic, Parry dismissed. None was found in the body, and the only evidence of arsenic, as found in the evacuation, was probably a mistake by Dr Taylor. Antimony poisoning too he dismissed. If it was present in any quantity it should have been found in the liver, and none was. The small amounts found in the body could have been impurities present in the various medicines that Isabella Bankes was given.

Was Isabella suffering from a bad case of morning sickness, known today as NVP – Nausea and Vomiting in Pregnancy? Clearly, it was a factor and could have led to the far more serious condition, *Hyperemesis Gravidarum*. The latter involves severe nausea and vomiting, dehydration and weight loss, and requires hospital treatment; but Isabella was also afflicted with diarrhoea which degenerated into dysentery. Either condition could have been fatal.

In 1932, a new type of inflammatory bowel disease was described by Dr Burrill Crohn, together with two colleagues, Leon Ginzburg and Gordon Oppenheimer, at Mount Sinai Hospital, New York. Crohn's disease, an inflammatory bowel disease, is defined in a recent *Lancet* article as a

> relapsing, transmural inflammatory disease of the gastrointestinal mucosa that can affect the entire gastrointestinal tract from the mouth to the anus.

Symptoms include fever, persistent diarrhoea, weight loss, nausea and vomiting, abdominal pain, and the passage of mucus and blood. Crohn's disease results from an 'inappropriate' response of the immune system in the gut.

In 1985 J F Fielding published a note in the *British Medical Journal* entitled *"Inflammatory" bowel disease.* Having summarized the post-mortem appearance of Isabella Bankes' body, which was described in detail in the paper by Dr Samuel Wilks, published in the *London Medical Gazette* in 1859, he concluded:

> ...the post-mortem findings leave little doubt but that Miss Bankes suffered from Crohn's Disease rather than irritant poisoning or "idiopathic dysentery", the early name given to idiopathic ulcerative colitis.

Much has been written about Crohn's disease, the causes of which are still not completely understood. One thing though is quite clear; there is a tendency for the disease to run in families. Isabella Bankes' father was known to have died of a condition, given on his death certificate as typhus, which culminated in severe diarrhoea. Louisa Bankes had stated in court that the whole family suffered from bilious attacks. It seems not impossible that their father too had Crohn's disease and passed on a predisposition for the condition to his children.

What really happened between Thomas Smethurst and Isabella Bankes during the eight months that they knew each other? Conflating the views of Sir Frederick Pollock and Serjeant Ballantine, Smethurst had identified Isabella as a vulnerable, impressionable woman, 'on the shelf', and in possession of money, and used his wiles to seduce her. He married her having told her that he was not really already married to Mary Smethurst. When he became aware that she was pregnant, he decided to get rid of her without delay in order to avoid the expense and inconvenience of a baby, and grab her money sooner rather than later. His brother James provided the arsenic and/or antimony, and when Isabella started to deteriorate sooner than expected, Smethurst had to rush through the will in order that he did not lose out on her property.

There is little doubt that this story, more or less, was the one initially believed by the overwhelming majority of all of those with knowledge of the case, including the newspaper-reading public, the jury in the murder trial and the trial judge. But there are a number of major difficulties with this interpretation of events. There was very little evidence that Isabella Bankes had actually been poisoned. No arsenic and only a small amount of antimony had been found in the body, and none was found in the liver. No poisons were found in Thomas Smethurst's possession; since he can have had no warning that he was about to be arrested, he had no chance to hide or dispose of anything incriminating. The specific symptoms of arsenic and antimony poisoning were absent from Isabella. The symptoms in life and post-mortem appearances although they *could* have resulted from poisoning, were equally consistent with natural causes. Richardson et al. as well as Baly and Jenner, noted that in poisoning the stomach becomes affected, whereas the large intestine generally does not. Isabella Bankes' symptoms were the exact reverse of that, entirely consistent with 'natural' dysentery. Many of the medical witnesses for the defence, and many medical practitioners who came forward afterwards, were quite familiar with severe vomiting and diarrhoea causing the death of pregnant women (although none of the witnesses for the prosecution apparently were).

Then there was the circumstantial evidence. Firstly, as became clear from the action for the probate of Isabella's will, her estate would only be worth a fraction of the apparent £1,800 due to the Chancery action. On the contrary, had Isabella lived, Smethurst would have continued sharing in the £140 a year from her uncle's will, a value that would have increased substantially had either of her sisters pre-deceased her.

Secondly, if Smethurst's intention had been to murder Isabella for her money, why did he leave it until the very last minute to make her will? Had he done so even a month earlier, no question could have arisen as to her 'incapacity' for deciding her affairs and the matter would hardly have been noticed. In having it made when he did, he not only drew enormous attention to himself, but he ran a significant risk of Isabella dying before it could be executed.

Thirdly, if Smethurst had set out deliberately to poison Isabella, why did he invite Dr Julius and his partner to come and treat her quite early on before she was very ill? There would always have been the risk – as indeed happened – that they would suspect poisoning and take the steps they did in order to prove it. The anti-Smethurst camp claimed that it was a deliberate ruse on his part, such that when Isabella died he could claim that she had been treated by other hands than his own and they would have detected poisoning. If poison had been Smethurst's real intent, the last thing he would want would be other doctors examining Isabella, checking her symptoms, asking awkward questions and risking exposing him.

But the fatal flaw in the Pollock/Ballantine view of events, is the fact that Isabella signed her will 'Isabella Bankes, spinster'. Either she believed that she was truly married to Smethurst, and his marriage to Mary was void, in which case she would have signed herself, 'Isabella Smethurst, wife of Dr Thomas Smethurst'; or she knew that the marriage was bigamous, and that she was still, legally, a spinster. If she had signed 'Isabella Smethurst', then since Smethurst's original marriage to Mary could be shown to have been valid – the register was presented in court – he could quite legitimately have been accused of fraud, and the probate action would have failed. Some might argue that if Friend Tomlin's assessment of Isabella as having a 'weak mind in business matters' was true, she might have been convinced, privately, by Smethurst to sign herself 'Isabella Bankes' still thinking herself to have been properly married. However, since Friend Tomlin was declared bankrupt not long afterwards, one has to question the probity of his judgement in such matters.

There was also the possibility raised later by Samuel Wilks, and taken up by Sir Frederick Pollock, that Isabella might have died from some substance given to her by Smethurst in order to procure abortion. Smethurst himself dealt with that possibility in his subsequent spat with *The Times*. Isabella's illness coincided almost exactly with the onset of her pregnancy. Smethurst could not possibly have known that she was pregnant when the poison, if it ever existed, was first administered (when she first started suffering from vomiting and diarrhoea). In any case, he was an experienced doctor, and as he graphically illustrated during *The Times* correspondence, there were other, simpler methods of achieving the same objective...

During the summing-up, the question of Smethurst forbidding visitors to Isabella and not employing a nurse for her was frequently cited as evidence that he wanted to keep the sick-room secret for his own dastardly ends. In fact it is fairly easy to see that it was probably to protect Isabella's modesty that this was done. Bowel and bladder function can be most distressing for sick people; Isabella was passing up to 15 bowel motions per day as well as being frequently sick. The last thing a 'genteel lady' wants under such circumstances is a trail of visitors in and out and being ministered to by strangers. It was also Smethurst's habit to give Isabella an opium enema following bowel movements. Clearly privacy was essential for such things.

Serjeant Ballantine's 'revelations' in his memoirs were just bunkum. The story about Dr Fresenius' article in *The Lancet* was nonsense, the charge that Smethurst was involved in the death of Julia Gibson's husband was complete fiction and Mrs Willis' statement about Julia Gibson's charges against the Smethursts was denied by her at the time. Mrs Gibson would, in any case, have been compelled to have appeared as a witness against Smethurst if any vestige of truth had been contained in any of the claims, since, as is clear from her statement, they had first been made to Inspector McIntyre before the second trial had started.

So much for motive and evidence, but what was the actual cause of Isabella's death? Modern medicine has identified Crohn's disease exacerbated by morning sickness as fitting both Isabella's symptoms in life, and the appearance of her body after death, and given the other conclusions regarding evidence and motive, it seems a likely explanation of her miserable end.

What about Smethurst himself? All the reports of his behaviour, both towards Mary, his wife of thirty years, and Isabella herself – much of it provided by hostile witnesses – stated that he was kind, generous and considerate at all times. In October 1859, Susan Freeland wrote to Dr Smethurst from Tunbridge Wells. Smethurst and Isabella had stayed with her for a while following their marriage and she wrote to him in prison following a letter which he had written to her:

> Sir, during the month you passed under my roof, I remember Mrs Smethurst (as I then believed her to be) complaining of sickness, and on her leaving the room, observing I thought her very fragile and delicate; I also recollect how anxious you were that she should immediately have flannel drawers, and of your ordering them for her; indeed, your devotion and attention was such, that she seemed to wish for nothing more, nor could anything exceed your gentlemanly bearing towards myself and every member of my household...

Mary Smethurst wrote to the newspapers when Smethurst was under sentence of death. With all the misery and anguish she must have suffered having to read about her husband's affair with Isabella Bankes, anticipating his execution within a few days, and having being been deserted by him, she nevertheless wrote detailing the kindness and attention she had always received from him. She talked about his humane character and amiable disposition, and related how he had provided for his invalid younger brother William.

Smethurst was, of course, a doctor, and he was conversant with the use of medicines including poisons. But he was well aware of how easily arsenic could be detected in dead bodies. In 1849 when he was editor of the *Water Cure Journal*, he described a case that had just been reported in *The Times*, where 'Mr' Herapath had detected arsenic in the body of a child that had been buried for eight years. The child's mother, Rebecca Smith, subsequently confessed to the poisoning of eight of her children.

However with all that, Smethurst was a self-confessed wife-deserter, perjurer and bigamist. The reaction of the public in court during the probate action made it clear how he was regarded, and any doubts that remained were surely dispelled by the unfortunate correspondence he had with *The Times*. Still, the accumulation of medical, chemical and circumstantial evidence surely indicates that whatever else he was, Thomas Smethurst was not a murderer.

Thomas and Mary Smethurst went to live in Hampton, just a few miles from Richmond where he and Isabella Bankes had spent their final weeks together. In 1864, Mary died of apoplexy and was buried in Hampton churchyard. The stone that marked the spot was engraved:

> Mary Smethurst, wife of Dr Smethurst, M.D., died 6th March 1864 aged 79

Of what Smethurst did next, little evidence has survived. There were no more letters to the press, apart from the altercation with *The Times*, and no more communications with *The Lancet*.

But Thomas Smethurst must have had something, because the year after Mary died, he married Anne Thomas, a dressmaker. He was now sixty; she was twenty-eight... 'Annie' Thomas was the daughter of John Thomas, a joiner and shopkeeper who lived in Golfa, a hamlet in the parish of Llansilin near Oswestry. At the time, Llansilin was in Shropshire, although the Welsh border appears to have subsequently drifted east somewhat, and Llansilin is now in Wales. The wedding took place at the Congregationalists' chapel in Oswestry, with Catharine Thomas, Anne's mother as one of the witnesses. Smethurst was described as a 'gentleman', and this time the marriage was by banns, Smethurst being in residence in Golfa. It is intriguing to speculate how it was that a retired (and notorious) doctor from London could have met and 'won' a dressmaker, more than 30 years his junior, living in a small hamlet on the Welsh border. Oswestry is only 30 miles or so from Budworth, where

Smethurst was born, so it is possible that now that Mary was dead, he was on his travels again. Perhaps he met Anne while passing through Oswestry on his way north. It is, however, interesting to wonder whether she and her family knew about his past. There could have been few people in the country unaware of the trial and subsequent furore, and even though it had all happened six years earlier, it is difficult to believe that no-one in Anne's community was aware of it.

Smethurst took his new wife to London, but he must have made an impression on her family before he left, because when her elder brother Robert and his wife produced a son three years later, the boy was named Robert Smethurst Thomas...

The Smethursts went to live in Scarsdale Terrace in Kensington, barely a mile from Rifle Terrace, where Thomas and Isabella had met seven years earlier. Thomas' disabled brother William lived with them, and it is notable that in the 1871 census, Thomas was still giving his age as six years less than it actually was.

In the end though, the calendar caught up with him; in 1873, Thomas Smethurst 'paid the final tribute to nature'. On 22nd October of that year, *The Times* ran a report of an inquest that had taken place the previous day:

> Dr Smethurst...The circumstances which brought the deceased into notoriety a few years ago [being] well-known to the public...

The Smethursts had moved, and were living at 2 Brompton Square. Anne Smethurst told the inquest jury that although Smethurst had been 'pretty well' he had been suffering from 'a number of diseases'. After a long walk on the Saturday he had been taken ill around 11pm, 'a sense of suffocation appeared to come over him'. Dr Pollard, their next-door neighbour, was called, but by the time he arrived, Smethurst was dead. Dr Pollard performed a post-mortem on the Monday and found the left kidney to be 'completely disorganized'; he also found congestion of the brain. Death by natural causes was concluded.

Evidently Smethurst had told his new wife at least something of his past, because on Saturday 25th October, 1873, he was buried next to his first wife Mary, in Hampton Churchyard. The stone was inscribed with the legend:

In affectionate remembrance of Thomas Smethurst, M.D., who died October 18th 1873, aged 68

In death at least, he couldn't lie about his age. He hadn't made a will, and Letters of Administration were granted to Anne on his estate which was valued at less than £100.

With such modest assets it might have been wondered what Smethurst had been living on since his release from Wandsworth in 1860. In 1859 he had made all his wealth over to his brother James in trust for his brother William, in order to avoid it being confiscated by the State. It couldn't be given back to him when he got out of prison, since that would quite likely have broken the terms of the 'valid consideration' and the money and assets could have been forfeit. All became clear the year after Thomas Smethurst's death by a rather unfortunate case in Chancery between William Smethurst, Thomas's younger brother as plaintiff, and James Smethurst, his elder brother as defendant. William, described as a person of 'weak mind', was represented by his sister-in-law, 'Anne Smethurst his next friend'. Among the papers relating to the Chancery case, was a deposition from Dr Pollard, the Smethursts' next-door neighbour; he was called upon to provide a professional assessment of William Smethurst's state of mind. He had known William Smethurst for some time and had seen him frequently:

He is of weak mind...and incapable of managing his affairs. He is not lunatic or insane but of childlike simplicity, harmless and affectionate in his disposition and easily controlled and influenced.

He went on to say that William was in the sole care of Anne Smethurst 'to whom he is most sincerely attached'. He added that Anne attended to him and watched over him with 'patient assiduity...'

The Chancery papers consist of charges and counter-charges between the two parties, but do clarify what had happened. In 1852 or thereabouts, James, Thomas and Mary Ann Smethurst (called their sister in the documents, but probably a cousin), had between them provided funds to purchase leases on three properties in Brompton, the rents for which, held in trust by James and Thomas, were to provide William with an income. In June 1859, just before his first trial started, Thomas signed all his goods and wealth over to James, and James became the sole trustee for the rents that provided William's income. In November 1859, just before his trial for bigamy, Thomas also signed over any benefits accruing from Isabella Bankes' will to James, since these too would be subject to confiscation should Thomas subsequently be convicted, as he was. When Thomas was released from prison, he went to live with his wife Mary and brother William, William's income from the rents, held in trust by James, paying the bills. Following the grant of probate of Isabella Bankes' will, James claimed he had received between £650 and £800 but could not remember exactly how much. Most of this was, he said, used to purchase annuities on his and William's life. Between 1865 and 1870, James purchased further annuities, using some of the proceeds from rents, which generated an income of £60 per annum. While Thomas Smethurst was alive, James allowed him to collect rents from the properties which he used to support himself, Anne and William.

Then Thomas died and it all went badly wrong. James was 72 years old by this time, William was 63; Anne was 36... James may have disapproved of his brother's young wife; possibly he thought she was a gold-digger. Perhaps she thought he was abusing the trust of his dead brother. In any event, according to Anne, James stopped all income to her and William bar a few shillings grudgingly given, and wanted her to pay rent on their lodgings. When William went round to James' lodgings to plead with him he was roundly abused by James' 'landlady', the redoubtable Mrs Gibson, who told him to 'go home and hang himself'. The suit called for James to respect the terms of the income of the funds in trust for William, and give him the money he was due; alternatively, new trustees should be appointed.

The response from James was that he hadn't threatened to charge rent, he had provided William with an income, and Mrs Gibson was not his 'landlady' but an 'educated lady of independent means'. He had also paid over £700 towards Thomas' defence during his two trials. It was obvious however from James' responses that he had no clear record of what monies were what and to whom they should be given. He was confused as to what was his own income, what was Thomas's and what had been placed in trust for William. It must also be admitted that describing Mrs Gibson as an 'educated lady', and remembering her background, was being less than completely honest.

The outcome of the Chancery case has not been recorded. It would seem though, that William and Anne Smethurst had an unassailable case against James, and since the value of James' estate when he died was only around £1000 (Thomas having been worth £3,500 plus Isabella's £800), it seems likely that some settlement in William's favour was made.

Anne moved back to Scarsdale Terrace were she lived with William for some years, and then in 1886, she married a neighbour, John Alexander Lockwood. Lockwood, a widower, was a retired surgeon from the US Navy, and was probably the same naval surgeon whom Herman Melville met on the USS

Constellation while in service in the Mediterranean.[3] Clearly
Anne had a penchant for older men; Lockwood was 71 when
they married, although she was a little economical with the
truth about her own age, being nearer 49 than the 42 she
put on their marriage certificate. The Lockwoods moved to
nearby Horton Street. They were still there in 1891 but then
disappeared from view. Possibly John took his new wife back
to Delaware in the USA where he had been born.

Julia Gibson, James Smethurst's long-time landlady, finally
died in 1879, and James was obliged to move out of the house
he had occupied for several decades. He died in Fulham in 1883
without having made a will. His brother William, as his closest
relative, inherited his money. The 1891 census found William
staying with Anne's brother, Robert Thomas, in Pendleton in
Lancashire. William died shortly afterwards in Pendleton. He
was 78 and Catharine Thomas registered his death. He too
died without making a will, and his assets of £507 3s 4d went
to his sister-in-law, Anne Lockwood.

Thomas Smethurst had led a full life. He married three times,
spent twenty years as a practising doctor, travelled around the
continent, set up his own water-cure establishment, wrote a
book, edited a journal, retired at the age of 50 on a comfortable
income, became for a few months the most well-known and
notorious person in the country, escaped the gallows by
the skin of his teeth, served twelve months' hard labour in
Wandsworth Prison and yet still pressed his claim to the
estate of the woman he had been convicted of murdering. After
all that, he was able to spend his last years living in relative
comfort with a young wife.

A search of that 21st Century fount of all knowledge, *Google*,
produces mostly records of Smethurst's trial for murder.

3   Herman Melville, the author of *Moby Dick*.

But a paper by Robin Price entitled *Hydropathy in England*, published in 1981 in *Medical History*, makes several references to Smethurst's 1843 book on the subject, with no mention at all of his subsequent turbulent history. Thomas Smethurst would have liked that.

APPENDIX 1 – Family Tree of Thomas Smethurst

He was related by marriage to the Evelyn family

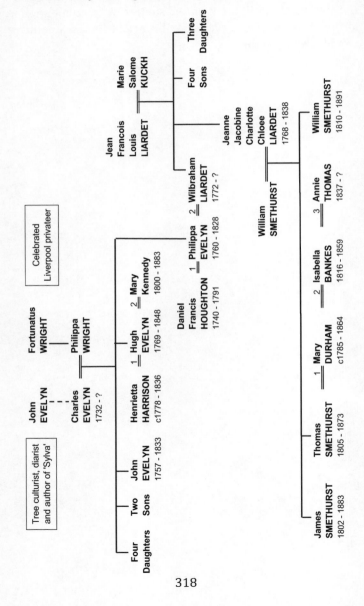

APPENDIX 2 – Family Tree of Isabella Bankes

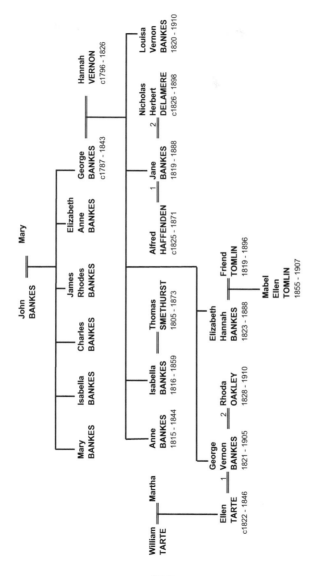

APPENDIX 3 – Thomas Smethurst's Letter to *The Lancet*

(From *The Lancet*, Page 246, 3rd September 1859)

"Audi alteram partem"[1]

THE CASE OF THOMAS SMETHURST, CONVICTED OF THE CRIME OF MURDER.
[LETTER FROM THOS. SMETHURST, WRITTEN BEFORE HIS TRIAL]

To the Editor of The Lancet

[The following letter was sent to us in June, when the writer stood committed to Horsemonger-Lane Gaol on a charge of murder. As it was sent to us by himself, and not by his legal advisors, we did not consider it prudent to publish it before the trial. – Ed. L.]

Sir, – Providence often sends unexpected relief in the time of utmost need. To this my attention has been suddenly called by an unforeseen communication made to THE LANCET for Saturday, 28th May last, by Dr. Letheby, of the London Hospital, touching the tests for arsenic when in solution with chlorate of potash, which seems from its importance to be of the utmost consequence to me in my critical position.

With the view of eliciting further aid, both *chemical* and *medical*, I request the favour of inserting in your publication a few facts connected with this most distressing affair, so far as the case will admit of out of court.

The deceased's usual state of health previous to her fatal illness. – Slight palsy of the head. Could not lie on the right side (uneasy). Constant acidity of the stomach. Tongue always furred. Womb complaint of some years' standing (compelled constantly to use injections of nitrate of silver). Hands and

---

1 "The other side should also be heard".

feet intensely cold, except when in exercise. Abdomen *always felt hot*, and was *frequently swollen*. Great flatulency existed. A spare feeder; could not drink beer, wine, or spirits without feeling uneasy in the *head* and *bowels*. Palpitation of the heart after walking quickly or making ascents. Could not eat soups, green vegetables, and many other things, as they produced flatulency. Could not ride in a coach without either feeling sick, or being actually sick. Bowels never right, generally constipated (blood and mucus frequently passing). Had a severe attack of *womb complaint* about five years since, then under Dr. Hoffman, of Margate. Had a severe attack of *bowel complaint* about four years since, at that time under the treatment of Dr. Thompson, of Eastbourne, for *one month* (said by deceased to be *similar* to her *recent attack*, but without sickness and loss of appetite).

Deceased's fatal illness. – Illness commenced on Monday, the 27th of March last, with diarrhoea and feeling weak; bowels acting about three or four times in the day and night for the first three days; slightly uneasy, but no actual pain; very little appetite. The next three days, diarrhoea and other symptoms much as before; but vomiting of *bile* now began, probably three or four times in the twenty-four hours, which seemed very much to increase her weakness. Dr Julius was then called in to attend. Lying on the right side would occasion vomiting; lying on the left side produced violent palpitation of the heart. Tongue much more furred than before the illness, but after the mineral poisons were administered exhibited the beef-steak appearance.[2] The brandy taken, however, about four ounces in the twenty-four hours throughout illness, no doubt played an important feature in the case; neither must the disease itself be forgotten. Lower part of the back (sacrum) tender, and very red from not being able to lie either on the right side or

---

2 By referring to the mineral medicines prescribed by Dr Julius and others as 'poisons', Smethurst had departed from what he had, no doubt, intended to be an objective and unbiased account. Such comments may have prompted the editor of The Lancet to delay publication.

the left side. No appetite whatever during the illness. Abdomen frequently swollen; much flatulence existed, but little or no pain. *Never complained of any pain*. Vomiting and diarrhoea continued throughout the illness from three to ten times in the twenty-four hours, but increased when the mineral poisons were taken to *fifteen motions*. Vomiting of bile persisted until about *five days previous to death*, when stringy mucus was brought up instead. Nausea and retching occasionally continued throughout the illness after the first week, which, however, always ceased after vomiting. From about the last fortnight to the fatal termination of the case the deceased was in a feverish heat, and could not bear any of the bed-clothes over the upper part of her person, although the nights at that time were very cold, in consequence of the chamber door remaining always open. About this period there was likewise some *slight* pain over the region of the *caecum on pressure*. As the disease advanced, the pulse rose from about 85 to 120.

Between the 18th and 29th April the mineral poisons were prescribed and administered – viz., acetate of lead, bismuth (forty-two grains), nitrate of silver, and sulphate of copper. The sulphate of copper (half a grain) was given on Friday, the 29th April last, which increased the motions from ten to fifteen in twenty-four hours; it was consequently suspended. A motion was taken away this morning (Friday) by Dr. Julius, at half-past ten A.M., before the sulphate of copper was taken; it was marked "No. 1," and examined by Dr. Taylor who said it neither contained bismuth, ARSENIC, nor ANTIMONY. A second motion, marked "No. 2," was taken on Saturday, by Mr Bird, the day *after the copper had been administered*, which is said to have contained rather less than a quarter of a grain of arsenic in four ounces, with traces of copper in it. No mention is made *here* of ANTIMONY by Dr. Taylor.

Autopsy (by Richard Barwell, Esq., F.R.C.S., Assistant-Surgeon to Charing Cross Hospital), May 4th, at half-past nine A.M. twenty-two hours after death. – Posterior part of the body much engorged by position; arms perfectly flexible; legs rigid; feet turned in and much bent, as though there had been spasm or cramp; back part of the body still warm; abdomen drawn in, and muscles seemed tense; tongue rough, and papillae prominent; fauces generally white; face emaciated, of a dark earthy colour; body generally emaciated. On removing the calvarium, the dura mater was rather more strongly than usual adherent to the bone; veins at the back of the pia mater engorged from position. Brain itself perfectly healthy in grey as in white matter; no change anywhere; the cut ends of vessels, on slicing white matter, very evident, and oozing; not even as much serum as usual in ventricles. Right lung engorged posteriorly from position; front pale; throughout crepitant, and perfectly healthy. Left lung: Idem. Heart: half an ounce of serum in pericardium; no inflammation of that membrane; heart and great vessels healthy in every respect; right ventricle contained a good deal of fluid blood; some clots in left ventricle. Abdomen: Liver large, pale, firm, fatty, speckled as usual; stomach and colon inflated; vessels of great omentum full. Stomach: Outside red at pyloric end; paler in centre; no aperture; duodenum very red; the small intestines generally inflated and minutely injected, and in spots roughened and glued by effused lymph, the result of peritonitis; gall-bladder distended. The bladder was empty. Kidneys healthy. Liver, stomach, spleen, intestines, uterus, and appendages were removed , placed in a jar, tied, sealed with six seals, and delivered to Inspector M'Intire [sic]. The uterus and ovaries were examined: the former was enlarged, and walls thickened; its cavity increased in size; contained a deciduous membrane, from which hung cord and foetus, two and a half lines in length; in ovary was Graafian follicle, filled with coagulum, and surrounded by effused fibrine. The deceased was in from the fifth to the seventh week of pregnancy.

Mr. Barwell's *subsequent examination May 5th, 1859, at Guy's Hospital, with* Dr.Taylor. – Stomach and intestines: Outside, red at pylorus, greenish in centre; *no aperture*; dark colour at cardiac end; duodenum very red; greenish-coloured spots; jejunum and ileum reddened; caecum and large intestines more approaching putrefaction; the peritoneal coat in some spots actually inflamed, with deposits of lymph that glued certain turns of intestine together. Inside stomach: Pale in centre, and towards pylorus corrugated; black at cradiac end from altered blood; contained a yellowish-brown, thickish fluid, with blood; no ulcers nor appearance of acute inflammation; coats firm. Dueodenum: commencement inflamed about three inches from pylorus; coats firm; no ulceration; slightly injected. Jejunum: Mucus membrane firm; in places minutely injected, the aborescent vessels showing remarkably well; the whole membrane rather more injected than normal. Ileum: the same appearance, except that it increased on approaching the lower part, and at last at about three feet from end; the mucous membrane was greatly altered, there being a deposit therein, and thickening; the membrane being at the same time roughened, and the glands less visible. It is remarkable that this change did not begin in the glands, as in the cases of fever and dysentery, but on the whole surface. Caecum: Upon the mucus membrane were many large spots, blackened by effused and altered blood, and many circular and some ragged ulcerations; the membrane extremely soft, (broken down,) and easily separable from muscular coat. Ascending, and transverse and sigmoid flexure of colon: These appearances continued decreasing throughout these viscera, and about the middle of transverse arch the mucus membrane became nearly normally firm, but still had black spots and ulcers; so on to rectum, which had been removed within one inch of aperture; in it were three spots of effused blood, and several ulcers. Spleen: Rather pale-pink, and soft.

Through the wild, imaginary brain of Dr. Julius, I am suspected and charged with having committed the horrid crime of murder – and that upon the life of one on whom my fondest affections were placed' and whose life to me was beyond all consideration: *the grounds alone, that his remedies ought to have arrested, but did not, the running stages of a fatal disease – diarrhoea and vomiting –* arising, no doubt, from long-continued chronic inflammation of the *liver and intestines especially*, as the autopsy clearly indicates. Our cohabitation was less than five months – 11th Dec. 1858, to 3rd May, 1859.

Although so cruelly and seriously charged, and *my life perilled by it*, I will not complain on my own account for the present, under existing circumstances. I do, however, proclaim my *entire innocence* before the whole world; and likewise declare, in the presence of Almighty God, that I am as pure as our Heavenly Father himself in this matter. At the same time, I cannot refrain from noticing and feeling the total neglect of the deceased by Messrs. Julius and Bird, and that for a *fortnight* (the time of their unjust suspicions), in not calling in other professional assistance, rather than *waste so much precious time* in hunting up matter to suit their own false impressions. It is indeed a most serious affair to *feel convinced that I was killing the deceased*, and yet *permit it to continue even until death occurred*, when a request to me to place the deceased entirely out of my charge would have met with a ready compliance at any time.

In conclusion, I am informed it has been stated I was not a legally-qualified member of the medical profession. I need only say I am a licentiate of the Apothecaries' Hall of London of twenty-five years standing; that I took my surgical education under Lynn, White, Guthrie &c., at the Westminster Hospital; and am doctor of medicine of the University of Erlangen of some years' standing, having been in the habit of visiting the Continent for many years. I may mention the late Drs. Pereira and Ashwell, and many other eminent men, as having taken these foreign degrees.

I have retired from the profession for the last six years.

Thomas Smethurst

June 1st 1859
Prisoner, Horsemonger-Lane Gaol

P.S. – The deceased's father died of a *similar attack of the bowels* in about nine days, although he had several eminent men in attendance. *He never ate anything during his fatal illness*. The deceased often said she was sure she was seized with her poor father's complaint, and would not get over it.

APPENDIX 4 – Glossary of Medical Terms

Much of this information was taken from *Materia Medica*, by John Biddle, published by Lindsay & Blakiston, 1868, Philadelphia.

Apothecaries' Measure

ap = Apothecaries' measure; imp = Imperial measure

Apothecaries units of mass:

1 grain*	=	0.06479891 grams = 64.79891 milligrams
20 grains	=	1 scruple
3 scruples	=	1 drachm
8 drachms	=	1 ounce$_{ap}$
12 ounces$_{ap}$	=	1 pound$_{ap}$
1 pound$_{ap}$	=	367.4098 grams = 0.82286 pounds$_{imp}$
1 pound$_{imp}$	=	1.21528 pounds$_{ap}$ = 453.592 grams

* '...the least portion of waight is commonly a Grayne, meaning a grayne of corne or wheat, drie, and gathered out of the middle of the eare...' (OED)

Apothecaries' units of liquid measure:

1 minim	=	1 'drop'
20 minims	=	1 fluid scruple
3 fluid scruples	=	1 fluid drachm
8 fluid drachms	=	1 fluid ounce
20 fluid ounces	=	1 pint
8 pints	=	1 gallon

An equivalence between mass and liquid measure may be derived in the case of water; 1 minim of water at 20 degrees centigrade weighs 0.91146 grains, and is approximately equivalent to a 'drop' of water.

Dr Taylor in his evidence said that he could easily weigh the 100th part of a grain, equivalent to 0.65 milligram.

Medicines and Chemicals

Acetate of Morphia is a water-soluble salt of morphine, used to treat the same conditions as opium.

Antimony is a quasi-metallic poisonous element. As *Tartar Emetic* or *Antimony Wine* it was used as a medicine.

Antimony Wine was made by putting 2 scruples of *tartar emetic* in 16 fluid ounces of boiling water, and adding 4 ounces of spirit. Four fluid drachms of this mixture contained one grain of tartar emetic. Alternatively sherry wine could be used instead of the water and spirit.

Arsenic is a quasi-metallic element, medically inert, although if swallowed it can oxidize becoming highly poisonous. It was used as a medicine, generally in the form Arsenius Oxide, or white arsenic.

Arsenius Oxide, see White Arsenic.

Bismuth, 'subnitrate of bismuth', used mainly to 'allay sickness and vomiting in chronic nervous affectations of the stomach...' Bismuth contained arsenic, which was 'removed' by treatment with sodium carbonate.

Calomel, 'mild mercury chloride', used to treat diarrhoea and dysentery.

Camphor, extracted from the Camphor Laurel tree. Used to treat dysentery.

Camphor Water, camphor, alcohol and magnesium carbonate in water.

Carbonate of Soda – Sodium Carbonate, used as an antacid.

Castor Oil, a laxative, extracted from the seeds of the Palma Christi or Ricinus Communis tree.

Catechu, a powerful vegetable astringent extracted from the Acacia tree.

Chlorate of Potash (Potass), Potassium Chlorate, $KClO_3$, taken internally, it acts as a diuretic, 'externally...it is an admirable (mouth) wash or gargle...'

Copper Sulphate, also known as blue vitriol, an astringent used for treating chronic diarrhoea and dysentery.

Corrosive Sublimate – Mercury Bichloride, used to treat secondary syphilis. In large doses it is a 'violent caustic poison', producing 'intense gastro-enteritis'.

Dover's Powder was invented by Dr Thomas Dover, an eccentric early eighteenth-century physician and privateer. In his book *The Ancient Physician's Legacy to his Country*, published in 1742, he detailed a preparation initially used for the treatment of gout, consisting of one part each of opium, liquorice and ipecacuanha with four ounces each of potassium nitrate and potassium sulphate. By the mid-nineteenth century, the potassium nitrate and liquorice had been omitted from the preparation.

Donovan's Solution is a solution of 'iodide of arsenic and mercury'. Used to treat rheumatism, scaly skin afflictions and syphilis.

Ether, ethyl ether, was prepared by treating alcohol with sulphuric acid. It was used as an 'antispasmodic...remedy in... cramp of the stomach and bowel...'

Fowler's Solution, potassium arsenate, is prepared by boiling arsenious acid with potassium bicarbonate. Uses similar to those of arsenious acid.

Gentian, the root of the Yellow Gentian plant, very bitter, used to 'relax the bowels' and to treat dyspepsia and gastric disorders.

Grey Powder consisted of three parts metallic mercury rubbed into five parts of powdered chalk (or one part mercury to two parts chalk). It was used as a 'gentle laxative'. Coincidentally Dr Dover proselytized the medicinal benefits of mercury (taken orally), to the extent that he was known as Dr Quicksilver; in his book, he reproduced a letter from a Captain Colt who reported that since taking an ounce or so of mercury per day under Dover's direction, he was almost entirely free of gout. He estimated having consumed 120 pounds of mercury over the previous nine years...

Hydrocyanic Acid – Prussic Acid – Cyanide , used to treat 'neuralgic affectations of the bowels...and...chronic vomiting...'

Ipecacuanha is a plant root found in Brazil; a 'mild emetic'.

Laudanum is tincture of opium, around 1½ oz of opium in 1 pint of spirit (ethyl alcohol); it provides about 1% morphine in alcohol. Uses as opium.

Lead Acetate, prepared by treating metallic lead with distilled vinegar, 'sedative and astringent', usually used in combination with opium to treat diarrhoea and dysentery.

Lunar Caustic – see Silver Nitrate

Magnesium Hydrate – Magnesium Hydroxide, in suspension in water it is called 'milk of magnesia'. An antidote for arsenic poisoning.

Opium is a narcotic extracted from the seeds of the opium poppy which contains morphine. 'Opium enjoys the widest range of therapeutic application.' It was used as the basis for the treatment of dysentery.

Quinine is extracted from the bark of the Peruvian Cinchona tree, mainly used for treating malaria.

Salvolatile, 'smelling-salts', ammonium carbonate in water.

Silver Nitrate, also known as Lunar Caustic, has a 'caustic or corrosive' effect; '...the most efficacious application that can be made to inflamed mucus membranes...'

Sulphuric Acid, diluted to around 10%, '...sucked through a tube to prevent injury to the teeth...', used among other things to treat choleraic diarrhoea.

Tartar Emetic, Antimony Potassium Tartarate, was prepared by 'boiling water and cream of tartar with oxide of antimony'. This process, 'tartarising', produces antimony in a water-soluble form.

White Arsenic – Arsenius Oxide, 'Arsenic', a poison, used 'with caution' in the treatment of malaria and other fevers.

Miscellaneous Terms and Definitions

Astringent, a preparation that causes the constriction of skin-cells and other bodily tissues (OED).

Caecum, a sort of 'pouch', separating large and small intestines; generally regarded as being the beginning of the large intestine.

Diphtheria, a bacterial infection affecting the throat, which includes the formation of a 'false membrane' within the lining of the mucus membrane.

Diuretic, a substance, taken internally, that tends to promote the production of urine.

Dysentery, severe diarrhoea with blood and mucus in the faeces.

Emetic, a preparation that induces vomiting.

Excoriate, Excoriation, damage to or removal of the surface of the skin.

Hyperemesis Gravidarum, extreme morning sickness involving dehydration and weight loss.

Injection, the first subcutaneous injection using a needle and hypodermic syringe was performed by Dr Alexander Wood in Edinburgh in 1853; such injections were only just starting to be investigated widely in 1858. 'Injections', as detailed in the treatment of Isabella Bankes, were intra-vaginal – douches, or intra-rectal – enemas. As detailed in the evidence given in court, either a glass hypodermic syringe or a rubber-bulb was used.

Marsh's Test, the first really sensitive test for the presence of arsenic, introduced in 1836. The material under test was boiled with acid and zinc which produced hydrogen. Any arsenic present combined with the hydrogen to form arsine gas. The arsine was burned, and precipitated the arsenic on to a sheet of glass as a 'black mirror'. Care was needed since arsine was highly poisonous.

MRCS, Member of the Royal College of Surgeons

MRCP, Member of the Royal College of Physicians

Mucus, the slippery secretion covering mucus membrane.

Mucus Membrane, lining mostly of internal organs, secreting and therefore covered with, mucus.

Oesophagus, the tube connecting the back of the mouth to the stomach.

Plaisters – Plasters, a piece of 'sheepskin, linen or muslin' spread with a mixture of lead oxide and olive oil to which is added a 'curative substance' (OED). The lead oxide mixture is adhesive at body temperature and acts to keep the medicine in contact with the patient's skin.

Purgative, induces bowel movements – a laxative.

Reinsch's Test, used to detect the presence of 'antimony, arsenic, bismuth, selenium, thallium and mercury' in organic material. In 1841, Hugo Reinsch published details of this test which was much simpler to perform than Marsh's test, although not quite as sensitive and not reliable for quantitative analysis. The suspect tissue was boiled in dilute hydrochloric acid in order to break down any organic matter present. A copper foil, gauze or wire was then introduced into the liquid. If any of the aforementioned metals were present, a thin metallic film would be deposited on the copper. Further analysis was then needed to identify the metal deposited.

Sudorific, a drug inducing sweating.

Tenesmus, the feeling of wanting to pass stools all of the time.

Typhus – 'Gaol fever', a bacterial disease transmitted by human lice, or rat-fleas.

Sources

Alfred Swaine Taylor, MD, FRS, (1806 - 1880) Forensic Toxicologist, Noel G Coley, Medical History, **35**: 409 - 427, 1991

Alumni Cantabrienses 1752 – 1900, J A Venn, Cambridge University Press, 1922 – 1954

Alumni Oxonienses 1715 – 1886, University of Oxford, Oxford & London, 1887

The Apothecaries' Act, 1815, a Reinterpretation, S W F Holloway, Medical History, 1966, April; 10(2) 107-129

The Ancient Physician's Legacy to his Country, Thomas Dover, C Hitch, London, 1762

The Arsenic Century, James C Whorton, Oxford University Press, 2010

Australian Dictionary of National Biography, National Centre of Biography, Australian National University, On Line, 2006 – 2013

British Pharmacopoea, General Medical Council, 1864

The Case of Thomas Smethurst MD, A Newton, Routledge, Warne & Routledge, 1859

Centenary of Hypodermic Injection, G A Mogey, *British Medical Journal*, Nov 28, 1953, 1180 – 1181

The Chemical Directory, Charles Wright & Co, London, 1852

Conspiracy, a Petition to Parliament etc, James Smethurst, J C Kelly & Co, Houndsditch, 1841

The Criminal Prisons of London, Henry Mayhew and John Binny, Frank Cass, 1862

Diaries of Sir George Cornewall Lewis, National Library of Wales

Dictionary of Trade Products, P L Simmonds, G Routledge & Co, London, 1858

Felons' Effects and the Effects of Felony in Nineteenth-Century England, K J Kesselring, *Law and History Review*, February 2010, Vol 28 No 1

From Grub Street to Fleet Street, Bob Clarke, Revel Parker, 2010

A General View of the Criminal Law of England, James Fitzjames Stephen, Macmillan & Co, London, 1863

The History & Topography of Hampton on Thames, Henry Ripley, Wyman & Sons, London, 1884

The History of the Evelyn Family, Helen Evelyn, Eveleigh Nash, London, 1915

Hydropathy in England 1840 – 1870, Robin Price, Medial History, 1981, 25: 269-280

Hydropathy or The Cold Water Cure, R T Claridge, James Madden & co, London, 1842

Hydrotherapia or The Water Cure, Thomas Smethurst, John Snow, London, 1843

"Inflammatory" bowel disease, J F Fielding, British Medical Journal, 290, 47 - 48, 5 January 1985

Inflammatory bowel disease: cause and immunobiology, Daniel C Baumgart, Simon R Carding, The Lancet, Vol 369, 1627 - 1640, 12 May, 2007

The Letters of Charles Dickens, British Academy, Pilgrim Edition, Vol 9, 1859 - 1861, Clarendon Press, Oxford 1997

The Life and Times of Sir George Cornewall Lewis, R W D Fenn, Logaston Press, 2005

The Letters of Charles Dickens, British Academy, Pilgrim Edition, Vol 9, 1859 - 1861, Clarendon Press, Oxford 1997

The Life of Samuel Johnson, James Boswell, Various publishers, 1824

Life of Vincent Priessnitz, Richard Metcalfe, Simpkin, Marshall, Hamilton, Kent & Co Ltd, London, 1898

A Manual of Pathological Anatomy, Carl Rokitansky, Blanchard & Lea, Philadelphia, 1855

Materia Medica, John B Biddle, Lidsay & Blakison, Philadelphia, 1868

Morbid Appearances in the Intestines of Miss Bankes, Samuel Wilks, Medical Times & Gazette, 264-265, Sep 10, 1859,

Murder by Poisoning, G Lathom Browne & C G Stewart, Stevens and Sons, London, 1883

Old Bailey On Line, www.oldbaileyonline.org, V 7, 2003-2012

On Poisons in relation to Medical Jurisprudence and Medicine, Alfred Swaine Taylor, London, 1859

The Oxford Dictionary of National Biography On Line, www.oxforddnb.com, Oxford University Press, 2004 - 2013

The Oxford English Dictionary On Line, www.oed.com, Oxford University Press, 2013

Pathological and Practical Researches on the Diseases of the Stomach etc, John Abercrombie, Waugh and Innes, Edinburgh, 1833

Personal Rememberances of Sir Frederick Pollock, Frederick Pollock, Macmillan & Co, London, 1887

The Principles and Practice of Medical Jurisprudence, Alfred Swaine Taylor, John Churchill & Sons, London, 1865

Read All About It, Kevin Williams, Routledge, London, 2010

Reasonable Doubt, Geoffrey de C Parmiter, Arthur Barker Ltd, London, 1938

Report of the Commissioners...into the Existing State of the Corporation of the City of London... Eyre & Spottiswoode, 1854

Reports of Trials for Murder by Poisoning, G Lathom Browne & C G Stewart, Stevens & Sons, London, 1883

The Rise and Fall of the Political Press in Britain, Steven Koss, Fontana, London, 1990

Sketches in London, James Grant, W S Orr & Co, London, 1838

Some Experiences of a Barrister's Life, William Ballantine, Richard Bentley & Son, London, 1883

A Topographical Dictionary of London, James Elmes, Whittaker, Treacher & Arnot, London, 1931

Transactions of the Associated Apothecaries and Surgeon-Apothecaries of England and Wales, Vol. I, Burgess & Hill, London, 1823

Trial of Dr Smethurst, Leonard A Parry, William Hodge & Co Ltd., London, 1931

Newspapers and Journals
The Times
The *Daily Telegraph*
The *Standard*
The *Daily News*
The *Morning Chronicle*
The *Morning Post*
The *Morning Star*
The *Observer*
The *Liverpool Mercury*
The *Illustrated Times*
The *Law Times*
The *Lancet*
The *British Medical Journal*
The *London Medical Gazette*
The *Water Cure Journal*
The *Saturday Review*

Picture Credits

1. Thomas Smethurst, from an image published in the *Illustrated Times*, 3rd September 1859.
2. Sir Frederick Pollock, Lord Chief Baron, © National Portrait Gallery, London, see note below.
3. Serjeant John Humffries Parry, from an image published in *Illustrated London News*, 24th January 1880.
4. Serjeant William Ballantine, © National Portrait Gallery, London, see note below.
5. Dr Frederick Gilder Julius, © www.thekingscandlesticks.com, by kind permission of Edward Fenn.
6. Dr Robert Bentley Todd, © Wellcome Library, London.
7. Dr Alfred Swaine Taylor, © Wellcome Library, London.
8. Dr Alfred Swaine Taylor and William Brande, © Wellcome Library, London.
9. Sir Benjamin Ward Richardson © National Portrait Gallery, London, see note below.
10. Sir George Cornewall Lewis, © National Portrait Gallery, London, see note below.

Cover picture *The Thames at Richmond*, 1867, by kind permission of the Richmond Local Studies Library.

Note: The photographs from the National Portrait Gallery have been cropped and processed to remove excessive defects with the gallery's permission.

Selective Index (Thomas Smethurst and Isabella Bankes are excluded since their names appear very frequently in the text)

A

Abercrombie, Dr John 200
Adams brothers 25
Allsop, Mr 299
Alma Villas 45, 48, 49, 53, 55, 69, 75, 78, 79, 97, 163, 257, 269
Ambrose, Lucy 43
Apothecaries Act 21
Apothecaries, Society of 21, 22, 26, 58
Archbishop of Canterbury 81
Aretaeus 24
Ashwell, Dr 325
Austrian Silesia 27
Authorized Version 179

B

Babington, Dr Charles Metcalfe 93
Bacon, Lord 175
Ballantine, Serjeant William 51, 53, 54, 56, 57, 58, 61, 65, 66, 67, 68, 72, 73, 74, 79, 81, 84, 87, 89, 93, 94, 95, 96, 99, 100, 103, 107, 110, 112, 116, 123, 124, 132, 133, 134, 136, 137, 143, 151, 152, 153, 160, 161, 171, 172, 174, 181, 183, 256, 257, 260, 268, 269, 273, 274, 292, 293, 294, 295, 296, 297, 298, 306, 309
Baly, Dr William 203, 204, 207, 218, 222, 223, 224, 229, 306
Bankes, Anne 41
Bankes, Charles 40
Bankes, George 40, 41, 77
Bankes, George Vernon 40, 41, 257
Bankes, James Rhodes 41, 43, 93, 262, 264, 266
Bankes, John 40
Bankes, Louisa 41, 42, 43, 46, 47, 48, 49, 52, 55, 62, 69, 70, 76, 77, 80, 91, 153, 159, 164, 236, 244, 255, 257, 261, 265, 266, 269, 270, 271, 275, 277, 279, 280, 305
Barber Surgeons, Company of 22

Barker, Dr 55, 81
Barry, Dr 215, 216
Barwell, Richard 50, 61, 86, 87, 88, 91, 97, 322, 323
Beasley, Mr 239
Biddle, John 327
Bird, Samuel Dougan 13, 45, 47, 50, 51, 57, 58, 62, 71, 72, 79, 80, 82, 83, 84, 85, 86, 91, 93, 95, 96, 159, 162, 171, 173, 174, 177, 183, 185, 186, 187, 190, 192, 195, 200, 202, 203, 205, 229, 259, 265, 271, 290, 301, 325
Bodkin, Mr 68, 73, 83, 99, 107, 123
Bowerbank, Dr Lewis Squire 94
Bramwell, Baron George William Wilsher 65, 239, 249
Brande, Professor William Thomas 104, 108, 110, 123, 133, 180, 190, 227
Brehon Laws 175
Brett, Dr 214, 215, 296
Briggs, Thomas 283
Bright, John 166, 220, 222, 223
British Institution 242
British Medical Journal, the 195, 305
Brodie, Sir Benjamin 113, 114, 115, 116, 230, 231, 232, 285, 289
Brompton Hospital for Consumption 82
Brontë, Charlotte 168, 185
Brunel, Isambard Kingdom 28
Burdett, Sir Francis 34, 35, 36
Butler, Samuel 176
Buzzard, Dr Thomas 47, 48, 58, 83, 86, 93, 96, 97
Byles, Judge 248

C

Campbell, Lord Chief Justice John 123, 169, 199
Cartaya, Pedro Maria 200
Carter, William 50
Caudle, William Adolphus Frederick 44, 49, 58, 77, 80, 86, 162
Central Criminal Court 173, 236, 237, 238
Chancery 259, 281
Charing Cross Hospital 50, 322

Chetwood, Jemima 49, 77
Claridge, Captain R T 28, 29, 31, 33, 36
Clark, Sir James 203
Clerk, Mr 73, 75, 76, 235, 239, 240, 241, 242
Cobden, Richard 166, 220, 221
Coke upon Littleton 175
Combe, Mr 235, 236, 237, 238
Cook, John 123, 133, 184
Cooper, Sir Astley 22, 23, 58, 113
Copland, Dr James 72, 94, 95, 135, 145, 173, 175
Cornewall, Harriet 197
County Gaol at Newington, *see* Horsemonger Lane Gaol 238
Court of Criminal Appeal 10, 193, 224, 250, 289, 299
Coutts, Miss Burdett 34
Cresswell, Sir Cresswell 255, 256, 282
Crimea 45, 48, 82
Crohn, Dr Burrill 305
Crohn's disease 305, 306, 309
Crompton, Mr Justice 65
Cutler, Edward 114, 115
Czech Republic 27

D

Daily Chronicle, the 51
Daily News, the 166, 167, 173
Daily Telegraph, the 165, 166, 167, 171, 173, 174, 179, 180, 182, 183,
190, 191, 193, 207, 221, 287
Darwin, Charles 36, 38
Davy, Sir Humphrey 110
De La Warr, Earl, *see* Sackville-West, George John 262
Derby, Lord 207
Dickens, Charles 9, 36, 43, 193
Disraeli, Benjamin 197
Doctors' Commons 43, 209, 264, 266, 268
Dodd, William 191
Dover, Dr Thomas 329
Downing Bruce, Mr 256

Dubois, Dr Paul 149, 186
Durham, Mary, *See* Smethurst, Mary 27, 62, 71, 74, 235, 239, 240, 241, 242, 243, 245, 246, 247, 251, 260, 262, 269, 272, 274
Dutch Mordant 99
Dymond, Mr 220
Dysart, Earl of 25, 178

E

Earl Spencer 114
Easter, William 235
Easton, Mr 71
Edinburgh Review, The 197
Edmunds, James 146, 168
Empress Maria Theresa 25
Erlangen 32, 33
Erle, Sir William 173
Evans, Mr 216
Evelyn, Phillipa 31
Evelyn, Sir Hugh 31
Evelyn, Sir John 31

F

Faraday. Michael 110
Ferguson, Dr Robert 207
Fielding, J F 305
Firth, Mrs 43, 263, 264
Follett, Mr 205
Forster, John 193
Freeland, Susan 309
Fresenius, Dr Karl Remegius 101, 293, 294, 309

G

Gadsby, Mr 37
Galen 24
General Medical Council 44, 116, 230
Gent, Leonard 290
George IV 81, 114

Gibson, Henry 214, 215, 216, 296
Gibson, Mr 72
Gibson, Mrs Julia Emma 208, 209, 211, 212, 214, 216, 217, 295, 296, 297, 309, 315, 316
Giffard, Hardinge 51, 65, 66, 73, 110, 117, 119, 120, 121, 136, 198, 222, 224
Ginzburg, Leon 305
Girdwood, Dr Gilbert Finlay 144, 145
Gladstone, William 197
Grabouska, Marian 43, 69, 74
Gräfenberg 27, 32, 33, 34
Great Northern Hospital 139
Grey, Sir George 203, 283
Grocers, Society of 21
Grosvenor Place School of Medicine 113, 114, 115, 116, 122, 129, 133, 139, 161, 173, 176, 177, 180, 199, 221, 223, 230
Gully, Dr James 36, 216
Güterbock 189
Guthrie, Mr 325
Guy's Hospital 48, 58, 61, 87, 109, 133, 141, 323

H

Habeas Corpus 234, 236
Haffenden, Alfred 41, 42, 270, 281
Haffenden, Jane 41, 42, 92, 257, 280, 281
Harvey, William 176
Hassell, Dr 162
Hatch, Henry John 10, 252, 288
Hay, James 26, 27
Henderson, Martha 242
Henry VIII 22
Herapath, Professor William 184, 186, 187, 190, 218, 219, 229, 290, 300, 310
Hesiod 5
Hills, Mr 162
Hippocrates 24
Hoffman, Dr 55, 321

Homoeopathy 28, 29
Hooper, Dr Robert 135, 175
Horace 278
Horsemonger Lane Gaol 9, 10, 50, 169, 198, 207, 235, 236, 238, 260, 326
Humphreys, Mr Charles Octavius 122, 146, 198
Hydropathy, *See* Water Cure 26, 27, 28, 29, 31, 33, 35, 36, 37, 178

I

Inner Temple 67
Instone, Thomas 72

J

Jackson, Dr 55
James, Edwin, QC 284
Jenkins, Miss 77, 255
Jenner, Sir William 203, 204, 207, 218, 222, 223, 224, 229, 306
Jenner, William 176
Johnson, Charles, *See* Laporte, Charles 243
Johnson, Dr Edward 34
Johnson, Dr Samuel 190, 191
Johnson, John Peter, *See* Laporte, John Peter 240, 241, 243, 244, 246
Johnson, Mary, *See* Durham, Mary 240, 241, 243, 244, 246, 247
Jukes, Constable John 48, 49
Julius, Dr Frederick Gilder 44, 45, 46, 47, 48, 49, 50, 51, 54, 56, 57, 58, 61, 62, 63, 69, 70, 71, 72, 76, 77, 79, 80, 81, 82, 83, 84, 85, 86, 88, 89, 91, 93, 97, 105, 107, 111, 112, 116, 131, 152, 153, 157, 159, 160, 162, 163, 164, 171, 173, 174, 177, 183, 185, 186, 187, 190, 192, 195, 200, 203, 204, 205, 217, 223, 228, 229, 259, 265, 271, 272, 290, 301, 307, 321, 324, 325
Julius, Dr George Charles 81
Julius, George 86
Julius, Rev Henry Richard 163

K

Keen, John 235, 237
Kidd, Dr Charles 175, 177, 182, 191

Kildare Terrace 43, 69, 74, 270
King Edward VII 298
King's Bench Prison 31
King's College Hospital 46, 60, 133, 207
Kinnerton Street Medical School 115
Knole Park 262
Kückh, Marie Salome 25

L

Lancet, the 14, 22, 23, 28, 29, 30, 31, 32, 33, 34, 35, 36, 55, 56, 62, 63,
100, 101, 114, 115, 124, 177, 184, 195, 221, 293, 294, 305, 309, 311
Lane, Dr Edward Wickstead 38
Lane, Mr 46
Lane, Samuel Armstrong 113, 114, 115, 116
Laporte, Charles 235, 236, 239, 240, 241, 244, 249
Laporte, Charles, Jnr 235, 244
Laporte, George Henry 240, 241, 242, 243
Laporte, John Peter 240, 242, 243, 244, 245, 246
Laporte, Mary Ann 243
Law Magazine, the 302
Lawrence, Sir John 73
Law Times, the 193, 250
Lázně Jeseník 27
Lehmann 189
Letheby, Henry 100, 101, 184, 189, 320
Lewis, Sir George Cornewall 11, 197, 198, 199, 203, 204, 205, 206,
207, 208, 209, 210, 211, 217, 218, 219, 220, 221, 223, 231, 234, 237,
253, 283, 284, 287
Lewis, Sir Thomas Frankland 197
Liardet, Charlotte Salome 25
Liardet, Colonel Charles 25
Liardet, Jean-François Louis, See Liardet, John 25
Liardet, Jeanne Jacobine Charlotte Chloee, *See* Smethurst, Charlotte
25, 26
Liardet, John 25, 26
Liardet, Wilbraham 31
Liebig, Professor 133, 176

Linck, Superintendant 215
Lister, Lady Theresa 197
Liverpool Mercury, the 299
Lockwood, Anne, See Smethurst, Anne 316
Lockwood, John Alexander 315, 316
Lockyer, Sergeant 215
London and Westminster Bank 74, 93, 239
London Hospital 320
London Medical Gazette, the 115, 305
Lynn, Mr 325

M

Marchant, William 54
Marsh Test 102, 110, 131, 332
Mather, Dr 215
Mayther, Mr, *See* Mather, Dr 211, 215
McCrosty, Alexander 74, 93, 239
McIntyre, Inspector Robert 48, 49, 50, 59, 83, 86, 91, 211, 236, 295, 309, 323
McMahon, Mr, MP 289
Medical Act 44
Medical History 317
Medical Times and Gazette, the 206
Medicine, Bachelor of 33
Medicine, Diploma in 23, 33
Melville, Herman 315
Merck process 184
Merewether, Mr 73, 256
Mesmerism 28, 29
Moor Park 37, 38, 39, 42, 47, 163, 261
Mordaunt divorce case 298
Morning Chronicle, the 114, 166, 168, 174, 177, 182, 191
Morning Post, the 166, 182, 250, 254
Morning Star, the 166, 169, 172, 173, 177, 183, 193, 220, 221, 222
Mount Sinai Hospital, New York 305
Müller Franz 282, 283, 284, 287
Murray, Catherine 86

N

Napoleon 94
National Archives 12
Newgate Prison 65, 72, 73, 169, 252, 282
New Surrey House of Correction 38, 248, 251, 252, 253, 254, 313, 316
Newton, Augustus 11, 12, 13, 204

O

Oates, Titus 179
Observer, the 169
Odling, Dr William 61, 62, 97, 99, 102, 104, 108, 109, 110, 160, 227, 228, 290, 300
Old Bailey 13, 56, 61, 64, 72, 123, 154, 155, 173, 210, 252
Old Palace Terrace 43, 54, 69
Oppenheimer, Gordon 305
Origin of Species 39

P

Palmer, Harry Smith 50, 91, 108, 169, 232
Palmerston, Viscount 197, 203, 207, 217
Palmer, William 116, 123, 127, 129, 132, 133, 157, 161, 167, 176, 177, 180, 182, 184, 186, 191, 199, 225, 230, 232
Parry, Dr Leonard A 12, 304
Parry, Serjeant John Humffries 65, 66, 67, 72, 73, 76, 77, 78, 80, 81, 84, 85, 86, 87, 89, 90, 91, 92, 93, 94, 95, 102, 103, 104, 105, 108, 111, 112, 127, 132, 138, 139, 140, 141, 142, 144, 145, 146, 148, 149, 150, 151, 157, 158, 159, 198, 222, 224
Patent Asphalte Company 28
Pedley, George 150
Peel, Sir Robert 66
Penrhyn, Edward 48, 49, 51, 61, 71, 83, 97, 105
Pereira, Dr 325
Phillimore, Dr 256, 257, 269, 272, 273, 276, 277
Phillips, Alderman 127
Physicians, Royal College of 21, 23, 113, 147

Pindar 34
Pollard, Dr 312, 313
Pollock, Sir Frederick, Lord Chief Baron 12, 66, 67, 73, 87, 116, 117, 118, 119, 122, 126, 127, 135, 136, 138, 139, 141, 147, 150, 154, 155, 156, 157, 158, 159, 160, 162, 164, 165, 170, 171, 172, 173, 174, 178, 179, 180, 181, 183, 198, 199, 204, 209, 217, 218, 219, 220, 221, 222, 223, 224, 225, 226, 227, 228, 229, 230, 231, 232, 233, 234, 249, 278, 283, 285, 286, 288, 300, 302, 303, 306, 308
Pollock, Sir George 73
Pollock, William Frederick 126
Price, Robin 317
Priessnitz, Vincent 27, 28, 29, 33, 35
Prince Albert 203, 205, 222
Prince of Wales, the 298
Probate and Divorce, Court of 253, 255, 281
Pythias and Damon 30

Q

Queen Charlotte's Lying-in Hospital 93
Queen Mary Hospital 147
Queen Victoria 154, 187, 198, 203, 207, 208, 209, 210, 217, 221, 237, 253, 281

R

Reinsch, Hugo 59, 333
Reinsch Test 58, 60, 93, 98, 99, 100, 101, 102, 110, 180, 184, 187, 189, 190, 201, 293, 300, 301, 333
Rembrandt 99
Reynolds, Henry 254
Richardson, Dr 106
Richardson, Sir Benjamin Ward 113, 116, 117, 118, 119, 120, 121, 122, 123, 124, 127, 128, 129, 133, 134, 139, 173, 199, 203, 204, 207, 221, 223, 225, 228, 301, 306
Rifle Terrace 39, 40, 41, 43, 51, 68, 69, 73, 91, 188, 205, 227, 235, 244, 252, 264, 266, 270, 312
Robertson, Ann 44, 45, 54, 55, 69, 74
Robertson, Miss Elizabeth 75

Robinson, Mr H G 235, 236, 237, 238, 272, 273, 274
Rodgers, Dr Julian Edwards 105, 129, 131, 133, 180, 183
Rokitansky, Dr Carl 135
Rosemont Road 45
Royal Academy 242, 243
Royal Institution 110
Royal Maternity Charity 146
Royal Pardon, The 252, 287, 289
Royal Society 58, 66, 67, 94, 109, 110, 114, 116, 230, 303
Russell, Lord John 203

S

Sackville-West, George John 262
Salter, Mr Talfourd 239, 242, 245, 272, 273
Sanitary Commission, the 38
Saturday Review, The 210
Schmidt 189
Scott, Sir Walter 207
Senior, Frederick 47, 53, 70, 77, 78, 256, 257, 258, 259, 260, 278
Shearman, Dr Charles J 189, 190
Shee, Serjeant 127
Sheridan, Henry Brinsley, MP 205, 273, 290
Sleigh, Mr W Campbell 239, 240, 241, 242, 245, 246, 247, 262, 272, 273, 274, 275, 280
Smethurst, Anne, *See* Thomas, Anne 312, 313, 314, 315, 316
Smethurst, Charlotte 25, 31
Smethurst, James 12, 26, 64, 187, 188, 209, 211, 213, 214, 215, 217, 221, 235, 251, 252, 254, 273, 292, 294, 295, 296, 297, 313, 314, 315, 316
Smethurst, James Mellor 47, 222, 261, 267, 268
Smethurst, Mary 9, 38, 39, 42, 43, 52, 64, 91, 112, 152, 162, 178, 187, 188, 189, 205, 206, 221, 226, 235, 236, 240, 244, 246, 249, 252, 253, 254, 255, 261, 263, 264, 265, 266, 267, 274, 280, 298, 306, 308, 309, 310, 311, 312, 313, 314
Smethurst, Mary Ann 314
Smethurst, William 25, 26, 64, 169, 214, 310, 312, 313, 314, 315, 316
Smith, Detective Sergeant 213

Smith, Dr William Tyler 147, 148, 149, 174, 185, 186, 187, 190, 195, 301
Smith, Joseph 235, 244
Smith, Mary 39, 41, 42, 43, 52, 68, 73, 205
Smith, Miss 215
Smith, Rebecca 310
Spencer House 27, 33
Spenser, Edmund 277
Sprice, James 43, 235
Squire and McCulloch 122
Stamp Duty 165, 166
Standard, the 166, 167, 173, 174, 190, 191
St Augustine 301
St Bartholomew's Hospital 114
Stephen, James 155, 187
St George's Hospital 46, 113, 114, 115, 181
St Mary's, Battersea 43, 71
St Mary's Hospital 115, 185
Stoltz, Professor 200
Sudder Court 222, 224
Surgeons, Royal College of 22, 44, 58, 87
Swabey, Dr 256, 257
Swift, Jonathan 37
Symes, Teesdale and Sandilands 253

T

Tanner, Detective Sergeant 213
Tarte, William 41, 70, 77, 79, 92, 280, 281
Taylor, Dr Alfred Swaine 13, 48, 50, 51, 53, 55, 56, 57, 58, 59, 60, 61, 62, 65, 67, 70, 71, 86, 87, 91, 93, 96, 99, 100, 101, 102, 103, 104, 105, 106, 107, 108, 109, 110, 112, 113, 116, 117, 123, 124, 129, 130, 131, 132, 133, 143, 144, 150, 152, 153, 160, 163, 168, 169, 172, 173, 175, 176, 177, 179, 180, 183, 184, 186, 187, 189, 190, 191, 192, 194, 195, 201, 204, 205, 206, 208, 218, 219, 223, 227, 228, 229, 272, 274, 289, 290, 293, 294, 297, 300, 301, 302, 303, 304, 322, 323, 328
Taylor, Mr C 27
Teetotalism 179

Tegart, Mr 26, 27
Temple, Sir William 37
Tennyson, Alfred Lord 36
Teutonic Hall 299
Thomas, Anne 311
Thomas, Catharine 311, 316
Thomas, John 311
Thomas, Robert 312, 316
Thomas, Robert Smethurst 312
Thompson, Dr 55, 321
Thomson, Inspector S 214, 215
Thudichum, Dr John Lewis William 117, 122, 133, 134, 135, 136, 137, 138, 139, 161, 175, 176, 177, 199, 203, 221, 223, 228
Thuggees 298
Times, the 12, 33, 34, 37, 165, 166, 167, 170, 174, 180, 182, 183, 184, 185, 186, 187, 188, 191, 194, 204, 210, 250, 255, 261, 268, 282, 283, 284, 287, 288, 289, 290, 291, 292, 308, 310, 311, 312
Todd, Dr Robert Bentley 46, 47, 51, 57, 60, 62, 72, 79, 80, 82, 83, 88, 89, 90, 91, 116, 123, 125, 133, 162, 163, 171, 173, 174, 176, 177, 185, 186, 190, 192, 200, 202, 205, 229, 271, 272, 290, 301
Tomlin, Elizabeth 41, 42, 92, 255, 257, 270, 271, 280, 281
Tomlin, Friend Jennings 41, 42, 255, 263, 270, 271, 281, 308
Tomlin, Mabel 42, 92
Tower Tavern, The 213
Treherne, Mr 262
Turner, Joseph Mallord William 242

U

University of St Andrews 113

V

Vernon, Hannah 40

W

Waddington, Horatio 198, 199, 208, 209, 218, 219
Wakley, Thomas 28, 29
Ward, Captain 298

Water Cure 28, 29, 33, 34, 35, 205, 316
Water Cure Journal, the 26, 37, 310
Watson, John 215, 216
Watson, Justice 174
Webb, Dr Francis Cornelius 118, 122, 138, 139, 140, 141, 142, 143, 144, 199, 203, 221, 223
Webster, Mr B 256
Westminster Hospital 26, 325
Wheatley, Miss Susannah 47, 70, 78, 259, 260
Wheatley, Susannah Angelina 45, 53, 54, 55, 69, 70, 75, 76, 159, 163, 265, 269
Wheeler, Mr 26
White, Mr 325
Whiteside, Mrs 220
Whitty, Mary 214
Wightman, Justice 67
Wilde, Sir James 282
Wilks, Dr Samuel 87, 88, 141, 206, 305, 308
Willes, Mr Justice 154, 174
William Hunter's School of Anatomy 113
Williamson, Mrs 92
Williamson, Sergeant 215
Willis, Laura 211, 212, 215, 216, 295, 309
Willis, Mr 212
Wilson, James 113, 114
Wilson, James Arthur 113, 114
Wood, Dr Alexander 44
Wooler, Jane 106
Wooler, Joseph 106
Wordsworth, William 207